MW00653700

Accidental Shepherd

Accidental Shepherd

How a California Girl Rescued an Ancient Mountain Farm in Norway

Liese Greenstelder

UNIVERSITY OF MINNESOTA PRESS
MINNEAPOLIS
LONDON

Published by the University of Minnesota Press
111 Third Avenue South, Suite 290
Minneapolis, MN 55401-2520
http://www.upress.umn.edu

ISBN 978-1-5179-1766-1 (hc)
ISBN 978-1-5179-1978-8 (pb)

A Cataloging-in-Publication record for this book is available from the Library of Congress.

Printed in the United States of America on acid-free paper

32 31 30 29 28 27 26 25 24 10 9 8 7 6 5 4 3 2 1

Contents

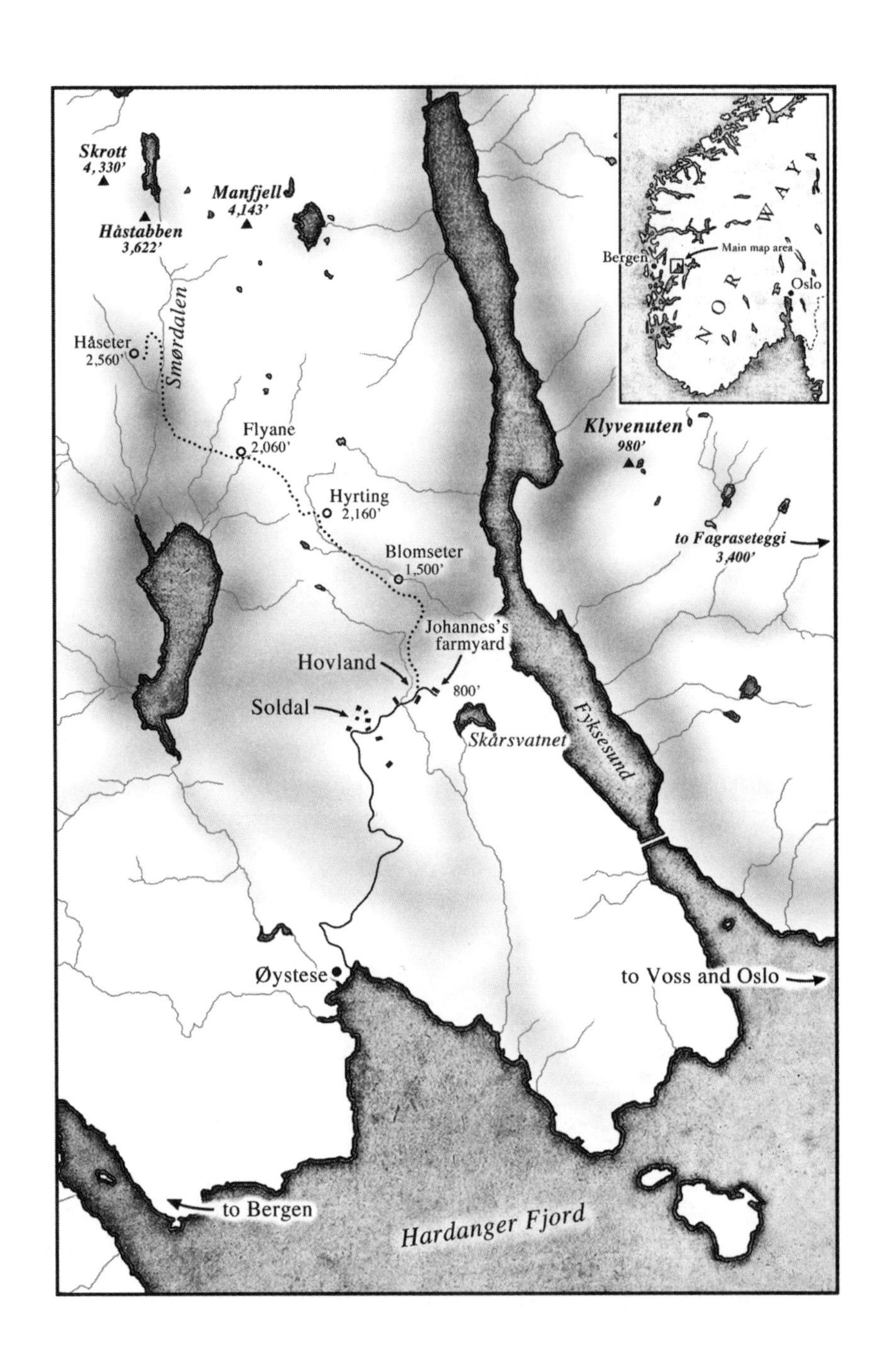

Skrott
4,330'
Håstabben
3,622'
Manfjell
4,143'
Bergen
Main map area
Oslo
NORWAY
Smørdalen
Håseter
2,560'
Flyane
2,060'
Hyrting
2,160'
Blomseter
1,500'
Klyvenuten
980'
to Fagraseteggi
3,400'
Johannes's
farmyard
Hovland
800'
Soldal
Skårsvatnet
Fyksesund
Øystese
to Voss and Oslo
to Bergen
Hardanger Fjord

Norwegian Friends and Neighbors

Note: I have changed the names of some people featured in this book.

Edvard: A young man who has helped Johannes with farmwork on weekends for several years. He is in his final year of studies at a maritime academy to become a ship's mate.

Einar: A farmer in Soldal.

Gunnar Hovland: One of Johannes's seven brothers. He lives just south of Øystese at the edge of Hardanger Fjord. Svein, his son, is ten years old.

Ingebjørg and Ola Mæland: Johannes's sister and brother-in-law. They live next door to Gunnar Hovland on Hardanger Fjord.

Johannes Hovland: Owner of the farm where I work; my boss.

Kari: A schoolteacher; one of Einar's three daughters.

Linda: My college friend from California who is studying agriculture in England.

Magnar: A farmer and a friend of Johannes.

Øystein Hovland: One of Torkel's three brothers. He spends weekends at his cottage on the edge of Fyksesund but lives at his job site farther north during the week.

Robin: A young man from the United States who applies for farmwork through the Norwegian Committee for International Information and Youth Work (NIU).

Sigurd Nesheim: A butcher who lives by Skårsvatnet.

Solveig, Alv, and Torgeir Hovland: Siblings who live on the first of Hovland's three farms.

Sverre Djønne: An acquaintance of Johannes who lives in Øystese.

Torkel and Inger Hovland: My closest neighbors; they live on the middle of Hovland's three farms. Their sons are Tormod (age thirteen) and Arne (age twelve).

September 22, 1972

Bella trotted ahead as Øystein and I made our way to an outcrop high on the rim of Smørdalen, "Butter Valley," a treacherous ravine named for the udder-engorging blanket of grasses and ferns that line its walls. Clouds had disappeared overnight, and the air was crystal clear in this chilly sunlight, making it easier to distinguish distant clusters of sheep from flecks of snow or patches of rock.

For three months the flock had been running free across these mountain slopes, grazing on nutritious grasses and forbs that grow above timberline. Now we needed to herd them back home before autumn snowfalls barred their return.

From our vantage point, we quickly spotted eight animals in three widely scattered groups. And then something else: a trio of whitish smudges on the steep and rocky south face of Håstabben, a stubby peak sandwiched between its two higher neighbors, Skrott and Manfjell.

"Are those sheep, do you think?" I asked.

Øystein pulled an old pair of binoculars from his pack and studied the cliffs.

"Yeah, a ewe . . . and two lambs." He steadied his back against a boulder to get a better read on the trio. "And it looks like they're *skorfaste*. If I'm right, it's going to be quite a job getting them out of there."

He stowed the binoculars and we began climbing. Before long, our feet were leaving tracks in pockets of snow that had fallen overnight, keen reminders of why it was crucial to bring the sheep home without delay.

Skorfaste. Not so long ago, I would have had a good laugh on learning that people of a mountainous country five thousand miles from my home had invented a word for "stuck on a mountain ledge." If I'd been told that I would soon be scrabbling up a boulder-strewn peak in that very country to rescue animals in just such a predicament, I'd have shaken my head in disbelief, for I knew almost nothing about Norway and I'd never touched a sheep in my life.

Yet here I was, a town girl from sunny California in the company of a Norwegian herding dog and a fifty-year-old man whose name translates to "Island Rock," setting out on a precarious mission after a September snowfall. And what for? Because I was the sole guardian of these three sheep, along with nearly a hundred others that were still ranging over these wild tracts. During the long winter ahead, the well-being of this flock would rest entirely in my hands.

What I couldn't yet know was that this bond would be mutual. The sheep's lives would depend on me, while I would rely on them for solace and comfort during those dark months when I would find myself *skorfast* in ways I could not have imagined when I'd first set foot in Norway just four months earlier.

1

The Best-Laid Plans

Thursday, May 18, 1972

No one was waiting for me. No Johannes. No horse. No wagon. While the driver retrieved my backpack from the undercarriage of his bus, I scanned the faces of people standing nearby. Some were waiting to board. Others were greeting passengers who had just arrived. No one glanced my way, not even the gray-haired man in rubber boots, the only person in this small crowd who was dressed in the baggy clothes and suspenders I imagined a sheep farmer might wear.

As the bus pulled away, I looked around at what seemed to be the heart of Øystese's modest business district. Behind me a bakery, a bank, and a few other buildings elbowed for space with meadows and woods. Across the street a scattering of rowboats fidgeted in the breeze sweeping over Hardanger Fjord. A wall of snow-covered mountains rose above the far shore, their peaks lost in gray clouds that blanketed the sky.

The bus stop crowd quickly dispersed, leaving me alone on a deserted street. This whole town must be sleeping in, I thought. Recovering, perhaps, from the same kind of revelries I'd witnessed in Oslo the day before, my first day in Norway. There the citizenry had celebrated May 17, *syttende mai*—Constitution Day, the country's biggest holiday—with parades and ceremonies in the morning and a spectacle of public drunkenness in the afternoon.

"Are you Liese?" a voice behind me boomed in Norwegian. I turned, and there was the man in rubber boots staring down at me.

"Johannes?" I asked, peering at him more closely now. He was a big man with bleary eyes, a large belly, and gray stubble shrouding his cheeks. None of this fit my image of the farmer who had hired me to spend the summer working for him.

He started talking in a loud voice, running the words of this foreign language together, pausing only long enough to take in a heavy breath. I understood nothing.

"Are you Johannes?" I asked again, using the formal term for "you" in Danish, a language I'd learned as an exchange student in Denmark two years before.

He may have supplied the answer, but I couldn't pick it out from his volley of words. So I tried something else. "Did you come with the horse?"

In our only phone conversation, I thought I'd understood Johannes to say that he would meet me at this bus stop with a horse and wagon. A poor connection rendered his bad English even worse. But I wanted to believe that he might actually have a horse. And I was charmed to think that my arrival could be special enough that he would put aside a truck or car in favor of a more stately mode of transportation.

"Could you please speak more slowly?" I said, breaking into his cascade of words. "I'm sorry, I can't understand."

During the few hours I'd spent in Oslo, I discovered that Danish was close enough to Norwegian that people could understand me as long as I vocalized all the consonants and vowels that Danes normally swallow. But my strategy wasn't working here. This voluble stranger didn't even acknowledge that I'd opened my mouth.

Suddenly two words popped out of his slurry. "Johannes," I heard him say, and "Voss."

So that was it! I'd switched trains in the town of Voss three hours earlier. Johannes must have driven there to spare me the last legs of my journey, then somehow missed me at the station.

"Is Johannes in Voss?" I asked. "Did he go there to pick me up?"

"Yes, he's in Voss, but . . ." The rest of his answer, like everything else, sailed over my head.

Bewildered, I let my eyes wander away from the heavy face hovering over me. With its old houses, small shops, and vista of mountains, fields, and fjord, Øystese was the prettiest town I'd seen since embarking on a nighttime journey across the southern half of Norway. Filled with excitement and anticipation, I'd spent most of the trip peering through a window at landscapes transformed by the soft glow of a northern night so short at this time of year that it never grew dark.

As soon as we'd left Oslo, evergreen forests began to take over.

They encircled fields, grew to the edges of towns, lined lakes and rivers, and swept like a black carpet to the ridgelines of steep hills that rose up on all sides. This was how I imagined northern Canada or Alaska might look, not the place where I was going to learn about farming. But I loved what I was seeing, and it made me even more eager to reach my destination and start exploring this country.

We'd been gaining elevation for some time when I spotted a white strip alongside the tracks. By the time we leveled out on an immense plateau, rivers had transformed to channels of ice, and snow covered the land. Here forests were gone, replaced by scattered thickets of spindly birches and willows, their branches naked and black.

The sky began to lighten about an hour later. Soon after that, we started our westward descent, leaving winter behind as quickly as it had overtaken us.

At six o'clock in the morning we pulled to a stop in Voss. I lugged my backpack across the platform and stepped into the smallest train I'd ever seen: a single red car that served as engine, coach, and caboose rolled into one. A handful of passengers had already boarded, all of them slumped in their seats, looking as if they'd spent an entire night celebrating the big holiday.

After poking along for an hour through forests and across meadows where the grass was not yet high enough to top a pair of work boots, we reached the end of the line in Granvin, a speck of a village on one of Hardanger Fjord's innermost fingers, nearly a hundred miles from where this expansive body of water meets the North Sea. Here I boarded a bus for the final leg of my long journey. Even then I was unable to close my eyes, for we were following a road that had been blasted into rock walls rising hundreds of feet straight up from the fjord itself. All I could do was stare in amazement at this landscape of waterfalls, cliffs, and mountains while telling myself how lucky I was to have come to such a beautiful and wild place.

Now I was doing my best to understand a man in knee-high rubber boots. The volley of words had not let up. Maybe he thought that if he just carried on long enough, I'd start to understand. The sole message filtering through his monologue was that something was wrong, possibly even terribly wrong.

With a few stilted sentences, I again implored him to slow down. But now, over his shoulder, I could see two other people approaching: a man and a woman hurrying toward us from a nearby building. As they drew close, the woman gave me a little smile.

"Good morning, Magnar," her partner called out. Startled, the man in boots turned. From his stiff nod and the set of his jaw, I could see that these two fellows were not friends.

"And you are Liese?" the woman asked, speaking in Norwegian I could almost understand.

"Yes. Good day. Good day," I replied in Danish, smiling at all three of these mysterious people, at a loss for what else to do.

The woman wore a flowered dress and pumps, her partner a gray suit and hat. City folks, I figured, old enough to be retired—not my missing farmer.

The men started talking, and neither seemed pleased with what the other had to say. As their voices rose, I strained to make sense of their argument. In the end, it was Magnar who backed down. Mumbling something in an angry voice, he turned on his heels and strode away.

The woman smiled at me again. "I'm Mrs. Evanger, and this is my husband, Mr. Evanger," she said, exaggerating each syllable to help me understand her Norwegian. "Please, come with us. We live right there." She gestured in the direction they had come from, toward a yellow, two-story apartment building just down the street.

"Have you had breakfast?" she asked. "You must be hungry."

"Well, I am, but just a little." At the moment, though, food was not my main concern.

"Please, might you know where Johannes Hovland is?" I asked, still hoping that by speaking slowly and formally in Danish I would be understood.

"Yes. He's in Voss, and . . ." Once again the crucial words eluded me.

There seemed no option but to abandon—temporarily, at least—my efforts to make sense of Johannes's travels. Shouldering my backpack, I followed the couple home.

It felt good to be in a house, in a kitchen with a lace doily on the table and hand-embroidered plaques on the walls. Mr. Evanger poured us a cup of coffee while his wife prepared bacon and eggs and set the table with cheeses, cured meats, jams, and slices of chewy-crusted bread.

They spoke slowly as we ate, asking questions about my home in California and the long journey to Norway. After a bit, I put down my fork and tried once again to crack the riddle of Johannes's whereabouts.

"You say that Johannes is in Voss," I began. "But I was just there and didn't see him. Will he come home today?"

"Good heavens, no! He won't be home for a long time. He had a *hjerneslag,* and now he's in the *sjukehus.*"

"*Hjerne . . . slag.*" A combination of the Danish words for "brain" and "blow." If Johannes had suffered a blow to his head, then of course *sjukehus* would be *sygehus* in Danish, literally, "sick house." Suddenly it all made sense. Johannes was ill. He was in Voss. In a hospital.

The more I listened, the easier it was to unravel the rhythms and patterns of the Evangers' speech. They explained that Johannes might not return home for weeks. He lived alone, they said, and there was no one to take over for him.

"Of course," Mr. Evanger hastened to add, "the farm is no place for a girl like you right now. It's too remote, and the work is too difficult."

His declaration crushed me. But of course he was right. Maybe, just maybe, I could handle living all alone in a remote house in a foreign country where I didn't know anyone. But it was ridiculous to think that I could also take care of an entire farm and a big flock of sheep—animals that were as unfamiliar to me as a new language. Having grown up in Mill Valley, a small town just north of San Francisco far from any dairy barns, John Deere tractors, or fields of wheat, I didn't know the first thing about agriculture.

2

A Tangle of Vines

My two sisters and I had owned a pair of horses for nearly five years, which was as close as I'd come to any kind of farming experience. I was ten when the mares were led out of a trailer onto a two-acre, fenced-in hillside across the street from our house, where the three of us would take turns feeding and watering them. From our home in a wooded canyon at the edge of Mill Valley, we could ride for five miles through forests and brushy grasslands to the Pacific coast or just amble along our twisting local roads to visit friends.

The summer job at Johannes's farm was supposed to be my introduction to *real* farming. I was twenty years old and had spent my teens marching for civil rights and against the Vietnam War. My list of favorite books included biographies of famous humanitarians like Albert Schweitzer and Gandhi. In my junior year of high school I decided that the best way to follow in these heroes' footsteps would be to work as an agricultural consultant in developing countries. My inspiration came from Yank Kaseroff, an old friend of my mother's who was a fishing adviser for the United Nations. Every few years when his travels brought him close to San Francisco, he'd drop by and regale us with stories from faraway places like Micronesia, the Philippines, and Ethiopia. His experiences fired my imagination and convinced me to follow his lead—not at sea but on land, working with farmers.

I felt as if I'd hit on the perfect career path that would fulfill everything I could want from a job: my desire to be of service to people in need, my hope to spend most of my work hours outdoors, and my dream of exploring the globe.

Knowing that I had a path forward provided me with a sense of calm during those last restless semesters of high school when the only thing on my mind was finishing up, getting out, and moving on to something new. It was during this time that I decided to apply to a competitive student exchange program in the hope of studying abroad for a year after I graduated.

When I learned I'd been accepted, I listed two developing countries in Latin America as my placement preferences, imagining that living in either one might serve as a steppingstone to my chosen career. Although program leaders made it clear that they endeavored to match each student with a compatible host family, it felt like a cruel joke when I was dispatched to Denmark, a country with one of the highest living standards in the world.

I spent twelve months there, knocking my brains out learning the language, trying to make a few friends, and going to school—called a *gymnasium*—six days a week with a small and insular class of fifteen students in their third and final year majoring in science and math. It wasn't until Christmas that I could speak Danish well enough to comfortably join in conversations with my classmates. On top of that, the grueling Monday through Saturday schedule with its brief recesses left little time for socializing.

Fall weather was cold and wet. Winter was even worse: dark and cloudy, with smatterings of snow that made everything sloppy rather than pretty and white. I stopped smiling in January. Not until mid-April, when sunlight broke through the clouds, did my spirits finally lift. By then, I was feeling at ease with the language, my classmates, and Denmark itself.

When I flew back home in July, I understood that my year abroad had endowed me with many gifts, including command of a rather esoteric language and a sense that I'd emerged as a stronger person from this first difficult period of my life.

Yet shortly after starting college just two months later, I discovered that almost none of my classes held my interest. Perhaps I'd been wrung out by the intense academic year in Denmark. Or the problem may have been that nothing I was studying—not chemistry, biology, anthropology, or political science—seemed to have anything to do with farming techniques in countries half a world away.

I barely made it to summer vacation before dropping out.

Back in Mill Valley, I joined my sixteen-year-old brother, Ben, the last of my four siblings still living at home. Our parents had little money to spare, but they did what they could to support their kids, including keeping the doors of our big old house open to any of us in need of a place to live.

Within a week, I set off to find a job, at the very time when unemployment was at its highest point in a decade. I applied to one position after another and left copies of my short résumé at a dozen restaurants and shops without hearing back from anyone. A month went by before I thought of checking out the Danish bakery in a nearby town. I got there at nine o'clock in the morning, early enough to find the owner drinking his last beer of the day and pulling the last loaf of bread from the oven. We spoke in Danish for half an hour, and right on the spot he offered me a position as a counter girl. Riding back home on my bicycle, I whistled every Danish tune I knew. At long last I had a job.

Later that evening darker thoughts flooded in. From high school, to Denmark, to college dropout, to salesgirl in a bakery. A tangle of vines had been creeping over my path, and I hadn't noticed until now that I'd lost my way.

I lay in bed staring at the ceiling until midnight, wondering how I could get back on the route I'd charted a few years earlier. If I wanted to learn about agriculture in developing countries, I told myself, as soon as I saved up enough money I could just hop on a plane and head to South America or Africa. The problem was, I wasn't brave enough to rely on a plan that involved traipsing into the countryside in a foreign land looking for someone to hire me.

Not for the first time I thought of my two eighteen-year-old friends who had gone to Mississippi in the summer of 1965 to support Black Americans asserting their right to register to vote at a time when all across the South people were being tear-gassed, beaten, and killed for doing the same thing. I was five years younger than the pair, and the thought of facing billy clubs and attack dogs paralyzed me. My hope was that bravery would grow on me, so that by the time I was their age, I'd be just like them, willing to lunge into the unknown, even if it was full of danger. Yet here I was at nineteen no closer to being that kind of person. Flying to a foreign country to look for work wasn't even particularly perilous. So why was I lying on this bed contemplating the ceiling and telling myself that it would be impossible to land a job in a place where I didn't know anyone and didn't speak the language?

For three months I boxed birthday cakes, sold fruit tarts, and scoured my community for people or resources that might help me find a farm job abroad. Finally, at a New Year's Eve party, a friend of my sister's who'd heard of my plight handed me a bundle of papers.

"I found this when I was looking for ways to live in Europe," he explained, pushing the package into my hands. "I didn't apply, so you can just take all this stuff."

A quick scan of the papers made my heart skip a beat. As soon as I got home, I sat down and read every word in the packet. Then I read them all again.

An organization called the Norwegian Committee for International Information and Youth Work (wisely referred to as NIU) was looking for people aged eighteen to thirty years to apply for summer jobs on Norwegian farms, where they would participate "in the daily life and work on the farm like a member of the family." In exchange for working a maximum of forty hours a week, each of these new family members would receive room, board, and a minimum of fifty kroner weekly for pocket money.

Even in 1972, the pay was a pittance. Fifty kroner was about seven dollars, the same amount I was earning for half a day's work at the bakery. Yet at this point, I would have been happy with no salary at all.

I didn't know much about Norway except that it was cold and mountainous. The Danes had taken a patronizing view of their neighbor to the north, speaking of it as a somewhat backward place, definitely poorer than their own socially advanced paradise. I remembered that my host father had once told me that unlike flat little Denmark, where tractors and combines rolled across monotonous fields of barley and wheat, Norway was a wild place, where farmers held on to tradition, cultivating plots of land hewn into mountainsides over the centuries.

I let all this roll around in my head for, oh, about thirty seconds and then decided that Norway would be the perfect place to launch my career in agriculture. If I were lucky, I might land on a farm with a diversity of crops and livestock. I could develop muscles and endurance while learning the first thing or two about agriculture in a place where the language and culture would be somewhat familiar. Armed with formidable newfound skills and strength, not to mention confidence, I might even grow bold enough to search for a more challenging situation in the fall. I spoke Spanish pretty well, so Spain would be a perfect second stop. And from there I could move south to find work in a real developing country somewhere in Africa.

Three days later my application was on its way to Oslo.

"We have now found a place for you on a Norwegian farm this summer," came the NIU's reply in March, just a week after my twentieth birthday. I was to work for Johannes Hovland, a sixty-year-old bachelor who lived on his two-hundred-acre sheep farm three miles outside of Øystese, a town on the western side of the country some fifty miles from Bergen. The farm had an "average" amount of agricultural machinery, and the work would consist of "haymaking, some cooking and housework."

This sounded just about perfect. On a small farm like this, I imagined, I'd be able to help with a greater variety of jobs than a larger farm might offer. I wouldn't even mind doing a little housework and cooking, so long as I wasn't expected to do all of it.

The last bit of information in the maddeningly brief description of Johannes's place sounded almost too good to be true: "The farmer has some beautiful flowers on the farm, also a little lake with water lilies. Many people come to see his botany garden now and then during the summer."

I'd been obsessed with native flora for years. My favorite biology assignment in high school had been to collect and identify thirty local wildflower species. Wherever I went, my eyes were always on the ground searching for interesting plants. With his flock of sheep and our mutual interest in botany, it sounded as if Johannes Hovland and I couldn't be better suited to one another.

3

Awe and Longing

The Evangers looked worried. I was standing at the living room window, my head pounding with lack of sleep and the struggle to comprehend this new, difficult language. From the kitchen Mr. Evanger offered to call the local "work office" to see if they could help.

"Yes, please," I said quietly, touched by his thoughtfulness. "That would be nice of you."

After making the call, he conferred quietly with his wife before turning my way and slowing his speech to a drawl. "He said he has a position for a maid at the hotel and for an assistant in a nursery school. He also knows a farm family on the other side of the fjord who may need some help. I think he's going to give them a call."

"Actually, we know them, too," Mrs. Evanger broke in. They were nice people, she said, and they always needed workers to pick strawberries in June. After that there would be cherries and other berries to harvest in July.

Only then did reality strike home. I was not going to Johannes's farm. No sheep. No botany garden. No intimate learning experience on the small farm I'd been dreaming about for two months. Instead, I'd be spending the summer on my knees picking strawberries. How much would that teach me about farming? I turned aside and squeezed my eyes shut. It wouldn't do to start crying in front of these kind strangers.

Sensing my anguish, Mrs. Evanger suggested from the kitchen that I call the NIU to ask about jobs on other farms. Swiping away tears before they could notice, I went for my address book.

Nora Thiis, NIU's director of farm programs, was distressed to learn of Johannes's illness and my predicament. She promised to do whatever she could to help, but she had only one available position left for the summer. If I wanted to take a train back over the mountains to a large grain farm near Oslo, I could start work right away.

The pounding in my head started up again. Now I had two options, and somehow both seemed like a defeat. The grain farm could surely provide more learning opportunities than a job harvesting fruit. But I didn't want to leave this wild and majestic landscape of mountains and fjords only to work in monotonous fields of barley and wheat.

I must have looked like a zombie as my mind stumbled through this maze, because Mrs. Evanger took a gentle tone when she posed a question.

"Liese, dear, would you like to visit Johannes's farm?"

Our three-mile drive followed a well-maintained dirt road that wound uphill through forests of birch and spruce before crossing an expanse of hilly fields surrounding a small cluster of farmsteads. After that, it narrowed to a single lane studded with potholes and rocks. Slowing to a crawl, Mr. Evanger navigated around a couple of bends to the crest of a small hill.

"Here they are," he announced, pulling to a stop in front of a closed gate. "The three farms of Hovland. That's Johannes's, the farthest in."

Strung out ahead of us lay three clusters of old buildings, some painted, others weathered and gray. All of them built atop rock foundations and roofed with stone shingles and slabs of rock.

"Hovland," Mr. Evanger had called this place. It took me a moment to understand that he was not just saying Johannes's last name but that Hovland must be the name of these three farms, as well. The word suddenly took on new meaning. It sounded old and strange but seemed to fit the panorama ahead of us, where scores of sheep and lambs ranged over green hills surrounding each farmstead. A massive mountain with two rounded peaks rose into the clouds behind the place that Mr. Evanger had named as Johannes's. Situated at the very end of our long, winding path from Øystese, his farm looked to be the last outpost at the edge of a mountain wilderness.

I stopped staring and jumped out to open the gate, a rickety affair of poles and wire fencing. A couple hundred yards farther on, we stopped at a second gate, somewhat shakier than the first. The third,

Johannes's, was by far the worst, barely holding together as I dragged it open and shut. We continued another two hundred yards and pulled to a stop where the road ended at the foot of a three-story house painted red and white. On our right, a series of terraces flowed downhill into a long flat meadow.

"Do you know about Johannes's garden?" Mrs. Evanger asked. "People come from as far away as Bergen to see it."

They led me to the garden's far end, where three little ponds were tucked among bushes and vines that were just beginning to leaf out. I wanted to dip down for a closer look at all of these wonders—terraces, ponds, new spring growth—but Mr. Evanger was already beckoning us as he veered toward the barn.

I stared up at the long, three-story building towering over us. Every part of it appeared ancient and gray, from its steep-pitched roof decked with jagged slabs of slate the size of table tops, to the middle story's dilapidated wooden siding, to the ground floor's wall of enormous rough-hewn rocks. What kind of machinery, I wondered—or what gang of giants—could have lifted all of these slabs and stones into place so long ago?

We passed through a portal in the massive rock wall, and entered a warren of ramshackle pens and stalls. Cramped, cold, and dark, the place felt like a cave. I detected a musty odor and then the familiar scent of horse manure. There were other smells, too, all foreign—some pleasing, some not so.

A burly ram reared up from his pen for a better look. Three ewes huddled together at the far end of another pen holding a wary eye on us. The dirt floor under this trio was elevated above our concrete walkway. And something about the dirt seemed odd, too. I bent down to examine it.

"That's manure they're standing on," Mr. Evanger said. "The animals spend all winter here, so it just keeps building up."

I jerked away and could feel my face burn. What an idiot I was to put my nose into a bed of manure in front of these people. "Oh, of course," I said feebly, hoping they wouldn't sense my embarrassment.

Mr. Evanger led us around a partition into a much larger chamber, this one even darker than the first. Now a chorus of nickering, lowing, and an odd mewling sound filled the air. I ran ahead, skirted a couple of empty pens, and stopped short.

Johannes did have a horse.

A beautiful dun mare, small and sturdy with ears pricked forward, stood in a stall craning her head in our direction. I flew down the walkway and stroked her soft muzzle. Just across from her, two cows loomed up from the shadows—one red, one black—tethered in adjacent stalls that were not much wider than the animals themselves. At the end of this row, a small red calf was emitting a warble of whimpers and grunts as he shoved his head through the rails of his pen, straining to catch a glimpse of us. I went to the little animal and scratched him around his ears and cheeks. He responded with such fervor I thought my heart would break. He was only a baby, yet penned up in complete isolation.

"A neighbor must be taking care of the animals," Mr. Evanger said, in his slow-down-for-Liese mode. "They have water . . . ," he observed, pointing to a full bucket in the mare's stall, "and they don't seem to be hungry."

"They must be taking care of milking, too," his wife added.

"Milk?" I asked stupidly. "There's milk?"

"Of course, dear," Mrs. Evanger said with a tolerant smile. "What do you think these are?"

I followed her gaze back to the cows. Only now did I see that the red one had a round, full udder with protruding pink teats. I felt my face go crimson. How could I have missed this? And how could I have looked at this animal and not immediately thought about milk? The black cow was different, though. Instead of an udder, there was something that looked like a small, furry animal hanging between its rear legs. I couldn't stand the thought of sounding even more foolish than I already felt, so for once I didn't ask any questions.

Suddenly I was overcome by the feeling that nothing was making sense. Why was I standing in this barn stroking a calf, letting a mare nibble my hand with her soft lips, and clapping these cows on their rumps, when tomorrow or the next day I'd be working in a strawberry patch or sitting on a train headed back to Oslo to spend the summer on a grain farm? A wave of sadness came over me as I took one more look around before following Mr. and Mrs. Evanger to the door.

Daylight came as a sudden reshuffling of the senses from the murky cavern into the pure light and fresh air of early spring. Right from the doorway I could take in a magnificent view of ridges, hills, meadows, and forests sweeping back to that long line of snow-covered mountains rising from the fjord's far shore miles away.

Standing there amid ancient rock walls in this ageless landscape, I felt as if I'd fallen back in time. How old could this farm be? One hundred years? Two? Maybe I was simply exhausted from lack of sleep, but I was struck by an overwhelming mixture of awe and longing as it dawned on me that I'd never been in a place more beautiful than this.

I sat in the back seat fighting to stay awake as we drove down the hill to Øystese. Something about the farm was nagging at me. But what was it?

The Evangers had been speaking quietly together in the front, when Mrs. Evanger turned to me with an invitation.

"Of course you'll stay with us until everything gets straightened out. We have plenty of room and we'd love to have you."

The offer came as such a relief that my voice faltered as I thanked them.

"Now, now, dear, don't you worry," she said in a comforting tone. "Everything's going to be fine. You'll love living with our friends on the other side of the fjord. And their farm is much more modern than Hovland, so you can learn a lot there, too."

That was it! Her friends' farm was "modern."

"I didn't see a tractor at Johannes's farm," I said. "Does he have one?"

Mr. Evanger started chuckling. His wife said something I didn't understand and gave him a sideways jab of her elbow.

"Good gracious, no," Mr. Evanger said, composing himself. "Those old mountain farms up there at Hovland, there's not a tractor on any of them. And for that matter, you won't find a car up there, either."

Taking a deep breath, I asked, "So, then, does Johannes use the horse for work?"

"That he does, young lady," Mr. Evanger answered. "That is exactly what he does."

At five o'clock, when I finally couldn't hold my eyes open any longer, Mrs. Evanger led me upstairs to a bedroom.

"Take a nap if you like," she said, patting the pillow of a narrow wooden bed. "Or just sit here and relax. Supper will be ready at seven."

I lay down for the first time in three days and slept for sixteen hours.

In the morning, Mrs. Evanger had a message for me. While I was sleeping, her husband's work had taken him to Voss, where he'd slipped into the hospital after hours to see his old friend. Johannes had told him that he wanted to meet me, Mrs. Evanger said. If I wanted to, I could catch a ride to the hospital with Johannes's sister and brother-in-law, who would be driving there this evening.

4

Johannes

Johannes Hovland lay propped up in bed. His left arm hung slack and the left side of his mouth remained rigid when he greeted us. By now, I'd understood that he hadn't suffered a blow to the head but rather a stroke in his brain's right hemisphere that had ravaged his left side. As if compensating for his foundered half, he shook my hand with a powerful grip.

"I'm sorry I wasn't at the bus stop to meet you," he said in an English that was so slurred and accented I could barely make sense of it. "My plan was to fetch you with the horse. But, you see," he said, sweeping his good hand over his limp arm, "it was not to be."

He was a lean man with broad cheekbones, a sharp nose, and gray hair styled in a way that reminded me of American forces in World War II: combed straight back from his forehead and cut short around the ears. I was most struck by his steel-gray eyes, which shone with an intensity that belied his condition. Even as he lay in bed, semi-paralyzed and draped in a gown, his presence charged the room.

In my budding Danish-Norwegian, I reassured him that the Evangers had been taking good care of me. When I mentioned that they'd taken me to the farm, he asked what I thought of his garden.

As I fished about for a response, his sister and brother-in-law, Ingebjørg and Ola Mæland, took over the conversation. The three of them spoke for a long time, moving from one topic to another, as far as I could tell. Eventually I recognized that Ingebjørg was trying to convince Johannes of something and that the discussion had turned into an argument.

"Enough!" Johannes exclaimed without warning. Turning from his sister, he trained his eyes on me.

"Neighbors have been caring for my animals this week. But they can't do this much longer." He was speaking slowly, working around the frozen portion of his face. "If I can't find someone to help, I'll have to send my animals to slaughter." He paused again, struggling for words. "And that will be the end of the farm."

The room fell quiet. In our silence, it dawned on me that nothing I'd seen or heard over the past thirty hours had penetrated my youthful skull. How could I have been so obsessed with my own problems without giving a thought to Johannes's? While I was weighing whether to spend the summer harvesting fruit or working on a grain farm, this farmer was lying in a hospital bed, teetering on the edge of disaster.

Now he was clenching his jaw, grappling in vain to contain his tears. I felt my eyes fill up, too. Ingebjørg reached out a hand to her brother, but he waved her away and turned back to me, straightening his shoulders and hardening his features.

"They tell me I'll be in the hospital for a month," he said. "Maybe a little longer. Someone has to care for my place during these weeks. I have no one to ask but you. Would you be willing to do this . . . stay at my farm until I come home?"

His words hit me like a shock wave. As the enormity of his plea sank in, my mind raced in a dozen directions. I'd never been able to turn down anyone who asked for help. But living alone on a far-removed farm while caring for a huge flock of sheep was magnitudes greater than any help I'd ever been asked to give.

"Please," he said, using that word for the first time. "If no one is there to keep watch over the animals, anything could happen."

He was staring at me with such intensity I had to turn aside to piece my thoughts together. How could I run his farm when I had no idea how to do it? There were cows to milk and a little calf to take care of, sheep in the barn, and all those ewes and lambs outside. The thought of being responsible for the welfare of this vast menagerie terrified me.

"You would just be a caretaker for the house and animals until I get back," Johannes went on, sounding even more desperate. "There's really no work to do until haying starts in July."

Now I remembered the farmer's draft horse—how she had nickered to me and let me stroke her muzzle. Here was one creature, at least, that I *did* know something about. Then I called to mind the moment I'd walked out of the barn and had been overcome by the beauty of Johannes's ancient buildings and their magnificent surroundings. The specter of that amazing place falling to ruin sent a chill through my core. If by living there for a month, I might truly make a difference, how could I turn down this man's anguished plea for help?

Three pairs of eyes were fixed on me as I took a deep breath and managed to stutter, "Y-yes. I . . . I'll do it!"

"Thank you," Johannes said softly after a long moment of silence. "Thank you."

Now the life started to return to his eyes as he began to fill my head with information. The most important job these coming weeks, he said, was to keep weeds out of the garden. As to the animals, the sheep that he'd already let loose in the fields could take care of themselves, and his neighbors could show me how to milk the cow and feed the other creatures still confined to the barn. "But don't let them touch the dog," he said sharply.

"Dog?" I asked in astonishment. "You have a dog?"

Her name is Bella, he told me. She was too young to be fully trained, so I would have to make her understand that I was her only master, and that meant not letting anyone else get close to her.

He was about to say more when a nurse appeared in the doorway to announce that our visit was too long; her patient needed to rest.

"I'm fine!" Johannes snapped. "Leave us be!"

This sudden change in temper astonished me. I snuck a peek at Ingebjørg; her face was red with embarrassment.

"Five minutes, no more," the nurse ordered. "Visiting hours ended ten minutes ago."

Johannes used our remaining time to pack me with information about the garden. By the time he finished, my list of tasks seemed surprisingly long but not particularly difficult. In fact, most of the jobs sounded fun.

To my relief, he also brought up the subject I'd been too timid to raise: He would pay me one hundred kroner a week, he said, double the NIU's minimum. More important, because the terms of my employment included room and board, I could use his account at a store in town to pay for groceries. I could even order them over the phone on Thursdays for delivery to the farm on Fridays.

Now he was ready to issue a final set of directives.

"You will be my agent, yes, my agent at Hovland. I give you *fullmakt* to run the farm as you will. If you need help, ask Magnar. Don't trust anyone else. And don't let anyone come with alcohol to the farm. There will be no alcohol there."

His decree shot through me like electricity, for not until he spoke these words did I truly grasp the significance of what was transpiring in this hospital room. *Fullmakt,* he'd said. "Full authority." An hour earlier I'd been prepared to cross the fjord to pick strawberries. Now I had full authority over a Norwegian mountain farm.

I was scared, excited, and ready.

I spent the night at Ingebjørg and Ola's house on the fjord about half a mile from Øystese. In the morning, Saturday, they drove me to Johannes's grocery store, where they introduced me to a man who explained how to call in my shopping list on Thursdays. We loaded two boxes with a week's worth of provisions and headed up the long, twisting road.

A hundred yards past Hovland's second gate, Ola pulled to a stop to talk with two boys sitting with their dog on the rock stairway of an old farmhouse: my closest neighbors, I thought to myself.

The older boy did most of the talking. He was in constant motion, asking questions, gesturing, laughing. He looked to be about fifteen and had dark hair that flopped into his brown eyes at every move. The younger boy, a brother, I assumed, had shy blue eyes, a hesitant smile, and blond hair nearly to his shoulders.

As we were about to leave, the dark-haired boy—talking so rapidly that I barely caught a word—picked up his dog and deposited it onto the car's back seat. She was a beautiful animal, small and husky-like with cream-colored hair, smart eyes, and a ready air. It was not until I got into the car myself and the boys were waving goodbye that I realized with a start that this was Bella, Johannes's dog, and that my responsibilities as farmer had begun.

5

Hovland

The Norwegian custom of introductions is to shake hands, say "good day," and slur your full name in a rapid murmur, about like the sound of water falling over rocks. But the visitor with a bucket in her hand who knocked on the front door early that first evening was an exception.

"Solveig Hovland," she said forcefully, crushing my fingers in her grip. As we stood in the entryway, she didn't give me a chance to ask how she might be related to Johannes, for she started by asking questions, then informing me that she was the person who had been caring for the farm's livestock over the past six days. And while she seemed relieved to have a replacement, she was clearly not going to gamble the welfare of the animals on a greenhorn like me.

"Why don't you put on Johannes's overalls," she suggested, plucking a limp mass of denim from a hook on the wall. "They're big, but you can roll up the cuffs."

The thought of wearing Johannes's clothes made me uneasy. I was in his house, but that didn't give me license to use his personal items. Yet here was a no-nonsense woman with outstretched arm proffering his overalls, leaving me no time to fret.

The old suit slipped easily over my clothes, and, except for being a bit too long, it fit almost perfectly. It surprised me to think that Johannes might not be more than a couple of inches taller than my own five foot four.

"If those are yours, put them on," my new teacher said, pointing to a pair of used rubber boots that Mrs. Evanger had given me as a going-away present.

Solveig was wearing her own work outfit: a beige kerchief, well-worn sneakers, baggy, hand-knit wool socks, and a frayed smock of blue twill that contoured around a large bosom and waist. She might be sixty years old, I guessed, about the same age as Johannes. Her face was broad boned and plain, framed by gray hair still tinged with brown that fell in loose curls around her neck.

As we made our way to the barn, I saw that she walked with a heavy gait, swaying a bit with each step in favor of her left leg. She told me that she lived with two of her brothers on the first of Hovland's three farms. They had a flock of thirty ewes, she said, and a herd of six cows, which the three of them milked by hand.

At the barn door, she sang out a greeting to the animals scattered about in dark stalls and pens. "Hello, hello, good friends! We're here to feed you. How are you today, dear ones?" A chorus of bleats, whinnies, and lows murmured an expectant reply to this call: a mysterious, soothing, and welcoming song, unlike anything I'd heard before.

"First we give them their hay," Solveig said. "It's easier to do the other chores after they start eating."

She was speaking in strong dialect, yet I could understand at least half of what she said, for her voice was bold and strong and she was good at using hand gestures to get her messages across.

Now she led me up a steep ladder-like stairway built against the back wall. As I climbed into the barn's hayloft, I felt like I'd entered another world. Unlike the gloom below, here it was bright and airy, with daylight squeezing through long gaps in weathered walls. A framework of hand-hewn timbers supported this wide, open space, which rose two stories high and extended from one end of the building to the other. Enraptured, I strode forward.

"Stop!" Solveig barked with such urgency that I froze with one foot in the air. "Look there," she called out, pointing to a spot on the floor ahead of me. "You'll fall right through that hole and break half the bones in your body. There's another rotten board just beyond it and even more over there, in the corner."

Most of the floor was strewn with hay, and at first I couldn't see what she was talking about. I looked back at her, and she pointed again. "A yard ahead of you." Now I found them. Fragments of holes and cracks in the wood almost hidden beneath the hay. In the far left corner there were no planks at all, merely a patchwork of sticks and poles layered so haphazardly atop the joists that only a ghost could safely tread over them. If I'd kept walking my straight path, I would have fallen through, landing on the cement floor below or, even worse, onto the railing of a pen or the side of a stall.

Terrified, I crept back to Solveig, retracing my steps as best I could, expecting at any moment to fall into a concealed chasm beneath my feet. These barn chores that Johannes had said would be easy all of a sudden felt like a minefield.

While she used a pitchfork to throw hay down the steps to the ground floor below, I inched my way over the loft. The route I chose proved sound, and I gathered a large armload of fine, sweet-smelling fodder. As I turned back, some marks on a pillar caught my eye. Peering closer, I could make out what looked like dates and initials—ancient graffiti chiseled into the timber in a fine old script. One number stood out from the others.

"Do you know what this number means, 1799?" I called back over my shoulder.

"That's the year the barn was built," she said. "But back then it was on the hill between you and the neighbor. Seventy, maybe eighty, years ago they had to move it."

I stared at her in astonishment.

"Don't look so surprised!" she laughed. "Our Hovland men have always been good carpenters."

We climbed back down the stairs, where my teacher explained how much hay to throw into each manger, measured by the armload. She took a moment to talk with every occupant, rubbing the three ewes around their ears, wrestling a bit with the ram as he swung his head back and forth, and stroking the horse's neck. With the sheep and cows she spoke in a high soothing voice, as if they were small children. She was more conversational with Begonia, Johannes's mare, addressing her as an old intimate. "Do you want to go outside now? Yes, I'm sure you do," she murmured. "You've been in the barn too long now, dear one."

Some of the animals also needed a ration of concentrated feed, she told me, pointing to a mixture of grain and minerals in a fifty-kilo sack labeled *kraftfôr*—"energy fodder"—sitting by the door.

"The cow is milking, so she gets the most," Solveig said, using a large tin can to scoop grain into a plastic bucket. "These three ewes will be lambing any day now, so they get some, too. The calf is too young to get anything but milk."

The cow that was lucky enough to receive two cans of coveted feed was the red one, the one with a big udder. She stood in a narrow stall near the barn's far wall, tethered on a rope so short she could move only a couple of paces forward or backward. Her young bull calf was penned up in a small enclosure just out of her sight. He seemed as desperate for attention now as he'd been when I first met him two days earlier. The full weight of his predicament hadn't dawned on me then. As I looked at him now I saw that he was a mere babe, locked up all alone, so close to his mother that he could smell and hear her but couldn't touch or even see her. He pushed toward me as I rubbed his head and talked to him in friendly tones. Later, after my neighbor had returned to her farm, I would come back to the barn and go into his pen to give him a good rubbing all over his gangly little body.

Now I stepped back to Solveig, who was standing by the cows.

"Why do they look so different?" I asked, pointing back and forth between the furry pouch hanging between the black cow's hind legs and her red companion's distended udder.

"Because this one is not a cow," Solveig answered matter-of-factly, tapping the black bovine's rump.

I was puzzled. "What is it then?" I asked, examining the four-legged, cloven-hoofed animal.

"Why can't you see, girl? It's a *kvige.*"

"A what? What's that?"

She heaved a sigh, and in the squint of her eye I could see that she was just beginning to grasp the enormousness of the effort it would require to school me.

"She hasn't had her first calf," she said slowly, pausing between each word to make sure I understood. "When she does, she will become a cow. She's not milking and not pregnant, either. So for now she gets just hay and water."

By the time I'd processed this statement—trying to understand why a cow was not a cow until it had borne a calf—Solveig had already moved on to Begonia, telling me that I was to give her an allotment of the energy fodder only on days when she was put to work.

While the animals ate their supper, we took water buckets from their pens and filled them at a tap just inside the door. After that, it was time to clean up. Solveig grabbed two shovels and led me to the end of the barn just beyond the calf's pen.

"Here's what we do with *møkk,*" she said, wresting a grimy wooden panel from the wall.

This new term was easy to decipher; it sounded just like "muck."

I peered through the narrow hatch and stifled a gasp, for it opened onto the peak of a mountain of manure rising from the floor of a deep, dark, and extremely grimy cavern. The massive stack was at least eight feet high and much wider at its base.

"Yes, you can gasp alright," Solveig said with a cackle. "It's been a long time since Johannes emptied his manure cellar."

She showed me how to scoop and scrape the bovines' runny piles and Begonia's firmer clods into a channel in the concrete floor, push all of it to the wall, and pitch it through the hatch, raising the mountain of manure higher still.

Now only one chore remained.

"Get some warm water and a rag from the house," Solveig commanded. "It's time to milk."

I ran to the kitchen and returned with a washcloth and bucket. Solveig plopped another bucket bottom side up at the red cow's right flank and sat down heavily. "First you have to rinse off her udder," she instructed. "You don't want to tickle her, so be firm. Rub the udder all over. Here, give it a try."

We traded places, and as I ran the cloth over four wrinkled pink teats, they slowly stiffened and elongated like the fingers of a surgeon's glove filling with water.

"There now," Solveig said, "she likes this, you see. She's letting her milk down."

"Do all cows have four . . . four of these things?" I asked, not sure that I knew the word for "teats." I was thinking of those drawings I'd made of cows when I was a kid, sketches that depicted udders bristling with enough nipples to feed a small herd of calves.

Instantly, I realized that this was probably the most idiotic question Solveig had ever been asked. Maybe she thought I was kidding, for she didn't bother to respond.

Now we traded places again. She sat down sideways to the animal. Facing its rear, she leaned her right shoulder into its flank while holding the milk bucket tightly between her knees. She smoothed her hand reassuringly over the udder once more, then grasped the two front teats and began milking with a rhythmic one-two, one-two motion. Slim white streams squirted into the metal bucket, their volume increasing with each stroke of Solveig's strong fingers. After a bit she got up and motioned for me to take over.

It looked easy enough, almost as if the milk just needed a little boost to get flowing on its own. Moving into position, I was suddenly aware that I was sitting beneath a huge animal, my head just inches from powerful legs and heavy cloven hooves.

I wrapped my fingers around the two front teats and squeezed one, then the other, in what I thought was a fine imitation of my instructor's performance.

"No, no!" Solveig scolded. "Don't *pull* on the poor animal. Use your hands, not your arms!" She showed me that she first clenched her thumb and index finger at the top of the teat, then carried through from finger to finger in a downward, wavelike motion.

I tried again, only to feel the cow's teats go slack beneath my hands. The big creature swung her head around, a few strands of hay poking from the corners of her mouth, her placid brown eyes sizing me up. I clapped her flank and spoke to her in English, murmuring reassurance and offering friendship. When she turned back to her manger and resumed feeding as calm as could be, I knew we were a team.

Soon the little squirts of milk I was extracting filled the pail nearly a half inch deep. I looked up at my mentor with a victorious smile, and in that blink of an eye, my new friend shot a rear hoof into my knee with such force the bucket flew into space. Solveig jostled me aside, and—as I grasped my leg and choked back groans—succeeded in cajoling the aggrieved animal into letting her milk down once again.

From the moment the little red calf had heard the first sounds of milking, he'd begun to cry for his dinner, squawking, grunting, and dancing about in his pen. Soon Solveig's bucket held a few quarts of frothing white liquid, which she ordered me to transfer into another bucket for the hungry baby. When I held this out to him, he thrust his head through the rails and drove his nose into his meal, snorting, lapping, and sucking it up with the fury of a pack of dogs fighting over a scrap of meat.

When the cow's udder was empty, Solveig took me back to the kitchen and showed me how to run our full bucket of milk through a cloth filter. As I examined the brownish film of manure and cow hair captured in the cloth, I realized that I'd been ignoring the undeniable fact that Solveig and I had just extracted milk from a less than clean udder into an open bucket in an ancient and grimy barn.

"This milk . . . ," I asked, searching for the right words, "uh, do people drink it?"

My neighbor's eyes clouded as she puzzled over this strange question. In a flash, she brightened up. Pulling a glass from a cupboard, she dipped it into the white liquid and handed it to me.

"Well, yes, there are some people who like it fine when it's warm like this. So you can decide for yourself what you think."

Doomed by my own stupidity, I took a sip—and felt a warm, thick liquid run down my throat.

"I think I don't much like it this way," I whispered, putting the glass down. At least the filter had done its job; I hadn't detected any nubbins of barn debris in my modest sample.

Busy with sloshing a couple quarts of milk into a smaller pail, Solveig didn't notice my discomfort. Now she grabbed the larger bucket, handed me the pail, and motioned for me to follow her outside. We descended the rock stairway alongside the house to reach the cellar door, which was set in the building's thick stone foundation directly below the kitchen windows.

Built into the hillside, this cave-like room turned the southern portion of Johannes's two-story house into a three-story building. A single bulb mounted in the ceiling threw just enough light for us to get around.

To our right and left, dusty floor-to-ceiling shelves were crowded with a miscellany of buckets, baskets, used machine parts, and cans of bent nails and rusty hardware. Potatoes sporting ghostly white sprouts filled two large wooden bins on the floor. Wizened apples filled a third.

"These are from Johannes's trees," Solveig offered, "and the potatoes are from Soldal."

I knew this name. In the morning, when Ola was driving through the cluster of houses and barns about half a mile down the road from Johannes's, Ingebjørg told me that the place was called Soldal, "Sun Valley." It was a pretty name and easy to remember.

She plucked a tuber from the bin and showed me how to rub off its long sprouts, advising that this would help keep the spuds edible for another couple of months. I also needed to sort through the apples at least once a week, she said, and discard any that had begun to rot.

Just ahead, something else stopped me short: a pair of plastic washtubs packed with fleshy, shapeless objects suspended in what looked like blood-tinged water. Whether it was horror or anxiety Solveig read into my expression, she rolled her eyes and shook her head before offering yet another explanation to this backward girl from California.

"That's the pig Johannes bought. It needs to stay in the brine a while longer before you can smoke it. Now, get over here, or we'll never be finished."

I glanced back into the brew and made out what looked like a slab of severed leg so humanlike it made me queasy. This was a ham, I realized. The leg of a pig. A shiver ran down my spine, for suddenly another term, "leg of lamb," seemed very real. Was this where some of those cute little animals grazing in the fields were going to end up?

The cellar was so cluttered and poorly lit that only now could I see that its rear wall had been excavated into bedrock. When I caught up to Solveig, she was standing in front of a little cavern hollowed into the rock wall some four feet off the floor. It looked to be a natural opening, large enough for a bear to curl up in. But rather than a bear, it held a small pool about two feet deep with water so clear that every fissure and jag in its stony bed was as sharp as a reflection in a polished mirror. I stuck in a finger; the water was cold as ice.

"Hold this steady while I get it adjusted," Solveig said impatiently as she set my milk pail into this amazing little pool. I stood dumbly by as she fiddled with one of several wires and hooks hanging from the grotto's ceiling. "There now," she said after looping a hook around the bucket handle. "Your milk will be cold in no time at all."

And then I understood. This wellspring hidden beneath Johannes's house was not a sacred shrine or a watering hole for local spirits and trolls: it was a refrigerator. We needed to chill the milk, and this was how to do it. Judging by the number of wires hanging above the fount and the small stack of buckets sitting beside it, I figured I'd be using the pool for any other food that needed cooling, as well.

Before leaving, Solveig let me know that she would be coming twice a day to help with milking for as long as necessary. But she wanted me to feed and water the animals on my own, then see how far along I could get with milking before she arrived and finished up. In exchange, she would take a few gallons of milk home each day to be sent to the dairy along with her own herd's output.

Back in the kitchen, I put a few potatoes on the stove to boil. This long and narrow room with a vinyl floor and plaster walls painted light green was centered at the very heart of Johannes's house. Earlier in the day, I'd discovered that all but one of the building's modern conveniences were clustered along the counter here: Johannes's compact electric stove; a two-gallon electric water heater mounted above a stainless steel double sink; and a short bank of cabinets and drawers.

The room's heat source—a black cast-iron woodstove—stood against the wall opposite the counter, right next to a dining table and three chairs, all made of plain, unfinished wood. Now I noticed that Johannes had mounted two framed prints of mountain landscapes on the wall above the dining set and a calendar with photos of European cities and mountains on the opposite wall.

The single indulgence in this utilitarian space was a makeshift sofa fashioned from a bed frame and a lumpy mattress wrapped in dirty red fabric. Johannes had positioned this well-worn berth beneath the kitchen's five narrow windows, which were set into a unique feature of the house: a three-story addition that had been pushed out from the middle of the building's long south wall. These windows—three facing south and one each facing west and east—served him both as daybed and command post, I imagined, for they provided a view over his entire garden, nearly half his farm, the wide vista beyond, and even a small sliver of the fjord itself.

The only other modern devices I'd discovered in the house were dim ceiling lights in each room and a telephone in the anteroom: the old-fashioned sort with a handle you had to crank to ring up an operator. Ingebjørg and Ola had both stressed that calls were very expensive, even to neighbors. So I knew to keep my hands off the instrument.

I tossed some slices of rutabaga and a piece of sausage into the pot. As I waited for the water to return to a boil, it hit me that for the first time in my life I would be living alone. And I was already enjoying it.

After dinner, Bella shadowed me as I walked back and forth checking out the seven small bedrooms upstairs. I chose a narrow chamber directly above the kitchen, because it had the same command post of windows. This higher vantage point encompassed an even greater view, including a little bit larger segment of the fjord. The room was furnished with two small beds lined up against the east wall and a woodstove and homemade chest of drawers along the west. I liked this simplicity and the light color and smooth finish of the room's beautiful hand-planed pine boards. But without a fire, my new sleeping quarters were cold, and my three windows were too small to let in enough light to cheer things up.

I opted for the bed farthest from the window because it was not quite as hard as the other. Its mattress—nestled in a wood perimeter that dug into the back of my thighs when I sat down to take off my socks—felt as if it was stuffed with straw. Both beds had been carefully made up with clean, well-used linens and coarse wool blankets encased in comforter covers.

"Come here, Bella," I called to the little dog, who had been watching me with anxious eyes. "Here, you can sleep here," I said, patting a small braided rug I'd brought from another room. Looking relieved, she circled her new bed three times and lay down. I lay down, too, and pulled the covers up to my chin.

Over the next few days I started to establish a routine. Rise at six thirty. Feed and water the animals in the barn. Start milking until Solveig came to relieve me. Feed the calf. Process the milk. Pour a share for Solveig. Suspend my share in the cellar's icy pool. Wash the cloth filter meticulously in hot water in the kitchen sink. Hang it to dry.

My last chore before breakfast took place in the woodshed, just beyond the house. There I split enough wood for my daily fire, a couple of armloads at least. Ola had shown me how to use Johannes's axe to cleave large rounds of hardwood into pieces small enough to fit into the firebox. He also demonstrated the remarkable property of birch bark. It ignited so easily and burned so hot that I needed only a single strip of bark, a few pieces of kindling, and a match to start the morning's fire.

With the blaze coming to life, it was time for a quick breakfast—usually oatmeal with chilled farm milk—before I had to go back to the barn to lead the two bovines out to pasture.

In the evening, I repeated these tasks. Morning chores took about two hours, evening chores a little less. As for the rest of the day, I decided to spend mornings doing garden work and afternoons cleaning out the barn and straightening things up in the outbuildings.

The place was a mess. Most of the pens' wooden railings were worn thin. Many were cracked, while others were broken all the way through. Gates were falling off their rope and wire hinges. Dirt and manure covered everything. The barn roof leaked, and the barn doors were barely holding together. What's more, I couldn't find a single tool in good working condition anywhere on the farm, not even a hammer.

In contrast to the disrepair of the outbuildings, Johannes's garden was like an only child lavished with attention. The apple of his eye, the jewel of Hovland, and the pride of Øystese, the garden had a reputation that extended throughout Hardanger all the way to the big city of Bergen more than two hours away. Johannes had built its rock-walled terraces, stairways, and ponds himself, pouring the concrete and setting each stone by hand, expanding the beds over the decades until they stretched nearly 150 feet along the hillside and 70 to 80 feet downhill toward the hay meadow.

Neighbors told me that Johannes spent his evenings combing through garden catalogs and botanical literature from around the world to find plants that might survive and thrive in a western Norwegian mountain climate. His collection now harbored more than 250 species of ferns, they said, and hundreds of species of alpine plants and water lilies, most of them only just beginning to emerge from winter dormancy.

Johannes had declared in the hospital that if the weeds were not pulled, the garden would be ruined. After spending four hours battling a wall-to-wall carpet of seedlings on my first morning of weeding, I understood what he was talking about. At this rate, it would take weeks to get through all the beds. Eventually I would learn that early in the previous winter, a midday weather report called for the temperature to plummet to well below freezing by midnight. Normally, a protective layer of snow would have been blanketing Johannes's garden, but at the time, the ground was still bare. Hearing the report, Johannes rushed outside and spent hours carrying loads of hay from barn to beds, spreading it in a thick layer over his botanical collection. The hay saved the plants, but it was also laden with millions of seeds, which were now happily germinating in a thick layer over every square inch of garden soil.

Every day for the next several weeks, I spent hours hunched down on rocks reaching far into flower beds to pluck out grass and other suspected weeds, blade by blade, plant by plant—while day after day, the rain poured down. Although the cascades took hours to penetrate my heavy-duty rain clothes, by the time they did, my fingers were so cold and numb that I had to run inside to get warmed up.

The job wracked me with indecision. Which plants were weeds and which were Johannes's beloved possessions? What should I do about that curled fern head just poking its way through the soil? Was it an endangered species from Australia or the ubiquitous Norwegian bracken fern? And how could I know whether that tiny trifoliate sprout was a transplant from the Himalayas or merely a common meadow plant?

At the end of the first week of this torture, just when I felt I was making a dent in the invading horde, I was crushed to discover a fresh blanket of seedlings and shoots sprouting up in the patch I'd cleared on my first day on the job. It looked as if this work was never going to end.

6

Wine and Stew

I first met Torkel Hovland when Bella and I took a walk down the dirt road toward Soldal just days after I arrived. His house was only six hundred feet in a straight line from Johannes's, but to get there, we had to swing around Johannes's long meadow and a grassy hill arising from its far side. This strange, undulating mound separated the two farms and was just high enough to block my view of both the house and the outbuildings of my closest neighbor, even from the elevated lookout of my bedroom windows.

I'd been warned that dogs were not allowed to run loose when animals were on pasture, so Bella kept pace at the end of a rope I'd fashioned into a collar and leash. Sheep grazing on both sides of the fence eyed us warily as I contended with Johannes's decrepit gate, and it was only after I'd closed it behind us that I noticed that, in contrast to my boss's grimy, long-fleeced ewes, my neighbor's animals were short-haired, white, and clean. Not only that, but these neighboring sheep seemed far less fearful of Bella and me than those on my side of the fence, which had the annoying habit of hurtling away whenever I made so bold as to come within twenty or thirty paces of them.

Torkel's barn was the first building to come into view as we rounded the hill. Built alongside the road, it was quite a bit smaller than Johannes's, was somewhat more weatherworn, and had a steep roof densely tiled with hundreds of huge irregularly shaped stone slabs. As I drew closer, I saw that it stood alone on the right side of the road. On the left, I counted one house and four smaller buildings.

"Good morning!" a voice called out, so close by that I had to stifle a scream.

I whipped around and saw a man sitting on the same wide stone stairway where the two boys had transferred Bella into my hands several days earlier.

"You must be Liese! I'm your neighbor Torkel." He spoke these words with such delight that I wondered whether he'd stationed himself in that exact spot just waiting for me to pass by. We shook hands and he welcomed me to the neighborhood. We'd been chatting for only a few minutes when he issued a surprising invitation.

"I was just on my way to the cellar," he said, gesturing to a low door in the farmhouse's stone foundation. "Come on down and take a look. You might find it interesting."

I looked at him nervously. He was an attractive man, straight backed and tall. Closer to fifty than sixty, I guessed, with a handsome, sharp-bridged nose, high cheekbones, and black hair tinged with gray that was just long enough to send a curl or two over his high forehead. For some reason I imagined that this was what a Viking looked like; and it seemed to me that following a Viking into a dark cellar wasn't a good idea, especially one that I'd only just met.

But then he smiled again—a smile devoid of guile that cast a halo of wrinkles from the corners of his eyes, a smile that melted all concern.

I followed him through the narrow opening and down a few uneven steps into a cramped, rock-walled chamber where a faint scent of yeast filled the air. Three large glass vessels sat on the floor with long plastic tubes snaking from their black rubber corks.

"I started this wine last fall and now it's ready to go," he said. "Shall we welcome you to Hovland with a nip?"

The offer startled me. Johannes's decree that there should be no alcohol on his farm fit neatly with a stereotype I held of farmers in general: that they were conservative, religious, and teetotaling. Now here was my next-door neighbor—until a moment ago a complete stranger—offering me a drink. Hours before noon. On a workday. I wondered how this tied in with local culture.

Torkel took no notice of my unease as he introduced each of his wines as if it were an old friend.

"This is my plum wine. Isn't it beautiful?" His gaze lingered on the vessel for a moment. "I'm not sure why, but this year it's deeper red than ever before.

"The brown one's pear. Not pretty at all, but so sweet you forget about the color at first sip.

"And this one . . . this one is gooseberry," he said with a flourish. "Golden green. My specialty. Hardly anyone makes it. Poor souls, they don't know what they're missing."

He picked two small glasses off a shelf and waved them toward the vessels.

"So which would you like?"

I was nervous. And embarrassed. I wanted to say "none" but didn't want to offend a good-natured neighbor at our first encounter. For all I knew, it was completely normal hereabouts to have a drink before noon on a workday. If I was going to fit in, I'd better not start by breaching etiquette. Besides, his wines sounded really good.

The one I wanted most was the gooseberry, because I'd loved these translucent green berries that grew on bushes in the garden of my host family in Denmark. But I saw that this was the wine Torkel had least of. So I pointed to the only vessel that was full to the top.

"I keep a glass down here because, well, because a winemaker's got to check how his brew is doing from time to time," he said as he siphoned russet-colored pear wine out of the big vessel. "But, of course, I have to keep a second glass here, too, because you never know who's going to turn up while you're checking."

We stepped back into the sunlight and sat on my neighbor's broad stairway while sampling his wares. The wine was sweet and good, with a mild taste of ripe pears and a little kick that made me glad our portions were small.

While we sipped, Torkel explained why he was taking this break from work. When Germany invaded Norway in the spring of 1940, he recounted, every young man who had ever served time in the military was immediately called up. His unit mustered in Voss, and he was put in charge of the horses used for transporting provisions. The town endured three days of bombing, but it was a horse that injured him. The damaged bones of his crushed foot never healed properly, and there were still times—like today—when the pain was so bad he couldn't work.

Although he spoke slowly, I had a hard time understanding his thick dialect, so I found myself asking time and again for him to repeat what he'd just said. He seemed amused by the challenge rather than annoyed. And this completely endeared me to him.

Soon our glasses were empty, and as I stood up to leave, he invited me to supper the next evening, saying that he would make soup for everyone. I looked at him and smiled.

I was bewildered at first as I met one person after another named Hovland or Soldal. The genetic ramifications of what I supposed were hundreds of years of intermarrying in the neighborhood were worrisome. I was set straight soon enough, however, when I learned about Norway's complex system of intertwined family and farm names.

From a time before the Vikings, most Norwegian surnames were patronymics. That is, the last name of a son or a daughter of a man named, for example, Olav would be Olavsson or Olavsdotter (or any of several variant spellings). Quite naturally, this system created a confusing legion of similar names. To clear things up, people started appending their farm name to the patronymic; so if Olav had a son named Jon who lived at Hovland, the lad would be known as Jon Olavsson Hovland. This custom also served as an address, for if Jon moved away, he would shed his old farm name for the new.

By 1923, when Norway finally required its citizens to assume fixed surnames, almost every family who lived in a city had already adopted a patronymic, while those living in rural areas had adopted their farm name. And here was the root of my bewilderment, for Norwegian farms are mostly grouped into small clusters. And each cluster has a name. Thus, the surname of all three families at the farm cluster called Hovland was Hovland, and—as I would soon learn—the surname of nearly every one of the dozen families in neighboring Soldal was Soldal. It was all quite confusing.

My father never cooked dinner for the family, and neither did any other father I knew, so I was pretty sure I'd misunderstood the second half of Torkel's invitation, the part where he said he would make soup. Yet it was his wife and two sons who came to the door to greet Bella and me the next evening.

All three shook my hand and recited their names, which I stumbled over before being able to repeat correctly: Inger, the mother, and Tormod and Arne, the two boys who had handed Bella to me the day I moved to Johannes's farm.

Bella pranced joyfully from one person to another, and soon she and the boys were running around the house in a game of tag. I stared uneasily at the trio, wondering how I could enforce Johannes's order that no one was to touch his dog.

"I think Bella needs to calm down and stay with me," I offered, without conviction. I called her to me and gave her collar a little tug as a reminder of where she belonged.

Now I looked around for the person who'd asked me to dinner. "Is Torkel still in the barn?" I wondered aloud.

"In the barn? Why no," his wife answered. "He's in the kitchen making supper for us."

I must have looked surprised, because she burst out laughing.

"It took some training, but he was a good learner. His soup is delicious."

She led us through the living room, where family photos and hand-woven tapestries hung on pine walls, and into the kitchen. There we found Torkel stationed at the stove, wooden spoon in hand. He extended a warm greeting and bid me to his side to admire his handiwork.

A colorful blend of finely diced carrots, rutabagas, potatoes, and meat filled the pot, exuding an irresistible smoky aroma. Torkel had grown the vegetables, he told me, and raised, slaughtered, and cured the lamb himself.

"And all of this is ready for us to eat right now," he announced.

We sat down at the kitchen table, a farm-built rectangle of pine draped with a red-and-white oilcloth. Torkel filled our bowls to the brim, and Inger pushed a platter stacked high with paper-thin rounds of crisp, wavy crackers. "*Flatbrød*," she said, when I gave her a questioning look. Flatbread. "Every few months I make enough to keep my boys happy, and after they've eaten them all up, I make more." The crackers were so dry, she told me, that they would never go bad, "if people would just keep their hands off them."

I savored one bowl of the delicious soup, then another, while getting to know my new neighbors. Tormod was thirteen. Dark haired and brown eyed, he was brazen and funny. There was hardly a moment when his mind, body, or mouth was not in motion. He asked questions and then questioned the answers, his eyes shooting open in exaggerated surprise at any revelation, squinting when he tried to follow my stilted language, and frowning when he was skeptical.

His brother, Arne, was two years younger and in many ways seemed to be Tormod's opposite: sensitive, quiet, reflective, gentlehearted. He blushed easily, and with his long blond hair, blue eyes, and angelic features, it was easy to mistake him for a girl. Both boys were intelligent and curious and seemed to share a strong sense of right and wrong.

Their mother, Inger, was a good-looking woman, plump in a girlish sort of way with curly black hair and bangs that she tossed back when they fell over her eyes. There wasn't much anyone said that she didn't turn around with a quip and a wry smile. She worked half-time in Øystese's small hotel, she told me, catching a ride down the hill every morning on the school bus and getting a lift home in the afternoons with a neighbor from Soldal.

As I listened to Inger's stories, I soon realized that I could understand almost everything she said without having to invoke my usual appeals of "Could you please speak more slowly?" or "Pardon me, what did you say?" When I asked her why this was, she explained that she hailed from Bergen, a place where people spoke with flatter tones and a grammar far more akin to Danish than Norway's other dialects.

Before leaving California, I'd learned that Norway had two official languages. I'd been hoping that Øystese was a place where *bokmål*, the dominant one, was spoken. *Bokmål* was so similar to Danish in its written form that I'd had little trouble reading an Ibsen play in Norwegian for a school assignment in Denmark. My understanding was that Norway's other tongue, *nynorsk*—spoken by less than a third of the population—was a few steps further removed from Danish.

My hopes of an easy language transition were dashed almost straightaway, when Mrs. Evanger informed me that Øystese and almost all of western Norway were deeply rooted in *nynorsk*. But no one actually spoke *either* of these two official languages, she said. Instead, almost every town, valley, and fjord in the country had its own dialect. With a hint of pride, she added that the local brand of *nynorsk*, dubbed *kvammamaol*, was considered one of the most difficult dialects for outsiders to make sense of. The reason that I'd been able to carry on a conversation with her and Mr. Evanger, she explained, was because they often substituted *bokmål* equivalents of *nynorsk* words they knew I wouldn't understand.

After dinner we moved into the living room, where Inger served coffee along with home-baked cookies and cake. Torkel capped off the evening with a small serving of plum wine for each of the adults.

"*Ja, ja,* Liese," he said as he walked me to the door. "Who would have thought that a farmer from Hovland would be making supper for a girl from California? And not just any girl but one who speaks Danish and milks cows."

As Bella and I walked back to Johannes's farm under the night's pale sky, I couldn't stop thinking about his words and about how happy I was to be a girl who milked cows and had Torkel and his family as my closest neighbors.

Instead of turning up the stone stairway to Johannes's house, I continued to the barn to check on his three pregnant ewes. Within those thick walls it was cold and calm. When Bella trotted over to greet them, two of the ewes rose heavily to their feet, their movements slowed by the unborn lambs in their sagging bellies. The third remained in place, with eyes half closed and forelegs tucked beneath her chest, chewing her cud with tranquil satisfaction.

Solveig had let me know that one of my most grave responsibilities was to recognize when lambing was imminent so that I could immediately call for experienced help. This was particularly important, she told me, because Johannes kept dala sheep, a breed notable for its robust musculature and stout head. It was not uncommon for a big, thick-headed dala lamb to get hung up in its dam's birth canal. If no one was there to assist, the young one could die, sometimes taking the ewe along with it. The sixty-plus lambs that were already frolicking, suckling, and sleeping in Johannes's fields were his principal crop; the death of any one of them—or any of those not yet born—would significantly decrease the farm's annual income.

So I had been checking on these expectant sheep at least seven or eight times a day, always hoping to find one of them pacing, bleating, or otherwise showing signs of labor. Tonight, as always, the ewes looked perfectly normal. So normal, in fact, that I guiltily considered dodging my middle-of-the-night inspection, a twenty-minute sojourn during which I did my best to remain asleep while pulling on boots and stumbling around the barn in a nightgown. But reminding myself that the loss of any lamb would be a minor catastrophe, I kept the alarm clock set at 3:00 a.m.

"One of your lambs disappeared last night," Solveig said without so much as bidding me *god morgon* when she arrived for morning chores. Usually I was happy to see her, because then I could scoot aside from the cow's flank and let her take over milking just when the muscles in my fingers and forearms were turning to jelly. Now her words were like a slap on the face.

"Didn't you hear that ewe of yours bleating all night long?" she asked. "I could hear her from my bedroom. Listen—she's still at it."

When Solveig explained important things to me, she spoke loudly, looking me straight in the face with her eyes opened wide and eyebrows arched high, determined to make herself understood.

I thought back to my 3:00 a.m. trip to the barn and realized that I'd heard the same persistent bleating that even now was floating in from the pasture. At the time, I thought nothing of it. The gentle cries blended well with other background noises constantly emanating from the flock. Now Solveig was suggesting that some of these bleats and baas held a meaning that I needed to learn.

We finished chores and then headed up the hill behind Johannes's house. Unlike the open meadow below his garden, here the pasture was scattered with low-growing trees and shrubs, which made our search more difficult.

When we finally spotted the grieving ewe, I was amazed that I'd been able to sleep through her lamentation. She was pacing the hillside, her head held high and ears pointed forward. After each long, forlorn bleat, she paused to listen for a reply. Hearing none, she moved on to another spot, looked around, then bleated again.

Leaving the ewe behind, we continued our search until we found what we were looking for—half of it, that is—hidden under a shallow ledge in a copse of bird-cherry trees. The little one had been neatly ripped in two around the midriff. There was no sign of its missing foreparts: no drag marks, clumps of wool, entrails, or scraps of flesh.

Only a human, I figured, could kill a lamb, cut it in two, and make off with its head and front legs.

Solveig knew better.

"This is the work of a fox," she declared. "Johannes is going to be awfully upset when he hears about it. He shoots every one of those critters that sets foot on his farm."

"But they're wild animals!" I objected. "Is that legal?"

"Legal? Girl, it's more than legal! They eat our lambs. So the county pays us to kill them."

I was shocked. Killing a fox would go against all of the conservationist values I'd grown up with. Now as we walked down the hill, I had to weigh which was more important: a fox's life or a lamb's.

7

Firstborn Son

On my second Sunday morning at Hovland, I walked out of the barn bursting with happiness. I'd just milked the cow all on my own for the first time and had a full pail of warm milk to show for it. Even though it had taken almost an hour—four times longer than Solveig's standard—this was my first real achievement on the farm: a much-needed victory for my battered self-esteem. Now I knew I would soon be good enough to take over the chore entirely, which would free up my neighbor from putting her own work aside twice a day to help me with mine.

Later that morning, after rain had been pouring down for two hours while I pulled weeds in the garden, I looked up to see a brilliant double rainbow stretched above the hill separating Johannes's farm from Torkel's. It was a beautiful sight that made my view from the garden even more extraordinary.

Johannes's farm was one of the highest in the area, sitting eight hundred feet above sea level and less than two miles as the crow flies from Hardanger Fjord. From the house, his fields spread out in all directions over hillocks and draws, a verdant carpet interrupted here and there by rocky outcrops and thickets of bushes and trees. Beyond his fields to the east, a forest of mixed hardwoods and evergreens took over. But my eyes rarely lingered on the trees. Instead, they skipped to three mountains rearing up behind them that were so close I felt I could reach out and touch their snowy peaks. The nearest was just two miles away: three-thousand-foot-high Klyvenuten, a rounded summit with a cloven face. Even more impressive was the massive, gray pyramid of Fagraseteggi, two miles beyond Klyvenuten and three hundred feet higher.

To the south, the view was just as spectacular: a panorama of farms, forests, and hills backdropped by snowy mountains rising from

Hardanger Fjord's far shore. Above all of this the sky formed a vast canvas of shifting clouds and sunlight that I never tired of watching.

Every day the landscape yielded new surprises: an unfamiliar bird arriving for the summer, a dusting of fresh snow on remote peaks, a new bloom in the garden, a wild orchid growing in a wet spot along the road. On this Sunday, two gray birds with long tails and striped breasts alit on a pear tree fifty feet from where I crouched in the garden, wrestling with weeds. When one of them let out a resonant two-note call, I could barely believe my ears. A male cuckoo was serenading me with his fabled song.

A few hours later, just as I was finishing chores, an unfamiliar car pulled up to the house. The driver, a fair-haired, serious man in his early fifties, introduced himself as Gunnar Hovland. He lived in town, he told me, and was on his way to the hospital in Voss to visit his brother Johannes. Would I like to join him?

Two weeks after the stroke, Johannes did not seem much better than at my first visit. A nurse told us that he'd hardly left his bed, and he still couldn't take a step without the support of two people. But his face seemed a little less rigid now, and his speech a bit clearer.

He was anxious to hear about the garden: which plants had emerged, which were in bloom, whether any had been killed by the early-winter freeze. He didn't seem to listen when I described how much time I was spending on weeding without making any progress, and he had little interest in talking about his sheep or cows. When I told him that between the garden and farm I was working ten hours a day, he said nothing at all.

My tale of the dead lamb, though, captured his attention. He ordered me to shoot the fox and provided details of when, how, and where to do it. Before I could object, or even ask why this was necessary, he moved on to a far more consequential matter.

The doctors were now telling him that he might not be strong enough to come home before July, he said, perhaps not even until August. After that, he'd need extra help for another month or two. Would it be possible for me to extend my stay until as late as September?

The question caught me by surprise, for until this moment I hadn't considered the prospect of him remaining in the hospital for more than a month or "a little longer," as he'd said at our first meeting. The summerlong chore of haying would be starting soon. It was an enormous undertaking that I couldn't imagine tackling on my own. Yet our original agreement had been that I'd work until mid-August, I reminded him, so of course I would stay until then. After that, I wasn't sure. Could he wait a few weeks for an answer?

On our long drive back to Øystese, Gunnar told me that he was relieved to know I was willing to continue at the farm for a few more months. "My brother doesn't get along with most people," he told me. "If you weren't here, I don't know who else would help him."

In the three hours I'd already spent with Gunnar, I'd noticed that, unlike his brother, he spoke in a calm, nearly detached tone, betraying only small signs of emotion. He looked a lot like Johannes, but where Johannes's eyes were volatile and gray, Gunnar's were steady and milky blue.

When we reached Granvin, the little town at the end of the fjord, he began to tell me more about his brother.

Johannes was the oldest son of twelve siblings, he said. Under Norwegian law, that put him first in line to inherit his parents' farm. But during the lean years of the 1930s, when Hovland's three farms could barely provide enough food for the big families living on each of them, hunger was the excuse Johannes needed to leave. He'd always dreamed of adventure, so at the age of twenty-four, he moved to Iceland. Eventually, he landed a job as a driver for the American embassy in Reykjavik, and it was here he learned English. When German forces occupied Norway during World War II, he stayed in Iceland and joined his country's navy-in-exile there.

Altogether Johannes spent more than a decade in the island nation. Not until 1947, two years after the death of his father, did he return home to assume his birthright. His siblings noticed right away that their big brother had grown moody and angry. When their mother died a few years later, his moods grew even worse. He couldn't control his temper, and no one knew what might set it off. One afternoon he got so mad at his fourteen-year-old brother that he chased him around the house in such a fury that the boy jumped out a window to escape. "And that was the last time my little brother ever set foot on the farm." Gunnar smiled fleetingly. "He ended up moving to Canada."

With each new piece of information I'd been given about my employer, my impression of him shifted. I'd experienced Johannes's commanding personality, even a little of his anger. But hearing that he'd run a fourteen-year-old boy—his brother, no less—off the farm and out of the country scared me, especially because Torkel's young son Arne had told me another alarming story about him, which I now relayed to Gunnar.

About a year earlier, when Bella was not yet six months old, she had turned up on Torkel's doorstep one evening. When Arne led her back to his neighbor and explained where she'd been, Johannes grew incensed. As the boy watched in horror, he picked up his puppy and flung her against the kitchen wall. Inger had later confirmed this account, adding that Arne had run home, crying uncontrollably all the way.

Gunnar shook his head sadly but said nothing.

Two hours before midnight, we reached Øystese and turned away from the twilit fjord to head uphill toward Hovland. Now Gunnar picked up the story again.

"My brother started gardening after our mother died," he said, "and I think that's what saved him."

At first, he planted showy flowers, filling the beds with roses, tulips, and primroses. When the garden was in full bloom, it was magnificent. People came from all over the region to see it.

By the early 1960s, Johannes was so obsessed with his hobby that he sold some of his dairy cows—not to make money but to cut back on farmwork to make more time for his flowers. After a while, though, he grew bored with cultivated plants. To the dismay of many, he started tearing out flowerbeds and building ponds for water lilies. Soon he was replacing his remaining ornamentals with ferns and flowering plants that were native to alpine areas around the world. To view the blooms on many of these species, visitors had to bend down low and look close.

"Everyone knows that Johannes has a temper," Gunnar said as he pulled up to the cellar door at the base of Johannes's house, "and he knows that he does, too. I think that's one reason why the garden is so important to him. He's a very smart person, so working with all those plants gives him a good way to use his brain. And that might be helping to keep him on a more even keel. I don't know where he'd be without them."

As I lay in bed that night, I worried about living alone in a house with a man who could terrify a little brother into fleeing the country. Yet so far, at least, I felt that Johannes was holding true to his word of giving me full authority over the farm. I even thought he liked me. In truth, I was so happy at Hovland that whether he was a nice person or not had no effect on my daily life. For the time being, I was just going to tuck my worries away, knowing that if he ever unleashed his anger on me, I'd simply pack my bags and leave.

8

The Hunt

I was longing for rain when the alarm went off at 3:30 a.m., but a glance out the window quashed my hope of using bad weather as an excuse to stay in bed. With foul thoughts swimming through my head, I dressed and went downstairs to get the shotgun.

I'd learned how to load it on my second day at the farm when the Evangers had driven up from Øystese with their son and his family. A large and enthusiastic man in his early thirties, the son knew that Johannes had two rifles and a double-barreled shotgun stored in a closet near the front door. Let's have some fun, he'd said, grabbing the shotgun and a handful of shells.

He led our little entourage into the field, showed me the proper way to load a shell into each barrel, and placed the weapon in my hands. It was heavier than it looked, and I gripped it awkwardly, holding it away from my body as I took aim at a treetop. I'd fired my mother's humble .22 rifle before and figured this qualified me to handle anything equipped with gunpowder and a trigger.

As the blast exploded in my ear, the impact of the big stock flying back into my shoulder knocked me off my feet. The young Mr. Evanger stood over me laughing. "Next time, tuck it into your shoulder," he said, picking up the weapon. "Like this, see? That way it won't kick back."

By now, the pain and bruise had faded, leaving their memory as a reminder of that lesson learned. I loaded a shell into each chamber and headed out the door.

The sun had already climbed above the horizon somewhere behind the clouds as I marched up the hill, brushing through grasses and flowers bent low with dew. Ten yards shy of the upper fence, I hunkered down at the base of a tree where I had a good line of sight into a creek hollow on my left and a boggy area stretching uphill above me. I propped the loaded weapon on my knees and scanned the tree-studded terrain. For half an hour I watched and listened, aware of the pungent odor of sheep droppings crushed into the grass at my feet and the opening notes of each birdsong wafting through this chilly dawn.

The fox appeared just as I was about to surrender to the call of my abandoned bed. Its red ears flickered above the grass as it nosed its way uphill from the creek, investigating rocks and mounds of dirt and pawing at tangles of plants growing against tree trunks. It didn't see me inch the gun to my shoulder or know that I was waiting for it to meander close enough for a clean shot.

Holding my index finger tense alongside the trigger, I steeled myself to destroy this beautiful creature, visualizing the sequence: loop my finger into the curve of cold metal; fire; carry my quarry down the hill; and then, best of all, receive praise from all of Hovland's farmers for a job well done.

I noticed that this curious animal seemed to be enjoying an early morning outing, intrigued by each new discovery. As I watched, the thudding of my heart settled down and the naturalist in me took over. I'd observed foraging deer, skunks, and birds before but never anything like this fox, a hunter capable of killing a lamb. This one had a scrawny body suspended above peculiarly long legs and looked considerably larger than pictures I'd seen of California's gray fox. Was it a male? Did males help rear the young? If I shot it, was I dooming a den of pups?

After a minute or two, it wandered just close enough that I drew a bead on its chest. Then it backtracked a dozen feet before drifting toward me once more. Now it was so close that I slid my finger onto the trigger.

At that moment the creature noticed me for the first time. It lifted its head high, alert, pointing the black tips of its ears straight at me as if it were a schoolteacher homing in on a noisy pupil.

My heart started thudding again as a question darted through my brain: What if this wasn't the actual lamb killer? The animal was holding its eyes on mine. Intelligent eyes filled with as much curiosity as surprise. A tilt of its head revealed a long black mouth crinkled in an impenetrable smile.

The natural world was dear to me: wild plants, wildlife, and wild places. Now here was the first native, four-legged animal I'd seen since arriving at Hovland, and I was fixing to kill it. Was I so beguiled by my budding notion of myself as a Norwegian farmer that I would do such a thing without question? I respected Johannes, yet I was aware that wolves, mountain lions, and other predators in my own country had been hunted down by ranchers and farmers even as their dwindling numbers no longer posed a threat to livestock. How did I know that this wasn't the case with foxes here in Norway? Since finding that first dead lamb, I hadn't heard that any others had gone missing from nearby farms.

If I were to avert my eyes, I would see a long fence a few yards above me: the border between these fields and an unpopulated landscape extending for miles beyond Hovland. Surely these tracts provided more than enough space for both Johannes's sheep and this fox.

Slowly, slowly, I eased my finger off the trigger and lowered the gun back to my knees. I needed more proof that killing this creature—and possibly a den of pups—was a fair trade for a lamb or two that Johannes might lose.

My quarry tarried another half second, then turned and leaped off toward the creek. The last I saw of it was the white tip of its tail disappearing into the woods.

9

Museum in the Living Room, Sheep Thighs in the Pantry

The house I was beginning to feel at home in was about one hundred years old and constructed in a style that was commonly used in western Norway until the early 1900s. That is, it was something like a log cabin, with timbers stacked one atop another. But in contrast to the round logs in Abe Lincoln's boyhood home, the timbers in Johannes's house were milled flat.

On exterior walls, overlapping horizontal boards covered these squared logs: a practical strategy that helped shed the nearly one hundred inches of precipitation, both frozen and wet, that fell here each year. On interior walls, what looked to my untrained eye like ten-inch-wide boards were actually the logs themselves, planed to a smooth finish.

I spent most of my indoor time in the kitchen. This narrow room never felt cramped, thanks to the magnificent vista its windows provided. One morning as I sat admiring the view, I noticed a milky blur—something like a cloud settling in after a storm—curling over the snow-covered ridgeline in the south.

"That's our glacier, Folgefonna," Torkel's wife, Inger, told me. "It's always there, winter and summer alike, but you can see it better now that the snow around it is melting." She explained that the white patch we were looking at was only a small nub of this eighty-two-square-mile glacier, the third largest ice field in the country. From that day on, Folgefonna was the first thing my eyes settled on whenever I glanced to the south.

The kitchen shared one of its long walls with Johannes's living room and the other with his bedroom: a chamber imbued with the close smell of an unaired space after a long winter. This room was so packed with his belongings—handcrafted heirlooms, stacks of papers and gardening catalogs, his clothes and bed—that whenever I entered I felt like I was invading his personal life. So I went there only when asked to retrieve a piece of clothing or any other item for him, and even then it made me uncomfortable.

The living room was fairly large, yet it felt gloomy and unwelcoming with its pale pine walls and darker floor and its small windows cluttered with potted plants that swallowed most of the light that tried to squeeze through them.

Johannes had transformed this formal chamber into his own little museum. Crowded on the floor and shelves were dozens of objects that his forebears had put to use in centuries past, almost all of them made of wood: a cradle, huge bentwood baskets, spinning wheels, blanket chests (one of them painted with the distinctive flowery swirls of Norwegian *rosemåling*), a hand-cranked wooden potato masher, wooden tankards, whisks made of twigs, and more. I examined them with reverence, running my hand over smooth surfaces, admiring sturdy joinery, and imagining a life with all of these items in daily use.

Here, too, were black-and-white photographs of Hovland ancestors and bygone wedding parties. Photos like these graced every house I visited in the neighborhood. I never tired of studying them, especially the party shots, in which scores of people are lined up on a hillside, every man in a suit, every woman in Hardanger's traditional costume of blouse, bodice, apron, pleated skirt, and belt, with stupendous embellishments of lacework, embroidery, beadwork, and flashy jewelry.

Two smaller rooms rounded out the downstairs floor plan: a closet by the front door where I kept my barn clothes alongside Johannes's three long guns and my favorite room of all: the pantry. This vented and isolated room stayed cooler than the rest of the house, so I stored almost all of my food there. I loved going into the pantry to survey its many treasures, like a bag of carrots mixed with sand and dirt (which is how they came from the store), canisters of flour and oats, and bowls filled with apples and potatoes that I replenished every so often from the cellar. One shelf was dedicated to *rømmekolle,* cultured milk. This yogurt-like substance became one of my staples as soon as Johannes's sister Ingebjørg taught me how to make it. Two or three times a week I poured a couple of quarts of milk, still warm from the cow, into one of

Johannes's flat-bottomed wooden bowls. After four or five days in the pantry, whatever yeasts and bacteria happened to be around at the time transformed the liquid into a delicate gelled mass with a layer of soured cream on top. The cream was considered a great delicacy, so I skimmed it off to give to visitors from town who prized it for its rich flavor as well as for the childhood memories it evoked. I kept the soured skim milk for myself and ate it for meals, snacks, and dessert, either plain or mixed with jam and *kavringar*—toasted biscuits—which I ordered with my weekly groceries.

Milk was the most abundant food on the farm. Fresh and soured, it constituted about a quarter of my diet, so I considered it a great stroke of luck that the cow's output was unusually low in butterfat. My neighbors disparaged her for this shortcoming, pointing out that the dairy paid a lower price for such milk. But I had never been a lithe young thing, and I was happy to trim some fat out of a diet that was otherwise heavy in meat, bread, and potatoes. Fresh produce from the store was so expensive—and I was so careful to limit how much of Johannes's money I spent—that I rarely ordered anything other than rutabagas, carrots, and the occasional cucumber. I especially missed being able to toss a salad together, for lettuce and tomatoes were pure luxury items.

Plum and strawberry jam were another of my staples. Johannes had cooked up barrels of both kinds the previous summer and fall, using strawberries bought from neighbors and plums harvested from his own trees. When I arrived at Hovland, there were about six or seven gallons of these preserves stored in open buckets on the pantry's floor and shelves. Before taking my first taste of the plum jam, I apprehensively scooped a thick layer of dusty blue mold from its surface and was delighted to find that the syrupy treat below was sweet and tangy, with a delicious plummy flavor.

Of all the wonders in my little pantry, nothing surpassed three dark haunches of lamb suspended from hooks in the ceiling. I first came face to face with this national delicacy when Ola and Ingebjørg led me into the house on my first day at Hovland. They had swept every surface clear of Johannes's clutter two days earlier, so the room was bare except for a gruesome object lying on the table. It looked like a mummified leg with a yellowed ball of bone protruding from one end and a chunk of flesh missing from its central muscle mass.

Oh, my lord, I thought, something must have happened to one of

Johannes's sheep; maybe he'd been conducting an autopsy when the stroke hit him. I felt embarrassed for Ola and Ingebjørg, so I kept my eyes down and pretended that I hadn't seen this hideous artifact.

But Ola had his eye on it. Hurrying to the table, he grabbed it up and apologized. "I'm sorry, we forgot to put this away." Then, instead of heaving it out the window, he pulled out a knife and carved off a thin wedge of dry, reddish-brown flesh. "Please," he said, pushing the meat toward me.

I must have turned white, because he withdrew the offer and popped the desiccated morsel into his mouth. Then he carved another for Ingebjørg.

"When we were cleaning up, Ola and I couldn't stop eating it," Ingebjørg said, apologetically. "It's hard to find *spekekjøt* this good." (Literally translated, *spekekjøt* means "cured meat." While this is the term my neighbors used, in most places in the country it's called *fenalår* or *fenadlår,* which translates to "livestock thigh.")

Not wanting to offend these good folk, I took a deep breath and tried a piece myself. It was salty, a bit tough, and studded with stringy tendons. When the Mælands' heads were turned, I spit a wad of sinew into my hand and stuffed it into my pocket.

Yet I couldn't help noticing that any visitor who was familiar with the house would, at some point, wander into the pantry in search of this cured meat. Like cavemen fresh from the hunt, they would carry a skinned leg back to the kitchen to shave off a few slices, waxing eloquent about its mouthwatering virtues. After a while I started concealing the haunches behind boxes and jars on the pantry shelves because I wanted to be able to dole this treasure out myself.

In Denmark I'd learned that it was a host's job to shower hospitality—food, that is—on every guest, even those who showed up unannounced. And here in Norway that tradition was even stronger. Johannes's *spekekjøt* was my ace in the hole, a delicacy I could always pull out to make any guest feel special. I even gave it a second chance myself. Once I got past the tendons and the meat's color of dried blood, I eventually grew passionate about its rich, smoky flavor and found myself carving off a little nibble almost every day, even when there were no guests to share it with.

The only heat sources in the house were four woodstoves. I washed my clothes in the sink, occasionally enlisting Tormod or Arne to help me wring out heavy items like jeans and sheets, took sponge baths in the kitchen, and, except for an occasional craving for a piece of hot toast, got along fine without any kitchen appliances.

On the afternoon of my first day on the farm, my anxiety over not being able to locate a toilet or pit privy had been put to rest when Ola pulled out his carpentry tools and built a makeshift platform in the sheep shed across the yard from the barn: a one-seater above a bucket. With some embarrassment and a good deal of gesturing and a short walk, he succeeded in explaining that, after use, I was to carry the bucket across the yard to the manure cellar and heave its contents into the pile.

I tried to maintain a sanguine air so as not to add to Ola's discomfort. But I felt my face redden as the implications of this arrangement began to sink in. The platform and bucket were not the problem. In fact, they were a bed of roses compared to digging catholes in the woods that I was used to from backcountry camping trips. No, the problem was the humiliation I was already experiencing at the thought of carrying a bucket laden with my own waste across a wide-open yard in plain view of the house and Johannes's long driveway. I was sure that anyone who chanced to see me would know exactly what I was doing.

10

Into the Wild

Our father had instilled his love of the outdoors into all of his kids. When we were young, he led us on hikes on Mount Tamalpais, a forested, twenty-six-hundred-foot peak that rose up behind our house. By the time I was ten, he was taking us on wilderness trips into the Sierra Nevada. My passion for botany and wildflowers came from him, too. On trips into the mountains, he taught us the names of plants he recognized and showed us how to distinguish tree species from one another.

So from the day I arrived at Hovland, I'd been longing to explore the mountains and plant life just beyond Johannes's fence line. Both Torkel and Solveig had been encouraging me to do this, too, because they wanted a first-hand report on conditions in the wild meadows above the farm.

They explained that as soon as enough snow melted and grasses had grown tall enough, we would release our flocks into those high elevation expanses. Right now the animals were pastured in home fields, areas that would be harvested for hay later in the summer. Grazing here, they were acting just like lawn mowers. If they stayed at home too long, their grazing would delay harvest and reduce yields. On the other hand, the sheep would thrive in the cooler climate at higher elevations and grow fat on alpine plants bursting with nutrition. Just as important, they would be harvesting their own fodder for at least four months, costing their owners nothing.

My chance to head into the hills finally came at the end of May. I set out in the afternoon with Bella at my heels. It was a good day for a walk. When the sun wasn't hiding behind large, puffy clouds, it cast a clean, cool light that brought the world into focus. Bluebells, buttercups, and pink mallows were blooming in the meadows, and newly unfurled leaves on alders and aspens shimmered like emerald fireworks.

A few minutes into our hike we came to a gate in the farm's upper fence, a reckless contraption of sticks and wire that belied its significance as the passageway between farms and *utmarka,* the outer lands beyond cultivation.

Below this portal lay fields, farms, roads, and towns. Above it were wild mountains that stretched forty-five miles north, intersected by only two roads and one inhabited valley before dropping into mighty Sognefjord, the largest and deepest fjord in Norway.

As I entered this backcountry, I was trying to hold on to the jumble of directions that Torkel had given me. There was a trail, he said, but it would be hard to find so soon after the snow had melted and difficult to distinguish from a multitude of paths that meandering sheep had created over hundreds of years. The main landmarks I was to look for were three clusters of cabins, each about a half hour's walk from the next. These buildings and the land surrounding them were called *stølar* or *setrar* (singular, *støl* and *seter*), places that for centuries had served as summer grazing grounds for a farm's cows and sheep and as summer residences for the women, called *budeier,* who tended them.

A *budeie* milked her cows morning and evening, let her charges loose to graze during the day, and kept them safe from predators by herding them into either a stone-walled enclosure or a cramped barn at night. Some made cheese, buttermilk, and sour cream that was sent back to the main farm every few days with boys who journeyed into the mountains on foot or horseback. Hovland's last *budeie,* Torkel told me, had been his youngest sister, Borgny, who closed the cabin door on this long tradition at the end of a summer some fifteen years earlier.

Just above the gate, Bella and I entered a narrow, rock-studded meadow that funneled into a canyon where Johannes had planted a forest of pine and fir. Farther along I sank almost to the tops of my high rubber boots in a bog that looked like solid ground.

After half an hour of climbing, I found the first two cabins perched in a grassy basin littered with large patches of rotten snow. This place was called Blomseter, the lower of Hovland's two *stølar.* The buildings stood side by side. One was painted a cheerful red; the other looked neglected and gray. Before moving on, I made a quick survey of the grasses and other plants sprouting up from the waterlogged meadow and found that they were not yet more than two inches high.

Western Norway's raw climate and long winters take a toll on its forests; although Blomseter was only fifteen hundred feet above sea level (seven hundred feet higher than Johannes's farm) it sat right at timberline. So now Bella and I left trees behind as we ascended a steep cleft, wading through leafless blueberry plants, tufts of heather, and neon-green spikelets of grasses and reeds emerging from winter dormancy.

"Which way, Bella?" I asked, when we came to a stream overflowing with snowmelt. "Did Torkel say keep left of the creek or right?" By this time, I had no idea if I was anyplace close to a trail, so I just kept slogging straight up the slope.

If my neighbor hadn't told me to look for them on a promontory above a wide bog, I would have missed the three cabins at Hyrting, Hovland's second *støl.* It was an ancient name, Torkel said, which meant something like "gathering place of herders." With walls weathered to the hue of withered grass and foundations made of rocks plucked from the mountainside behind them, the three buildings were almost indistinguishable from their surroundings.

From where we stood, the view took in all of Hovland and Soldal, a long stretch of the fjord and its convoluted shorelines, and mountains in every direction. But the sky ahead was filling with dark clouds, and I was so intent on my explorations that I turned my back on this vista and pushed onward toward the clouds.

The going was easier now. Bella and I had climbed another 650 feet in elevation and were on a broad bench of a long, high mountain, picking our way over uneven terrain strewn with patches of exposed bedrock and fields of melting snow. We jumped rivulets and squished across small peat bogs until we came to an overlook with yet another vista. To our left the bench plummeted into a deep, wide valley, which opened up a sweeping scene of mountains and lakes beyond this broad rift. Most spectacular was a colossal rampart of bare rock several miles long with a vertical face incised by jagged clefts that channeled fingers of snow to elevations far below.

At Hyrting I'd been transfixed by the solitude, but the wildness before me here was deeper still. The only signs of civilization in this majestic panorama were two clusters of cabins, one many miles away, the other a group of three buildings on a grassy shelf a hundred feet below us. This must be Flyane, I figured, the last of the *stølar* that Torkel had described.

A sudden gust of wind pushed a bank of mist over the cabins. The clouds had already dropped lower, and now a few beads of rain blew against my face.

"Come on, Bella!" I called. "Time to go home."

The storm moved in fast. Rain was coming down hard as we loped past Hyrting and started picking our way more carefully down the steep slope to Blomseter. By the time I closed the gate to *utmarka* behind us, we were wet to the bone. Gazing down at Johannes's house and a broad swath of his fields where ewes and lambs were hunched up against the storm, I was struck by how much tamer this landscape now looked than it had just hours earlier.

I hadn't gone far in my frantic dash down the driveway that evening before I caught sight of a lean, gray-haired man wandering my way, hands in his pockets.

"Solveig sent me," he said shyly before I could spit out that I needed help because one of my pregnant ewes was acting strangely. "She came by earlier this evening, guess you were still on your walk. She said it looked like your ewe was getting close." He glanced past me to the barn behind us. "Thought you might need a hand."

I'd already met Alv a couple of times. A younger brother of Solveig, he was in his midfifties and as unassuming as she was self-assured. The two of them lived on their farm along with another brother. It had surprised me to learn that Solveig was single; since our first meeting, I'd imagined this matronly woman surrounded by a flock of children, showering them with the same love and attention she bestowed on Johannes's livestock.

Nothing in Alv's demeanor demonstrated urgency. I suddenly felt foolish for losing my head and tried to conceal my alarm, hoping that he hadn't already noticed. Feigning a casual air, I matched his calm pace as we returned to the barn.

"She's pretty far along," he said as soon as his eyes landed on the ewe. "Should be less than an hour now."

The animal was still standing, but now she was scraping at the floor, her motions fast and mechanical as she gouged out a little basin in the hard-packed manure. I noticed that her breathing was shallower and faster than normal. Alv stood quietly, taking this all in.

"She's doing fine," he concluded, after a bit. "The best thing to do is to stay out of her way as long as nothing's wrong."

I waited for him to expound on this statement; all the other people I'd met had made it their mission to cram as much instruction, information, and local lore into me as possible. When none was forthcoming from Alv, I stole him a glance. There at the railing, it seemed, he was not so much watching the agitated animal in the pen as avoiding looking my way. A barn jacket hung loosely on his thin frame. The flat cap he wore was pulled down low, shadowing his features. Yet I detected a handsome kindness in his face, exaggerated by a downward cant of his eyes and a fan of fine lines radiating from their corners. I found myself thinking that he actually looked quite dashing—like a horseman in riding breeches, perhaps—with that tilt of the cap and the way he'd tucked those loose-fitting trousers into his high rubber boots.

We didn't make any small talk over the next hour as we stood side by side watching the ewe grow more and more agitated, pacing in circles, digging at the manure floor, getting to her knees to lie down, changing her mind and standing up. Yet he did occasionally offer instruction where it would be most useful.

As the time approached, the ewe finally lay down on a bed of hay that Alv had thrown down for her. Her contractions were clearly visible now, sometimes so strong that they made her groan; at one point she let out a squeal that sounded almost human. This lamb *must* be born soon, I told myself.

"There now, that's exactly what you want to see first," Alv said a minute later, in such a placid tone he could have been talking to himself. "Two feet and a nose."

What I saw emerging from the ewe's swollen vulva was a dark jumble with no distinguishing features. She was straining hard with each contraction, and soon more of the mass emerged. Now it looked like a slime-encased cylinder. But through this film, I could just make out the outline of a tiny head cupped within two outstretched legs. Another contraction, and more of the cylinder appeared. The ewe strained yet again, and this time a limp bundle slid out into the world. What I saw now was a lifeless body sheathed in a membranous sack.

I turned to Alv, bewildered, searching for words to ask what had gone wrong. But before I could suck in my breath, the dank mass shuddered, shook its little head, and gulped for air.

"I thought it was dead," I said, almost in tears.

"Oh no, no, it's fine," he said reassuringly.

Now the ewe rose to her feet. She examined her newborn with a sniff or two, then set to work licking the membrane from its nose and body with unwavering determination.

"See now?" Alv said. "Some lambs just need a second or two to think about what comes next, I guess. Others come into the world kicking." A bashful smile lit up his pale blue eyes and turned the little wrinkles at their corners into smiles, too.

I'd once watched a cat give birth. The kittens popping out of her looked unpleasantly like limp blind rats. This birth was different. Almost immediately the lamb shook its head and opened its eyes. Within minutes, it was swaying back and forth on four long wobbly legs, even as its dam determinedly licked life into it. When it fell on its side, my heart melted and then bonded—both to the feisty little creature and to its mother, who was taking such good care of it.

Alv told me what to watch for and directed me to not leave the barn until I knew that the newborn was successfully nursing. Pronouncing the lamb in perfect health, he headed home.

Within an hour the tiny creature metamorphosed from a wet rag to the fluffiest, most pink-nosed little lamb I could ever have imagined. It tottered this way and that, poking its nose into its mother's knees and belly and exploring all her other woolly features until it found a teat. I followed Alv's directive and waited until I saw the lamb's long tail wriggling like a worm on a hook, a sure sign that milk was flowing to the right place.

As I walked back to the house, my pleasure was tempered by the memory of those chunks of pork swimming in the pinkish brine in Johannes's cellar. How long did this new little lamb have before it ended up there, too? I'd heard that the annual slaughter took place in October, but I didn't know which animals got put on the chopping block. In any case, I'd be gone by then, so I could just push this unsavory topic out of my mind.

11

Drunken Driving

The first time Edvard came to the farm, we barely spoke. The tall young man simply appeared at the barn early one morning, introduced himself, said he'd been asked by Johannes to help clean up around the place, and went to work hauling manure with the horse and cart for most of the day. I was pulling weeds that morning and found myself standing up to stretch more often than usual in order to catch glimpses of him. He was incredibly attractive.

"He's a nice boy," Inger responded when I asked if she knew this mysterious stranger. "I'm friends with his mother, and his sister is a friend of our daughter."

Edvard, she told me, had worked at sea for three years and was now attending maritime school. After graduation, he'd be well on his way to becoming a first mate.

"Why would someone who's going to maritime school spend a weekend hauling manure at Johannes's farm?" I wanted to know.

"I'm not really sure. He's a little shy," she ventured, "so maybe he likes the solitude. And I do think he considers Johannes a friend, because he spends a lot of weekends here."

I had just started milking when Edvard darted into the barn on the following Saturday morning, my two-week anniversary at the farm. Greeting me with a quick "*god morn*," he lifted Begonia's harness from its stand by the door and turned to leave. I'd been dying to see him again and needed to get his attention before he disappeared. So I blurted out the first thing that came to mind.

"Hey, do you need help with the manure today?"

"Sure," he said, over his shoulder. "Come down whenever you want."

Then a crazy idea popped into my head.

"I could make *middag* for you afterward, if you'd like."

Now he turned around, holding the ungainly harness in both arms, and looked at me as if he didn't know what to say.

"Well, that is, if you were thinking of staying until then," I faltered. "Maybe you weren't. But if you were, I could make something . . . nothing very fancy, I don't think."

He was twenty-five years old, well over six feet tall, with lively brown eyes and curly brown hair that spilled over a high forehead. He looked at me and smiled, a charming, lopsided grin.

"Sure," he said. "At noon?"

I returned his smile and felt myself blush. "Yeah, noon," I assented, wondering what had come over me. Norwegian farmers took *middag*, their midday dinner, very seriously, and I didn't know what to cook.

I hurried through chores, then grabbed a quick breakfast before joining Edvard in the meadow below the house. Our job was to remove dozens of piles of manure that Johannes had hauled there a few months earlier. It would have made fine fertilizer if he'd pitched it over his dormant fields and harrowed it into the earth right away. But grass had begun shooting up even before he was felled by the stroke. Now this new green growth was so tall that it would be destroyed if these black piles of muck were spread and harrowed into it. So all this manure had to be carted to the edge of the field and stacked up for later use.

The garden, I knew by now, was Johannes's first priority. That's what accounted for this unspread manure, the barn's leaking roof, the hayloft's rotten floor, farm tools in disrepair, run-down sheep pens, and rickety gates. I was just barely keeping up with the combination of farm and garden work, and this was supposedly the slack season. It wasn't hard to imagine that during busier times of the year there were not enough hours in the day for Johannes to maintain both garden and farm in tip-top condition.

Edvard didn't say much while we shoveled heavy, wet manure into the cart. He didn't seem unfriendly, just ill at ease around me. With Begonia, on the other hand, he was perfectly calm and assured, guiding her with steady hand and voice from one stack of manure to the next. After we'd loaded several piles into the rubber-tired wooden cart, he handed me the lines.

"It's your turn now," he said. "You won't be able to run this farm if you don't know how to do this."

I tried to stifle a silly grin. Here I was on a Norwegian farm about to learn how to work with a draft horse.

Begonia was a Norwegian fjord horse, stocky and strong like the rest of her breed. In a land of steep and treacherous terrain, where pasture was scarce and feed in short supply, fjord horses had been bred to be surefooted and steady and to thrive on scant rations of low-quality fodder. They are willing workers and quick learners and rarely object to any task assigned them, from pulling a cart or harrow, to dragging a log, to carrying a rider across the mountains.

Like most fjord horses, Begonia was dun in color, with a downy white muzzle as soft as rabbit's fur and a black dorsal stripe that ran from her forelock through the center of her white mane all the way into her tail. Farmers highlighted this feature by cropping manes to stand erect, with the black stripe sandwiched in white like a ribbon of chocolate running through cream. The best barbers also managed to tailor a graceful crest into the mane, giving their steeds the sturdy-necked look of a Trojan horse.

The lines I was now holding were not the fancy leather versions depicted in old paintings of stagecoaches and such but rather two long, frayed ropes tied together at their ends that stretched from Begonia's bit, through two rings in the harness above her shoulder, all the way to the rear of the small cart she was hauling.

I took my place beside the mare and held the lines the way Edvard had, one in each hand. I called the animal's name softly. *Begonia.* It sounded odd at first. Not quite fitting for a sturdy horse hauling a heavy cart.

"Move back," Edvard told me. "Don't stand right next to her or you'll be in the way when she turns. You have much better control when you walk beside the cart or all the way behind it."

He took the lines and demonstrated by driving down the meadow, slaloming around the manure piles, then circling back to where I stood.

"She's a good horse, but she doesn't always listen," he said, handing her back to me. "You need to let her know that she can't get away with anything."

I stood beside the cart, took a deep breath, and slapped the ropes over the horse's back. She took a step forward, then stopped. I slapped again. Nothing.

"She's not going to go anywhere unless you tell her to," Edvard said with a smile. "Here, I'll show you. Keep hold of the lines."

With that, he smacked his lips together, producing a loud kissing noise that launched Begonia into a handsome clip. I'd heard him make this sound earlier. Now I realized that it must be the Norwegian equivalent of "Giddyup!"

Guiding horse and cart around manure piles wasn't as easy as my instructor had made it look. Begonia was so sensitive that unless I applied precisely the same tension to both lines, she swerved one way or the other, heading in whichever direction she sensed a stronger pull on the bit.

When I wanted her to turn, I quickly discovered, I couldn't just pull harder on one line; I also had to release all tension on the other. Plus I had to keep out of the way of the cart that was careering along beside me and at the same time avoid the manure piles scattered like moguls across the field.

I drove like a drunk, veering one way and then the other, plowing through manure and quick-stepping out of the way of the cart's tires. When I approached the fence, I wobbled Begonia through a wide turn and headed back.

By the time I reached Edvard, my arms were shaking. I pulled firmly on both lines; Begonia slowed for a moment then continued ahead at full speed. I tried again, this time calling out a resolute "Whoa!" while tugging back as hard as I could. She kept going.

Edvard ran up from behind, took the lines, pulled back, and rolled his lips to make a noise that sounded like high-pitched machine gun fire. The mare jerked to a stop.

"I guess I should have told you how to stop her before you got going," he said. "I just thought everyone knew how to do that."

I gave the machine-gun call a try but couldn't get my lips to roll. At my second attempt, Edvard tried not to laugh. There was no way to save face, so I just looked my teacher in the eye and told him I'd practice on my own.

Edvard and I worked together for a couple of hours before I headed back to the house to make dinner. The biggest meal of the day, *middag* was always eaten at noon on surrounding farms. I'd gotten into the habit of making my own simplified version of local fare by boiling rutabagas along with potatoes and a small chunk of salted pork from the cellar. So that would have to do for today, as well. To add a special touch, though, I harvested ten fat stalks of rhubarb from Johannes's garden—the only edible plant that grew there—and turned them into a compote, to be served with homemade cultured milk from the pantry.

The pleasant *middag* hour I'd envisioned was not to be, however. Another friend of Johannes's had shown up just before noon to help out. Artur greeted Edvard warmly but avoided looking me in the eye. Over dinner, I sat silently by as my two guests conversed with one another. Before returning to work, though, both of them cleaned their plates, which I took as a good sign.

Late in the afternoon, just as I headed to the house to make supper for my two-man crew, shafts of sunlight pierced through the clouds for the first time in days. My spirits soared to see wet slate roofs glimmering in the light. This sudden burst of joy astonished me, because I was already so happy at Hovland that it didn't seem possible for a ray or two of sunshine to make me happier still.

As I laid out supper in the kitchen—bread, cheeses, canned liver pâté, jam—I pondered over the source of the nearly boundless well of energy I'd been experiencing since arriving at the farm. I'd been working every day of the week, running between house, barn, and fields from one job to the next, and enjoying every minute of it.

The easy answer was that my work was new, exciting, fulfilling, and interesting, while all of the people I was meeting were friendly, kind, helpful, and—when I could understand them—quite funny. On top of that, I was surrounded by the beauty of an ancient landscape of buildings and farms and, of course, those magnificent mountains all around. Even the miserably wet weather barely dampened my spirits.

Deeper down, I realized that at Hovland I was a blank slate, judged only by the work I was doing and my interactions with neighbors over these past few weeks. No one could fault me for whatever errors I'd committed in the past. Instead, my neighbors were supporting, helping, and instructing me, because no one wanted Johannes's farm—or the new girl who was running it—to fail.

Every day I was also enjoying living alone more and more. I'd grown up with four siblings, spent a year with a Danish family, the next with a roommate in a college dorm, then a summer of house sharing before moving back home. Now every night when my work was done, I was free to read books, write long letters, or do whatever else I pleased without interruption. It was a marvelous and liberating feeling.

Around eight o'clock that evening, Torkel and a nephew of his strolled over to say hello. One of my pregnant ewes had been showing signs of lambing, so I immediately asked my neighbor if he would look in on her. Edvard and Artur, who had gone back to hauling manure after our supper together, had just called it quits for the day. So all five of us traipsed into the barn together. Twenty minutes later a lamb was born.

"Mother and baby are healthy," Torkel declared after clambering into the pen to inspect the little one. "It's time to celebrate Liese's second lamb!" He turned to his nephew, a young man about my age. "Go back to the house and fetch a bottle of plum brandy—on the top shelf in the cellar."

"No. We can't do that!" I blurted out. "Johannes doesn't want alcohol on the farm. He won't allow it."

On top of Johannes's edict, I wasn't sure myself if I wanted to sit down with a bottle and several men I barely knew. It had already been a long day, and I worried that alcohol could make it much longer.

The four towered above me, disappointed and incredulous.

"You don't need to worry about that," Torkel objected. "Remember that Johannes put you in charge here. So this isn't his decision now." He smiled at his neat logic, confident that it would win me over.

I glanced questioningly at Edvard.

"Don't worry about Johannes," he said, his brown eyes brimming with amusement. "Whenever I work here, he gives me a dram afterward."

That Johannes was not a teetotaler was news to me. Now I wondered why he demanded that I be one. How strange that at our first meeting he had banned alcohol and given me *fullmakt* almost in the same breath. *Fullmakt.* Complete authority. That was the word he used, and I had been taking it seriously, watching out for his farm and animals as if they were my own. When I tried to come up with a reason why it would be an abuse of my authority to take a nip with friends—or obey an irrational command—I came up blank.

"Alright. We can have the brandy." The words seemed to lift a weight from my shoulders. "But just one drink."

The nephew sprinted away and returned at a run ten minutes later carrying a bottle filled with a viscous brown liquid that immediately found its way into glasses I'd procured from the kitchen.

As we stood in a circle by the barn's stone foundation sipping Torkel's tasty concoction, I was amazed to see how quickly this group of rather quiet men grew animated and jovial. Artur, who had not made eye contact with me all day, asked what state I was from and how I liked living at Hovland. Torkel told a story about a particularly lively lambing he'd once assisted. The nephew laughed. It was Saturday night, and everyone was having a good time.

No sooner had the last drinker's glass turned bottom up than Torkel lifted the bottle for a second round with a grand gesture and big smile.

"No," I said quickly. "We agreed on just one glass."

All four men looked at me in surprise. Their combined gaze made me feel small.

"Oh, come now. There's no harm in drinking up the drop that's left," Artur argued with a frown.

For some reason, I looked to Edvard again. Maybe because I liked the way he seemed to be standing apart from the others, enjoying their company yet observing them rather than falling in with them. He returned my glance with a smile that told me I was on my own.

I felt that a lot was at stake here and that any hesitation on my part would create a crack for this crew to wedge open.

"No," I repeated firmly. "No more."

My drinking mates, sensing that I meant it, put the bottle away.

Later I reflected on what had been at stake. To begin with, I was a girl living alone—no good could possibly come from letting four men leave the farm that night with stories about how they'd talked me into an evening of drinking. There was more to it than that, however. Something about being able to hold my ground, even among this friendly group, eased a burden of insecurity I'd been carrying. For two weeks now I'd been struggling to understand a new language, learn new skills, and navigate through a new culture, all while living in another person's house, dependent on strangers for help and advice. I couldn't be sure who to listen to, who I should obey, or even what I should be doing each day. I was unsure of myself and didn't know where I stood. By standing firm against these four men and by formulating a response to Johannes's unreasonable demand, I began to feel less like a guest here and more like master of the house and farm.

After everyone left, I made my final evening inspection in the barn. The new mother and baby were fine, but now my third pregnant ewe was looking puzzled, cocking her head and pulling straw into little mounds with her hoof.

I knew that Torkel and Inger, like many other families in the area, did not have a telephone. So without hesitating, I flew down the road to their house and bounded up their stone stairway two steps at a time. It was past eleven, but Inger answered my knock and invited me into the living room, where she and her husband had been enjoying a cup of tea. Torkel listened to my description of the ewe's behavior and concluded that it would be a while before any serious action took place.

"No sense heading back to a lonely house," Inger said, pushing me to the sofa. "If you'll sit down, I'll get you some tea."

My good-hearted neighbor accompanied me back to the barn at midnight. At this northerly latitude, the sky was never completely dark for a month or two around the summer solstice. So Torkel and I walked up the road through a dusky light that transformed trees and grazing sheep into mystical presences: a light so spellbinding that despite the cold, I'd been writing my letters at night sitting outside on the garden steps.

We found the ewe pacing in short, fitful circles. But delivery was still a ways off, Torkel said, displaying not even a hint of irritation. We should both get a few hours of sleep, he advised, before I checked on her again. If things were livelier then, I should fetch him without delay.

For once it was easy to get up when the 3:00 a.m. alarm sounded. With my head clouded by thoughts of an exhausted ewe unable to deliver a large-headed lamb, I couldn't bother to get dressed. Instead, I threw a sweater over my nightgown and slipped into rubber boots before hurrying to the barn.

Outside it was light enough to see the long ridge of mountains rising from the fjord's far shore. But it was gloomy within the barn's cold stone walls, and the smell of lanolin, straw, and manure hung heavy in the air. The pregnant ewe was still pacing erratically, but now a slimy string trailed from her rear end to the floor. Alv had drawn my attention to this same thing when we'd stood by while the first ewe was in labor. What was it he'd told me then—that this string was a sign that birth was imminent? I raced back down the road, expending precious minutes fumbling with the loops and wires of Johannes's infirm gate.

Standing at the base of my neighbors' house, I wasn't sure what to do. I didn't want to wake Inger and the boys, but my ewe might need help any second now. After wavering a bit, I grabbed a pebble and threw it against the couple's bedroom window. Four or five tosses later, Torkel appeared and raised the sash.

"The fetal water is hanging out of the ewe!" I whisper-shouted, describing the situation with a term I'd heard Alv use during the first birth. He whispered back that he'd be along in a minute, and I sped back to the barn without waiting.

Torkel had attended barn births since before he could walk, so as soon as he arrived, it took only a quick glance to fix the time of delivery.

"Still about an hour off," he said.

I felt terrible. What an idiot I'd been to lose my head and wrench my good neighbor from bed. How he managed to smile at that point, I don't know. But there it was: that guileless smile casting its halo of wrinkles from the corners of his eyes.

"Looks like we're going to get to spend some more time together, Liese," he said. And instead of fussing, he did what he could to put me at ease, to make it seem as if this were something he'd done dozens, perhaps hundreds, of times before. No, there was nothing odd about hanging out in a barn at three thirty in the morning with a foreigner—a young woman he barely knew—clad in boots, sweater, and nightgown.

We decided to go to the house, where the wait would be more comfortable. Seated at the kitchen table, Torkel fished a pouch of tobacco and papers from his jacket pocket and rolled a cigarette.

"*Ja, ja,* Liese," he said softly, "how do you like the job?"

"It's exciting," I replied, "and fun. At least so far."

"You're here at the best time for a farmer. The animals are outdoors taking care of themselves. There's not much to do except wait for the grass to grow. When the haying starts, it's going to get harder."

"I wish I didn't need so much help from you and everyone else," I told him. “I feel like I’m causing lots of trouble. I’m sorry. And I’m really sorry that I got you too early now. I just don’t know what I’m doing.”

He dragged on the cigarette and smiled. “Don’t worry. I’m used to getting up at night for my sheep, and I’m happy to get up for yours, too. We’re going to make a good farmer out of you soon enough. I’m sure of that.”

We sat in drowsy silence for half an hour longer before going back to the barn to witness another untroubled birth. Torkel walked home and I went upstairs to bed, hoping for an hour’s nap before morning chores. My last thought before falling asleep was that if anyone ever asked me what characterizes a gentleman, I’d tell them the story of my neighbor Torkel, who stayed awake all through the night to help me because I didn’t know what I was doing. And how he never made me feel bad about it.

12
Exodus

Early in June, on a cloudy evening just after supper, fourteen able-bodied souls assembled by the barn door. The crowd included Ingebjørg and Ola along with four of their children and Johannes's brother Gunnar along with his wife and three children. We all listened intently as Gunnar, in his calm and detached manner, outlined the strategy for our evening endeavor: *saueslеppet,* the releasing of sheep to the mountains, one of the most significant events of the farming year.

An expectant air had permeated the neighborhood for days now. Lambs were growing bigger and gaining the strength they'd need to endure the rigors of life above timberline, while reports were trickling in that forage conditions at higher elevations were improving.

"Our sheep spend November to May crowded into cold, dark barns," Solveig had told me. "But during their summers in the mountains, they're as free as every other wild animal. We're free then, too . . . free of having to care for them, and our fields are free from their grazing. As soon as they're gone, you'll be watching your grass grow higher and higher. By the time Johannes gets home, you'll be making hay."

That sounded good, but now as I watched the crowd assemble, I was wondering why it would take so many people to herd forty-five ewes and some seventy lambs through a gate.

"We'll spread out along the far side of the fields and advance inward—very, very slowly," Gunnar ordered. "We have to keep every animal moving or we'll run into problems."

He turned to me, the least experienced of the group. "It's important to go slowly. We don't want to frighten them. The best strategy is to keep far behind, so they hardly know you're coming after them." I nodded, and he did that little half smile of his, where his eyes—blue as glacial ice—remained immobile.

He sent Martha Johanne, Ola and Ingebjørg's nine-year-old daughter, high up the hill to open the gate for us, and he told me to keep Bella tied in the yard; Johannes's young dog had strong herding instincts but as yet no training. Then he split us into three teams, assigning his ten-year-old son, Svein, and me to a group under Ola's direction.

Each team was sent to a different corner of the farm's lower fields, with orders to assemble our widely scattered flock into a single group. My team's measured sweep went well at first. Staying far behind the knot of sheep gathered ahead of us, we let them think it was their own idea to move upslope. Soon we found ourselves on a parallel path with Gunnar's team and their dozen animals. As our groups merged, a couple of ewes began to suspect that something was amiss. First one and then another paused to look back.

"Stop," Gunnar commanded quietly. "Don't move until they settle down."

We held our positions for a couple of minutes until a few animals began nibbling on nearby plants, at which point our captain deemed it safe enough to resume our slow uphill march. But we didn't get far. A ewe, startled by some unseen terror, suddenly bolted away. And as she did, every one of her companions followed suit.

We humans had no option but to trudge back to our initial posts to start the operation anew. Working even more cautiously on this second attempt, it took us nearly an hour to gather ewes and lambs into a single flock. At that point, with a long line of people proceeding at a snail's pace behind this group of more than one hundred animals, the going got easier. When the fence with its wide-open gate came into view, my fellow herders and I exchanged tentative smiles of success.

We were less than thirty yards shy of our goal when the flock halted. I froze, too, waiting for the lead animals to spearhead a stampede to freedom. Surely all of these ewes harbored memories of summers past when they were at liberty to wander wherever they chose, from one sweet mountain meadow to the next.

But now they were glaring suspiciously at the fence ahead. For half a dozen heartbeats neither human nor animal moved. Then a big ewe snorted, another stamped her foot—and the entire flock exploded, bursting away in every direction like the birth of a universe.

In a flash, we abandoned our go-slow strategy and tore after our quarry. With hearts racing and feet pounding the ground, we had no other thought than to run the ewes down one by one and drag them through the gate.

The chase lasted another hour. Working in pairs we pursued small groups of animals, driving them uphill, leaving them no time to think about which way they were headed. Ola instructed Martha to stay by the gate and pull it closed behind each ewe and lamb we forced through it. From every corner of the farm came the sounds of wailing sheep, whistles, yells, commands, and full-throated curses.

By the time Svein and I reached the gate again—now with two ewes and three lambs careering ahead of us—a few sheep were already huddled on its far side. Our young gatekeeper was at her post and pulled open the portal just at the right moment. I braced myself to tear after any sheep that might turn aside, but to my amazement, not one of them wavered as they joined their companions in *utmarka,* the outer lands, on the other side. Martha shoved the gate closed, and we three comrades-in-arms saluted each other with cries of victory.

Each new group of animals ran through the gateway more willingly than the last. Apparently the open country that had so terrified them a short while earlier now looked more inviting, populated as it was by their friends and neighbors.

At ten o'clock that evening, when the night sky was still light enough to read a book by, we escorted our last holdouts into the mountains. Everyone headed home, and I went inside and collapsed into bed. Images of galloping sheep kept me awake for at least an hour as a question rolled uneasily about in my head: If getting the sheep to leave was this hard, how could Johannes ever get them back home again?

For a couple of days, the familiar bleating of ewes and lambs carried downhill to my ears. But soon the animals drifted farther upslope, finding their way to favored mountain haunts.

My life was quieter and lonelier without the sheep. Over these past weeks, I'd grown fond of various ewes, particularly the older, calmer ones and those with recognizable traits who I'd endowed with names like Ragged Right Ear and Bleats Like a Bullfrog. So I was happy to keep my two favorite ewes at home for another fourteen days. These were the pair that had been the last to lamb. During our weeks together, they eventually lost their fear of me and actually seemed pleased to have me around. It didn't hurt that I spoiled them with extra rations of grain, which they learned to eat straight from my hand. They even let me pick up their infant lambs the day Alv came to brand them, Norwegian style.

He handled this task with the same calm skill I'd witnessed at earlier encounters. As I held the small creatures for him, he used a razor-sharp knife to shear off the tips of both ears and carve a small half-moon into the margin of the right. Every farm had its own distinctive earmark, and this was Johannes's. The lambs flinched at each cut, then shook their heads in short bursts for a minute or two before getting on with their day as if nothing unusual had befallen them. As soon as these two grew strong and fleet enough for the rigors of mountain life, it would be my job to shoo them and their mothers out the gate, too.

If not for the bottomless task of weeding, Torkel would have been right about this being an easy time for a farmer. Every sheep pen was finally empty, and Begonia was outside, too, grazing happily in a large fenced pasture beyond the hayfields. Even the ram was gone, taken away to the slaughterhouse. Genetics determined his fate. For two years he'd sired the farm's lambs. Now that his oldest daughters were ready to be bred in the fall, the flock needed a new alpha male: one from a different bloodline, to avoid inbreeding.

Of course, I still had to milk twice a day, a task that Solveig had only recently allowed me to manage on my own. For another week, she informed me, I should continue milking in the barn. During the day, I was to turn both bovines into the fields that the sheep had just vacated. Then in another week or two—when the grass was high enough—I would transfer both cow and heifer to the pasture where Begonia was now grazing. At that point, I would start milking in a little shed out there, about a hundred yards from the barn. Begonia, in turn, would move into a forest just below the pasture.

This left only the calf as a full-time barn resident. Born just a few weeks before I arrived, he was still a baby, only bigger now, with silky, red hair; a wet, sensitive nose; and an aching desire for contact with other warm beings. Each time I entered the barn, the little creature's soft, throaty cries beckoned me to stroke his neck and rub his ears. Bella couldn't resist him, either. Whenever she squeezed into his pen, he responded by alternating between dancing in excitement and nuzzling up to her, confused, it seemed, as to whether the dog was his friend or mother.

When people first settled Hovland two or three thousand years ago, the hillsides would have been blanketed by forests and scattered with stones and boulders. Clearing the land was a backbreaking, never-ending task on which the farms' survival depended. Trees and shrubs were burned, boulders smashed apart, and rocks and stones plucked from the earth and piled in mounds or stacked into foundations and walls. Over the centuries, Hovlanders pushed out in all directions, eventually breaking every bit of ground that could support a crop.

The story of these efforts was written in Hovland's fences, which demarcated not Johannes's and his forebears' capacity to clear the land but the earth's limits in yielding up cultivable tracts. Solveig's instructions to move livestock from one fenced enclosure to another were designed to take advantage of every nourishing leaf and blade on Johannes's farm. During summer months, his fenced forest produced just enough fodder for Begonia, his pasture just enough for the cows. Before we herded his sheep to the mountains, they had been grazing on his fenced hayfields: the only acreage he owned that could produce this vital crop. Now that the red cow and the young black cow (which I'd eventually figured out was called a heifer) were grazing on these fields, they too were gobbling up the precious grass, which was why I needed to move them to their pasture next door as soon as conditions were right.

A dearth of good land was one jaw of the vise squeezing Hovland's farmers; the other was a growing season that didn't start until May and petered out toward the end of September. The average temperature in July, the year's balmiest month, was a mere 55 degrees Fahrenheit. By October, the average temperature at Hovland dropped to a miserable 41 degrees: not so bad for hardy crops like potatoes, carrots, and rutabagas but too cold to produce enough grass for more than one harvest. In contrast, farmers with land at lower elevations—like the fields around Øystese only a few feet above sea level—could squeeze two and sometimes even three hay harvests into a season.

A dismal corollary of the short growing season for crops was the long period of barn confinement for livestock. Weather was so raw and forage so sparse in late fall and early spring that animals could fend for themselves only during the warmest five or six months of the year. From November to May they had to be housed inside, where day after day they consumed the farm's hard-earned supply of feed.

Although cultivated land was scarce, *utmarka* was vast. During the summer months when sheep (and, decades earlier, cows) roamed the mountains, they harvested their own feed, relieving farmers of the burden of doing it for them. This was a remarkably efficient method of converting wild plants into wool, meat, and milk. Access to mountain forage almost doubled the number of animals that Hovland's farms could support.

"You'll need to check on your sheep at least every couple of weeks," Gunnar had solemnly declared after we pushed the last ewe out the gate that evening. "With this flock, it's not always easy. Some of these ewes range far beyond Hyrting."

He must have misread the excitement these words stirred in me, for he was quick to add, almost by way of apology, that many of my neighbors enjoyed this task more than any other. I had to stifle my laughter over the good fortune of landing in a neighborhood of mountaineering farmers and of holding down a job requiring treks into a wilderness that I longed to explore.

13

Attack of the Mad Heifer

I did my best to hide how awkward I felt when walking through Soldal's cluster of houses, where I knew hardly anyone and no one waved or smiled at me. My destination was a three-walled shed known as the milk ramp, which stood across from Soldal's last farmhouse, right where the broad, hilly shelf that this little community sat on took a downhill dive toward town. Three days a week local farmers left their double-handled steel milk cans here to be collected by a truck from Øystese's dairy. The shed also served as a shelter for kids waiting for the school bus. Most importantly for me, this diminutive building was where I got my mail. Mounted on its north wall were two rows of green metal boxes, one for each household at Hovland and Soldal. In the middle of the top row was a larger box painted bright red and secured with a padlock. Emblazoned with the word *POST* in gold letters, it was for outgoing mail.

I slipped my letters through its slot before lifting the lid of my green box. Inside was an envelope addressed to me from Johannes. I opened it on the spot and pulled out its entire contents: five one-hundred-kroner bills. If he meant this as pay for the four weeks I'd been working, it was more than the one hundred kroner per week he'd offered at our first meeting. A momentary feeling of pride washed over me with the thought that this extra pay could be a token of my boss's approval. And I was overjoyed to finally have some cash in my pocket, for almost everything here seemed to be about twice as expensive as at home, and my money had been trickling away.

I first noticed that something was wrong with the heifer on a Saturday afternoon. The big black animal was pacing the hillsides and mooing loudly. She also began to take an unnatural interest in my comings and goings. Whenever I went into the field, she followed me like a dog, sometimes brushing her head against me. I couldn't tell whether she was being affectionate or aggressive, but it hardly mattered, because she was so strong and reckless that she could kill me either way. Her behavior worsened each day, to the point that each time I needed to enter her domain, I'd wait until she was out of sight to sneak in and execute the task at hand.

On Monday I'd just finished checking on my two ewes with their young lambs, when both the cow and the heifer trotted into sight from behind a thicket of saplings. Grunting her usual greeting, the younger animal lurched toward me, tossing her head dangerously close to mine as if I were a long-lost friend. I tried to maintain a dominant attitude, giving her a deep-voiced warning and a firm punch on the neck.

She backed off, and I turned to leave. But in a trice, she reared up behind me, landing her forelegs onto my shoulders. How I was able to stay upright I'll never understand, for at least two hundred pounds were bearing down on my back. I staggered forward, dipped, and twisted left, expecting to be pushed to the ground by her weight or to be knocked senseless by one of her heavy hooves. Somehow, though, I found myself in the clear and, miraculously, intact.

"You stupid, dumb cow! Get away!" I screamed, smacking her on the neck and shoulder. With a low murmur, she turned and trotted off, and I retreated to the other side of the gate.

"Sounds like she's *stutagalen,*" Solveig said when she dropped by that afternoon. "You'd better be careful around her for a while."

"*Stutagalen?*" I asked. "Do you mean she's *gal,* mad?" I knew that in Danish, the word for "rabies" was *hundegalskab,* a combination of the words for "dog" and "madness."

The possibility that the heifer might be rabid was horrifying. I reviewed the encounter, thinking out loud to Solveig. "She didn't try to bite me, and my skin isn't broken anyplace." If the heifer did indeed have rabies, at least for the time being I was all right.

"How can I tell if she's *gal?*" I asked somberly. "What should I look for?"

"You just have to wait a couple of days and see if she changes," Solveig replied. "But don't worry. I'm sure she's fine."

It seemed odd that after suggesting this animal could be incurably ill and I was in danger of my life, Solveig was not taking the matter more seriously. Perhaps, I told myself, she didn't know enough about the disease to be afraid of it.

I didn't follow her advice to not worry. The house, garden, and outbuildings were a little island surrounded on all sides by cow and heifer territory. Unless I was going to wall myself off indoors, almost everything I did required entering their perilous domain.

For the next two days, whenever I went outside I carried a stout stick and watched for the heifer as if I were a field vole scanning for hawks. Keeping tabs on her from a distance, I scrutinized her muzzle for drool or any other telltale signs of the dread disease. On Tuesday I was relieved to see that she was considerably calmer, and by Wednesday, she was back to her old self. Solveig stopped by that afternoon, and I gave her a full report.

"Sounds as if she definitely was *stutagalen,*" she said. "You should write down the dates and tell Johannes about it. My guess is he'll want to get her inseminated next time around."

I looked at Solveig blankly. What was she talking about? Get the heifer inseminated next time she had rabies? My mind raced through the possibilities. *Gal* meant mad—that I was sure of. But what, exactly, did *stut* mean? When it suddenly dawned on me, I felt my face turn red.

"*Stut,*" I said, with contrived casualness. "Is that a boy cow?"

"Of course it is, girl!" Solveig said, ratcheting her voice into that special range she reserved for addressing idiots.

Now everything fell into place. *Stutagalen* didn't mean dog madness; it meant bull craziness. The heifer was not rabid but in heat. And since there were no boy cows around, she'd taken a fancy to me instead.

In mid-June, I traveled by myself on my third trip to the hospital, a journey that took four hours, starting with a 5:30 a.m. walk to Øystese, followed by the bus and little train. In my hand I held a long list of questions.

"You've finished weeding, right?" Johannes asked first thing. The statement startled me. I'd sent him a letter a week earlier saying that it was impossible for me to keep up with the weeds. I'd spent hours combatting them, yet only half his garden was clean. Endless days of rain were partially responsible: precipitation seemed to nourish the most invasive plants while hampering my efforts to deal with them. On top of that, the repetitive actions of weeding and milking—especially in chilly, wet weather—were taking a toll. My fingers turned white and cold whenever I worked in the garden, milked the cow, or held a pen, and sometimes even when I was doing nothing at all. Yet it didn't seem to matter what I said or wrote to him. His brain was like a woodworking shop, cutting apart my sentences then piecing them back together into whatever shape suited him.

He'd made some small improvements since our last visit, which he demonstrated by wiggling his left thumb and bending his left leg ever so slightly. So when a nurse appeared at the door to ask if we'd like to move to a nearby balcony, she and I were able to shift him into a wheelchair without too much trouble.

Outside a thin layer of clouds blanketed the sky, and the air was mild and comforting. Our view from this aerie stretched over the town's slate roofs across a large lake to a narrow band of farms at the foot of a long, snow-covered ridge.

"It's a nice house you're living in, isn't it?" Johannes asked quietly, without really asking. "You should have everything you need there."

"Yes, it's a beautiful house," I answered, surprised by the sudden realization of how much I'd grown to like his place.

"Is there anything you miss from home?"

"Not really, no. I'm having a great time at Hovland. I'm making friends and working a lot. There's no time to miss anyone."

A glint of sun broke through the clouds. I turned toward it and squinted, feeling its warmth on my face.

"Oh, but yeah, there is actually something I miss. My piano. When I was at home, I played it every day."

His thoughts had already moved elsewhere.

"I've been meaning to tell you, I hear that Edvard has been coming to my farm. And other men, too." His voice was flat now. "I don't want them visiting when you're there alone."

I looked at him with a blank face. All the good will from our pleasant talk slipped away. How dare he dictate who I was allowed to see? And didn't he realize that it was only because of the efforts of good-hearted people like Edvard that his farm was staying afloat?

Yet I was afraid to incur his anger, so I bottled up my feelings and mumbled that I had a train to catch, tacking on a few words about how much time Alv and Edvard had spent helping him.

As I wheeled the farmer back to his room, I tried to get answers to at least a few of the questions I'd come with. The most valuable piece of information I gleaned from the visit was that I needed to call the insemination technician right away to let him know we'd soon need his services. "Keep your eye on the creature every day starting next week," Johannes told me. "Then call him back as soon as you catch the earliest signs."

14

Worlds Apart

Johannes's question about whether I missed anything from home had me thinking about my family and friends during the four-hour trip back to the farm. The last time I'd seen my mother was on April 12, when she and my sister Sara had taken me to San Francisco for the first leg of my long journey to Øystese. Plane fare was far more than I could afford, so I'd charted a five-week route at a fraction of the cost: overland to New York, from there a cheap flight to Luxembourg, followed by various trains, ferries, and buses. I slept on board sitting up and made seven stops along the way to visit far-flung friends, including a two-week stay with my host family in Denmark.

We left Mill Valley before dawn with Sara at the wheel. A storm was rolling in as we crossed the Golden Gate Bridge, then wound along San Francisco's waterfront to a gargantuan tangle of water-spewing concrete tubes. Normally we would have made a couple of jokes about this new municipal sculpture. Instead, we said not a word as we studied a loose-knit group of young people milling around the clunky, oversized van parked just ahead.

Mom broke the silence with a deep sigh and a question. "Are you sure this is what you want to do?"

When I nodded, she sighed again and opened the door.

I was about to cross the country in a remodeled bookmobile, one of those libraries-on-wheels that make weekly visits to schools and rest homes. I'd discovered it on a ride-sharing board: only forty dollars from one coast to the other, even less for me because I'd be jumping ship in Ohio for my first visit.

Mom, Sara, and I held together as we surveyed the van and my soon-to-be fellow passengers. Men and women alike wore their hair long in ponytails or hanging loose—not unlike my own, which was pulled into a short brown braid. Almost all of us were dressed in blue jeans and nondescript tops, but a sprinkling of paisley knee patches and hand-embroidered shirt collars testified to the lingering spirit of the 1960s.

Considering that I was about to jump into a hippie van on the first leg of a three-year round-the-world trip, Mom was remarkably sanguine. Perhaps she was remembering how she'd eloped at age eighteen, then spent more than a decade hanging out with poets, writers, artists, and other Bohemian types in various corners of the country. Or maybe watching her five children come of age in the Bay Area of the sixties had thickened her skin. She and our father had stood at our sides as we threw ourselves into the politics of that era: unionization of farmworkers, civil rights, and protests against the Vietnam War. And they'd watched us steer through ground zero of the countercultural revolution of drugs and free love. They must have known that we'd dipped our toes into all of it. Now, in 1972, she was probably breathing a bit easier, recognizing that we'd made it safely through those heady years and that our experiences were standing us in good stead.

As I stepped into the bookmobile, eager to be setting out, my mother delivered her one imperative, her single admonition.

"Write," she said. "Write me a letter every week. If you don't have time for a letter, send a postcard, just one line to let me know how you are. You know how much I'll worry if I don't hear from you."

By the time my parents moved to Mill Valley in 1951, my big brother was eight years old, my sister Anne was two, Sara was just a few months old, and Mom was pregnant again, this time with me. The last of my four siblings, Ben, was born just before I turned three.

Mom and Dad were not the cuddly kind of parents who showered their kids with praise, yet we knew they loved us and would stand by us whenever we needed them. Mom read us bedtime stories every night when we were little, and Dad shared his love of books by choosing just the right one for each of us at birthdays and Christmas.

Both of our parents instilled a sense of social justice in all of us. They told us about the Holocaust that occurred before we were born and about Jim Crow laws and voter-suppression tactics that were still rampant in the South. We knew they had friends whose lives had been upended by red-baiting inquisitions of Senator Joseph McCarthy and the House Un-American Activities Committee. At a time when gay people had to conceal their sexuality to avoid discrimination, violence, and even arrest, our parents were open with us about which of their friends were gay and about the bigotry they faced.

As I moved into my teens, protests against the Vietnam War were ramping up, and Sara and I started going to San Francisco for marches and sit-ins. We felt fortunate to have parents who supported us, for many young people returned from marches to violent confrontations with parents who were dead set against demonstrations and every other aspect of the burgeoning counterculture. We even knew of fathers who threatened sons for growing their hair long. In contrast, Dad marched with me a few times, and as an ACLU board member, he defended everyone's right to protest. By the time I was fifteen, he had grown his hair long, too.

While we were growing up, our parents' friends, a mélange of artists, filmmakers, writers, and poets, played an outsized role in our lives. At least half a dozen of the rather eccentric people who befriended Mom during her peripatetic years had also moved to the Bay Area, while Dad's earliest contribution to the mix consisted of three classmates from his years at Reed College who were prime forces behind the Beat movement in San Francisco. Two of them, poets Lew Welch and Gary Snyder, were frequent guests in our home.

For a while in 1956, Gary and his friend Jack Kerouac lived across the street in a little cabin at the top of a steep trail. Kerouac memorialized this place and time in his book *The Dharma Bums.* Our mother even appeared on a few pages as "a gal named Jane."

In 1962, Mom and Dad went in with four other families to buy a fourteen-acre parcel that encompassed a rundown tavern, eight or nine decrepit little cabins, and Muir Beach, a one-thousand-foot crescent of sand tucked into endless hills of coastal scrub. By then Mom was eager to do something besides mothering her flock, so she started working as landlord of the cabins and manager of the tavern's bar and snack bar.

For a few years we four kids accompanied her almost every weekend. The twenty-minute drive took us over a long shoulder of Mount Tamalpais, then down a treacherously curving road through air scented with a minty, sage-like aroma wafting in from the hills. Reaching the tavern, a long, low building at the edge of the beach, the earthy smell of land gave way to a kelp-scented breeze blowing in from the sea.

We helped out wherever we could: sweeping floors, selling candy and chips, flipping hamburgers, washing dishes. During the first few years, the place rarely attracted a crowd, for the beach was tucked into a cove that not only held onto fog but seemed to nurture it as well.

In 1965, Mom opened a restaurant there and named it Wobbly Rock, after a meditation-on-life poem by Lew Welch. She had a vision for the place and refined it with the help of a young chef named Sandy Stewart, who specialized in Italian and French cuisine. Their plan was to serve dinners only, on Friday, Saturday, and Sunday evenings, offering a menu of just two or three entrees and desserts, all designed around the freshest ingredients available that week.

Wobbly Rock's entire waitstaff consisted of us three sisters, with Mom and Sandy coming out of the kitchen to pour wine, chat up guests, and bask in the praise showered on them by ecstatic diners—for Sandy truly was a great chef.

"Serve from the left, pick up from the right," Mom commanded. We worked for tips and occasionally spilled a plateful of food on a diner's lap. Fortunately, we were young and just cute enough that guests (most of them) found us charming rather than incompetent.

Throughout high school, I felt I was straddling two worlds, not completely at home in either. On one side were my parents with their intellectual, artistic, and Bohemian friends; my weekends at Muir Beach; the days I spent hanging out with my sister Sara and her hip friends; and demonstrations against the war in Vietnam. On the other side was school. My four best girlfriends inhabited this side. All five of us were academic nerds, expecting no less from one another than our class's top grades. I spent more time with them than with anyone else outside my family. We didn't talk about boys, and none of us had a boyfriend.

School and my friends won out in the end. I always knew I was heading to college, which was odd, because our parents never pushed any of us in that direction. In fact, they never pushed us in any direction at all. Nor did they tell us what *not* to do. So I always felt that any decision I needed to make was mine and mine alone.

15

A Swim in Skårsvatnet

Toward the end of June it finally got hot. Windows were thrown open in all of Hovland's houses. Livestock disappeared into thickets of trees at midday to wait out the heat. I weeded in cut-off jeans and a T-shirt, wilting along with Johannes's plants under the bright sun. Every time I passed a thermometer on the house's north wall, I took a look. It didn't seem possible that a paltry 77 degrees could feel so hot.

Edvard appeared midafternoon. He was on summer vacation now and had visited several times this past week, always finding work that needed doing. There was an alternate route to the farm, and that was how he came. It led up a trail through the forest where Begonia now resided, then crossed into the cow and heifer's pasture at the farm's eastern border. This path bypassed Soldal altogether, for, like me, Edvard wasn't comfortable walking through that intimate cluster of farms whose residents tended to observe strangers rather than greet them.

He could show up at any time, always unannounced. But I didn't mind; I loved his smile and the gentle way he worked with Begonia and played with Bella. And I appreciated his patience in teaching me to drive the horse and the humor he'd found in my predicament the night of the brandy incident. He was a tall and handsome enigma who came to work without pay for a man who had almost no friends. And I'd been crazy about him since the day we met.

Trying to figure out how he felt about me was pure torture. Some days I was sure I was his motive for coming to the farm. Other days I was sure I was wrong, especially after Inger told me that he'd been helping Johannes for years. He did seem to enjoy spending time with me. At the end of each work day, I would make a meal for us both, and we'd sit in the kitchen taking our time with food and conversation.

On this hot day, he found me sitting in the shade on a garden step taking a break from weeding.

"Want to go for a swim today?" he asked. "The lake's warming up, so I brought along my swimming trunks."

My heart skipped a beat. He'd never proposed that we do anything together.

"People go swimming there?" I asked, trying to sound casual.

"It's the best place to swim for miles around. That's where everyone goes. If we quit a little early, we can get down there before the sun drops too low."

I told him I'd love to, and he headed to the barn to get to work.

Actually, his question surprised me in more ways than one. The thought had never crossed my mind that people in Norway *ever* swam. It had been rainy and cold for most of June; icy water ran in the creek at the farm's border; my vista from the garden still took in plenty of snow; and water in the fjord was freezing. Even on this hot day, until Edvard had mentioned it, the concept of swimming had been as remote as the North Pole.

When we called it quits for the day, I ran inside to grab a towel and an extra set of clothes; I didn't have a swimsuit, so I'd have to jump in wearing shorts and a T-shirt. Edvard tied a rope to Bella's collar and we headed out, backtracking the way he'd come, through the pasture and down the forest trail.

As we walked, I gave an account of my recent trip to Voss. When I told him how upset I was over Johannes's statements about men visiting me at the farm, he burst into laughter.

"Poor Johs," he said, using his nickname for the farmer. "He's not a bad person, really. He just thinks he can control what other people do. He can't, of course, so there's no sense in you worrying about what he says."

I was dubious, but Edvard's reassurance helped quell my anxiety over defying Johannes's directive. Then again, Edvard laughed about a lot of things. His face always held a half smile and his brown eyes a slight glimmer, making me think that he was eternally entertained by the goings-on around him. There was a slight detachment in his manner, too, as if he had carved out a small gap between himself and everyone else, a space that allowed him to stand back and observe, perceiving things that others couldn't.

This was my first time on the forest trail, so I was astonished when we popped out of the woods after a short walk, and there was Skårsvatnet just across the road right in front of us, a lovely little grass-fringed lake set in a shallow basin of forested hills.

Edvard led me to a broad rock that sloped gently into the tea-colored water. Along the shore to our left, meadows ripe with grass wound through stands of trees and snaked around two farmsteads before giving way to a leafy forest lining the far shore. On our right, a patch of potatoes, cabbages, rutabagas, and carrots ran in straight rows down to the water's edge. A year's supply for a family, with some left over to sell, Edvard said. Farther away we could see a long red building. This was a community hall, he explained, used mostly for meetings, dances, and parties.

Edvard dove in first and had already reached the opposite shore a couple hundred yards distant by the time I started inching my way in. I was self-conscious about my figure and how a wet shirt would highlight the little paunch at my belly. But those thoughts disappeared as soon I got used to the cool water, which felt wonderful as long as I didn't let my legs dip into the chilly layer just below the surface. I swam a little but mostly just lay on my back, drifting with eyes closed, relaxed and weightless, savoring the sensation of immersion after weeks of living in a house with no shower or tub.

Bella ran back and forth along the shore, tracking us with a worried eye. We called her, but no amount of cajoling could get her into the water.

"She's probably never gone swimming before," Edvard said. "I'll bet she'd like it if she gave it a try."

He waded to the bank, picked up the little dog and tossed her in. She swam back to shore with short, desperate strokes. "She probably just needs time to get used to it," I suggested. He pitched her in again, and this time as she floundered back to land, she fixed us with such a look of misery that we both felt like criminals. Apparently swimming was not in her genes.

After a while the sun slid behind a hill, taking its warmth with it. We toweled off and sat next to each other on the long smooth rock, watching circular ripples spread in the water where fish were feeding on the evening's insect hatch. Edvard's hand was resting on the warm stone just inches away; I felt each beat of my heart and an odd wooziness in my stomach as I imagined that hand slipping over mine.

"They say there are eels in the lake," he said quietly. "They live here for a year or two and then swim down the creek to the fjord and all the way to the Caribbean."

"That's amazing. I wonder how they can find their way back."

I thought about the eels while I waited for his hand to move. When it didn't, I looked down at my own fingers and willed them to slide to his. But they were glued in place, too.

"Well, I'd better be getting home," he said after a bit.

We pulled dry clothes over our wet swimming outfits and went our separate ways. As I pushed through low-hanging branches on my way back up the trail, my mind was filled with this tall fellow who appeared so often at the farm and who was so kind to me. I realized that he was the only person I felt comfortable talking with about my thoughts and experiences since arriving at Hovland, and I let my mind brood over questions that were growing all too familiar, wondering what he thought of me and whether it was for my sake or Johannes's that he kept coming back to the farm.

Later that week, Johannes's brother Gunnar showed up at the house bearing a large radio. It belonged to Johannes, he said, and had been in the repair shop for nearly two months. That evening, I searched for news in English on the old, wood-cased instrument, switching between shortwave, AM, and FM as I dialed up and down the long tuner. I had a lot of catching up to do: the war in Vietnam was ongoing, and Richard Nixon was running for reelection against a Democratic Party that was making a mess of choosing its nominee. When I eventually found both the BBC's evening news broadcast and its classical music program, my world was complete. From then on, news and music filled the kitchen of the old farmhouse for an hour or two every evening.

16

Of Cows and Manure

"Your friends tell me you've become a fine milkmaid!" a loud voice called out. Startled, I looked up from milking to see Øystein Hovland, one of Torkel's brothers, striding my way over the barn floor. It had been more than a week since I'd met this powerfully built man who had volunteered to repair Johannes's hay wagon for me. Now I was so surprised he was actually following up on his offer that my only response was to ask if he'd had breakfast yet.

"I wanted to get here as early as possible," he replied. "I thought if I found you in the barn, I could make coffee for both of us while you finished up."

Such an unexpected offer from a near stranger confused me even further.

"No, no," I managed to spit out. "Let me do that. I'm almost done here."

"Well, I'm going to the kitchen right now, so you might as well tell me where you hide your coffee."

"It's in the cupboard," I called out as he disappeared around a corner, "just above the stove to the right!"

By the time I got to the kitchen with my bucket of milk, Øystein was sitting at the table over a pot of coffee and a spread of food he'd foraged from the pantry.

Øy and *stein:* island and stone. I'd never heard the name before I met him, but it seemed a good fit for this handsome man with a long, angular face framed by wisps of white hair. He was in his early fifties, I figured, possibly a bit younger. I'd learned that he worked at a hydroelectric power plant about seven miles north of his cabin, which sat just above Fyksesund, a narrow branch of Hardanger Fjord straight down the mountainside from Hovland. On weeknights he slept in barracks at the plant. Then on Friday and Sunday evenings, instead of spending three hours on buses and trains circling around the mountains that lay between his home and work, he spent six hours hiking right over them.

That a man (one I barely knew) would make breakfast for me impressed me deeply. Even so, the meal turned out to be somewhat awkward. Except for discussing work that needed doing, neither of us seemed to know what to say to the other.

We finished eating and he disappeared into the barn's upper loft, where the farm's horse-drawn vehicles were stored. By dinnertime, *middag,* he'd restored Johannes's hay wagon to good working condition, ready for summer's harvest. Promising to return in a week to do more, he left on a trail leading downhill from the pasture a hundred yards north of the trail that Edvard ascended when he visited. I accompanied him that far, and as I watched him making the steep descent to Fyksesund, I felt myself hoping that he was serious about returning.

The heifer came into heat again on the first Sunday in July. Troublesome as always, she chose a day when it cost twice the standard rate for a house call by the insemination technician. He arrived late in the afternoon, bearing a clunky canister filled with liquid nitrogen and long thin tubes of frozen bull semen.

The operation was brief. I held the heifer's muscular black tail to one side while he carefully manipulated a rod loaded with semen along her vagina and into her uterus, at which point he depressed a plunger to deposit the payload.

As he was washing off, the technician informed me that this procedure's success rate was only a little better than 50 percent, so I'd need to keep a close eye on my charge over the coming weeks. If she didn't come into heat again, he told me, I'd have a calf in nine months.

This high-tech intrusion on the farm was jarring, and I was filled with questions. Where was the bull that supplied this semen? What was its breed? Why did Johannes want to use artificial insemination instead of the real thing?

It was a Sunday afternoon, and my guest was in no hurry. He leaned against his van in the farmyard, lit a cigarette, and told me the story.

In 1935, a group of Norwegian dairy farmers organized a breeding association with the hope of producing a healthier cow that gave more milk. Before then, each region of the country had its own favorite breed. The problem was that people had formed a rather romanticized notion of what their particular kind of cow was supposed to look like, so animals were being bred for appearance rather than performance. The new organization took the radical approach of ignoring a cow's superficial traits to focus on attributes that actually affected a farmer's bottom line, like milk production, meat quality, and resistance to udder infections.

This approach involved crossing Norwegian breeds with each other, as well as incorporating foreign breeds like Ayrshires and Friesians into their gene pool, undertakings that traditionalists regarded as nothing short of sacrilegious.

Meanwhile, advances in artificial insemination had created a reliable means of distributing bull semen without distributing the animals themselves. So much so that for the past ten years, it had been possible for every cow in Norway to be inseminated by a prize bull without any of the animals leaving their home fields.

Snuffing out his cigarette, he went on to explain that both my cow and my heifer were enrolled in the national breeding program, along with 90 percent of all of Norway's cows. That was why he was permitted to come to the farm today: only enrolled animals were eligible to receive a tube of the precious semen from his canister.

"Well, then, what kind of cows are these?" I asked him. "Are they all mixed up, or do they have a name?"

"Why, they're *norsk rødt fe,*" he said with surprise. "Norwegian red cows. You didn't know?"

During his visit, the technician had found something new for me to worry about: my cow, apparently, had stubby teats.

"How do you manage to milk her?" he'd asked.

When I gave a demonstration, he shook his head in pity.

"Look how cramped your hands are up against the udder. You're just barely getting three fingers around a teat. The udder is small, too. I'm not sure it would be worth Johannes's time to get her inseminated again."

The stubby teats were more than just a bother. The combination of three-fingered milking twice a day and weeding in cold, wet weather was making the numbness in my hands worse. Sometimes I'd wake up in the middle of the night and my whole arm would feel dead. As the circulation returned, the pain was so intense all I could do was grit my teeth and whimper.

Solveig was sympathetic. In her decades of farmwork, she was no stranger to this kind of injury. She volunteered to take over evening milkings for me and insisted that I stay out of the garden until my hands improved.

To substitute for garden work, I took on a new chore: mucking out Johannes's sheep pens. Confined indoors for five or six months from fall to spring, the ewes compacted everything that landed under their hooves into a dense, adobelike material. Most farmers cleaned out this accretion of hay, manure, and dried urine every spring; Johannes hadn't done so for two or three years, and the buildup was nearly half a yard deep.

Mucking was odious work. The only way to sink a pickaxe into this layered, fetid mass was with a full-force, over-the-head swing. A lucky stroke could dislodge a bathmat-sized roll of the gunk an inch or two thick. More often than not, the blade simply embedded itself into the manure, and I'd have to twist and pry it out, ending up with only a small chunk of pay dirt for my effort. At this rate, it took at least fifteen minutes to fill a wheelbarrow.

Like soil at an archaeological site, the manure was stratified, its color, texture, and odor varying with depth. The upper strata were dark brown, with a strong, yet tolerable, manure smell. Six inches deeper, the smell acquired a hint of decay. At ten inches, a pallor came over the material, and fumes of sulfur and rotten eggs washed through the barn. At fifteen inches, the mass turned bluish gray and reeked of ammonia along with sulfur. Below that, I was too dazed to take note.

Before starting work each morning, I hitched Begonia to the manure cart and tethered her at the barn door. After four or five wheelbarrow loads from pen to cart, I drove to a site about 150 yards away and tipped the cart's contents into an ever-growing pile.

Working with the horse—and with Bella, who never strayed far from our side—was the best part of this job. The more time we spent together, the better we liked each other. Begonia was constantly on alert for my commands, even as she was forever testing just how much she could get away with before I joggled her into obedience with a verbal reprimand and quick tug of the lines.

One afternoon, as the three of us were driving back to the barn, Edvard showed up.

"Here's something you haven't seen yet," he said with a big grin. "Watch this."

Snapping his fingers over Begonia's back, he called out to Bella.

"Bella, come! Up, girl. Up, up!"

With a flying start, Bella leaped into the cart then bounded onto Begonia's back, where she promptly sat down.

"Bella! Up! Up!" Edvard cried again, with another snap of his fingers. Still sitting, the little dog leaned back and waved her front feet in the air.

"No, Bella, not like that," Edvard said sternly and snapped his fingers even higher over her head. "All the way up, Bella. Up, up!"

Wonder of wonders, my own little Bella rose onto her hind legs and stretched herself into a standing position for a second or two before dropping back to all fours.

"Good girl!" Edvard said, patting the little dog affectionately. "Good little Bella."

It was an electric moment. I couldn't fathom why Edvard hadn't shown this trick to me earlier, for I knew without a doubt that I would show it off to everyone within hailing distance anytime I had horse and dog together.

When I first started cleaning out the pens, I thought it would be a job with a beginning and an end, as opposed to the eternal work of barn chores and weeding. Yet ten days after I started, only two pens were completely free of manure. By that time my fingers had almost recovered, so it was a relief to quit mucking and take over evening milking from Solveig again. One job I wasn't going back to, however, was weeding. The fields were finally ripe for harvest. And with summer haying season upon us, the garden's weeds were now free to grow as they pleased.

17

Alv's Revolution

In the first week of July, Klyvenuten, the mountain that dominated my eastern vista, lost the last vestiges of snow nestled in its deep cleft. I'd been watching this long white remnant of winter dwindle away since early June. These past couple of days of hot weather—forerunners of a three-week dry spell—had hastened its demise. Snow was retreating from peaks on the far side of Hardanger Fjord, too. There the glacier Folgefonna—which had previously blended in with its white, snowy backdrop—was now an eye-riveting landmark draped like a saddle over the ridgeline.

The garden, too, was transformed. Ferns and bushes hung gracefully over its stone stairways, and most of Johannes's diminutive alpine plants were coming into bloom with showy flowers typical of high-elevation species. Now when I visited the largest pond, I could appreciate Johannes's mastery of horticulture. Here an exuberant mix of terrestrial greenery encircled the dark water, which itself was crowded with aquatic irises, lilies, bulrushes, and arums. I visited this pond daily, delighting in the botanical profusion that swept me away from any worries that might be weighing me down.

In the hayfields, millions of stamens dangled from grasses in full bloom, shifting the once-green tapestry to a flaxen hue. Where spring's ephemeral flowers had earlier lined every field and road, summer's coarser flora now stood tall: tufts of fragrant yarrow, stalks of angelica bursting with white umbels, bluebells nodding in the wind, and spikes of purple foxgloves. Here and there, a thick stem of curly dock marred this dazzling landscape, an irritation to farmers too busy with summer's work to dig out the invasive weed.

My little red calf was growing up, too. A few days earlier I'd turned him loose in the pasture with the cow and heifer and he exploded with happiness. Running for the first time in his life, he flew across the ground as hard and fast as his legs could carry him. Since then, whenever I went to the pasture he raced around me in long loops, stopping every now and then to let me rub his head. He loved to jump, and once he flew right over Bella's back. Ever since arriving at the farm, I'd been rough-housing with him in his pen. Now that he was getting bigger, I realized that this was a bad idea. On his second day in the pasture, he'd suddenly wheeled around behind me and playfully butted me to the ground.

The cow couldn't have been more different than the unpredictable heifer or the wild calf. With an udder that dragged halfway to the ground, she ambled from one patch of grass to the next, moving at her own slow pace. Whenever I was in the pasture, she followed me around like an affable pet. She loved it when I scratched her under the chin, an act that triggered outbursts of sweet-smelling belches. Now that she knew me better, she was letting her milk flow more easily, too. The time I spent milking each morning and evening in the little shed in the pasture dropped to an almost respectable twenty minutes.

On July 8, Ola Mæland drove to Hovland to get me started on summer's most important mission: harvesting and curing enough grass to nourish Johannes's livestock through six dark, cold months.

In a country where summer rains often last for weeks, curing green grass into dry hay can be especially problematic. Ola's main task today was to teach me everything I needed to know about the *hesje,* Norway's homegrown solution to this dilemma. The concept was simple enough: use poles and wire to build a fence-like structure, then hang layers of fresh-mown grass over each wire. When executed correctly, the upper layer sheds any rain that falls, allowing inner layers to dry in a week or two.

Our first job was to unload Johannes's gas-driven, walk-behind mower from his brother-in-law's vehicle. This unwieldy contraption looked like a brawny, self-propelled rototiller, except that its working end was outfitted with a five-foot-long cutting bar rather than tines. Ola had taken the two-wheeled machine to his basement workshop months earlier for repairs and a tune-up and was now returning it.

Machines like this had begun replacing long-handled scythes on farms around Øystese in the early 1950s, he told me. Now every farmer had one. Johannes's Swiss-made Bucher was about fifteen years old, he guessed, but fresh out of the shop, it was going to run like new. With just a couple pulls of the starter rope, Ola was off and running, guiding the mower in long sweeps across the hillside, leaving broad swaths of fallen grass in his wake. After cutting a tidy little patch, he led me to our next endeavor: searching for Johannes's stash of poles that form a *hesje*'s framework.

"He's supposed to store them up there," Ola said, pointing to an ancient open-walled shed sitting halfway up the farm's steepest hill. "But he has a bad habit of leaving them outside. Let's go take a look."

Breathing heavily from our climb, we found that Johannes's habits hadn't changed. "A few poles stacked in the trees over there, but none under the roof," Ola muttered. "And the rest of them lying around who knows where. At least his wire's here."

A year or two of exposure to rain and snow had taken its toll on more than half of the slender eight-foot poles that we located under various trees. Crafted from hardwood saplings, fewer than thirty were still usable. We lugged all of these and several spools of wire to our patch of mown grass. And now it was time to build a *hesje*.

"You want the poles in a straight line about five feet apart," Ola instructed. "And they have to be set deep."

He grabbed a digging bar from a pile of tools I'd assembled and thrust it into the earth, then deepened the hole he'd just created with another four or five well-aimed jabs. Satisfied with his work, he picked up a pole and rammed it into the hole to set it firmly in place.

My attempt to duplicate this process failed miserably. I had to raise the digging bar up high and plunge it down as hard as I could just to sink it a few inches deep. Where Ola had hit his mark with each thrust, my dozen futile stabs described a pattern not unlike that made by darts around a bullseye. The same went for my attempts at setting the poles. I just didn't have the combination of strength and marksmanship the job required.

Not until Ola had set the last pole did I get a real job. One person could string a *hesje* alone, he explained, but it was easier with two. He had me walk ahead paying out wire and circling it around each of the uprights. He followed behind, positioning the wire before pulling it so taut it bit into our wooden poles. The most important part of my job, he told me, was to keep the line free of kinks and loops that could break under a heavy load of grass.

With the wire strung and several long poles fastened against it for bracing, we had a long, empty, six-stranded *hesje*.

"I hope you like to rake," Ola said with a wan smile, as he picked up one rake and handed me another, "because you're going to be doing a lot of it this summer."

It didn't take long to learn what lay behind this ominous remark. All of our mown grass had to be moved to the wire-and-pole structure, a feat that was far more difficult than it looked. Raking was easy at first. But the greenery quickly accumulated as we advanced toward our *hesje*. Soon it was matted into a big green roll that felt as heavy as a corpse. At this point, Ola grabbed a pitchfork from our tool pile to demonstrate how to spear balls of grass and fling them forward.

Raking, spearing, and flinging, we eventually consolidated the grass into an elongated pile at the foot of our *hesje*. Now we were ready for the final, crucial step: hanging it over the wires.

"You've got to fluff it up first," Ola said, lifting an armload. "If it's too compacted, it's going to start rotting before it can dry out."

Working through the balled-up mass with his fingers, he pulled it apart with rapid fluttering motions until a pile of untangled strands lay at his feet. He took the pile up again and, with one quick sweep, spread it over a bottom wire between two poles of our drying rack.

By the time Ola finished coaching me through my first armloads, it was time for him to head home to Øystese for supper. As we walked to his vehicle, I stared back at the six little patches of grass swinging from our drying rack—and quickly calculated that I had another 108 empty spaces to fill. Around us, spreading out in every direction were acres of grass waiting to be harvested. In this vast green sea, the patch that Ola had mowed was the tiniest of islets.

Ah, yes, I thought to myself. This is going to be a long summer.

The biggest event that occurred at Hovland in July was embodied in an object that was actually quite small: a little one-axle, two-wheeled, 12-horsepower tractor, the first motorized vehicle of any kind on these three farms.

It was Alv who brought it home one afternoon, along with a tiller, a mower, and other attachments. The most notable of these was a fused-together driver's seat and cargo box mounted atop its own two-wheel axle. With the two axles hooked in tandem, Alv had himself a rudimentary pickup truck capable of hauling just about anything on his farm that needed hauling.

When Arne had shown up at my door that afternoon breathless with the news of Alv's purchase, I hurried down the road to see for myself. I knew I was being selfish, but the mere thought of such a revolutionary change at Hovland almost made me cry. One reason I so admired my neighbors was because they had remained aloof from many of the enticements dangled before them by the modern world. I saw the people of Hovland and Soldal as custodians of a profound well of knowledge about this particular place that had been amassed by generations before them, a well that enabled them to survive on little plots of land in an ungentle climate by nurturing their livestock, raising their crops, knowing how to put wild plants to use, and availing themselves of all that the mountains had to offer.

Of course, serious inroads had already been made into this way of life, particularly since the end of World War II. But my neighbors had come of age before the war started, and they still harbored the skills and insights of their forebears.

Alv's new machine was only one of many elements that were slowly eroding that deep reservoir of cultural expertise, yet it seemed like the biggest one. Walking across the fields of Hovland every day, I was getting to know the farm, discovering its surprises and idiosyncrasies. I could see where there were problems with soil and plants, and I had a feeling for where magpies, foxes, and other wildlife might be hanging out. A tractor would change that relationship, I worried. Seated high up, drivers would read their fields like an eye chart, scoring better on the big things while missing everything else. Soon, I imagined, they would be bulldozing copses, outcrops, and anything else on their lands that might stand in the way of an impatient tractor driver.

I knew I was an impractical romantic, but I loved how close we were at Hovland to our animals and fields, and I was proud of how little we needed to buy from the outside. Of course, we were nowhere near being self-sufficient, but as long as we had horses working for us, we weren't paying for tractors and machinery that required endless amounts of gas, diesel, and maintenance.

On the other hand, I could also see how a lifetime of heavy labor had burdened every one of my neighbors. Some had pain in their hips, others in their backs, knees, feet, or hands. After just a couple of months on the farm, I was already feeling the pain myself. If I slung grass over a *hesje* for as little as two hours, my back would be in agony. Sometimes I'd wake up in the middle of the night with so much pain in my arms and hands they felt like they were burning.

This tractor would surely make it easier for Alv, Solveig, and their brother Torgeir. Alv was already fifty-five. If the tractor could delay the day when his body gave out, it would give him more years to tend the land he loved. Solveig's hips had long since been worn down by farmwork. And Torgeir, a good worker with reduced mental capacity who had lived his adult life under his siblings' care, walked with a chronically bent back after a farm accident. The tractor might also make it easier for the trio to stay competitive in a system of farming that was rapidly changing. It would probably even allow them to hold their heads a bit higher when they ran into neighbors who were already a decade or so ahead of them in adopting new farming technology.

When I reached their barn, Alv stood with his siblings by their new machine, his shy smile wider than I'd ever seen it before. So I couldn't help but share in his happiness. I oohed and aahed over the smooth curves of his little tractor and watched in fascination as he demonstrated its controls and explained how each implement worked.

A motion in the woods above the field caught my eye. I looked up to see Stella, the farm's fjord horse, trotting to the fence. She may have heard the motor humming and approached for a closer look. Like Begonia and the rest of her breed, the mare thrived under harness. But like Alv, Stella, too, was getting old. So perhaps if she understood what all the commotion was about, she would have been as happy as the rest of us.

18

Driving Begonia

On the evening of the second Tuesday in July, Torkel dispatched his brother to lend me a hand with Johannes's buggy. I was pleased to see Øystein again, for everything about him fascinated me: his stiff formality and proud bearing; his strong-boned good looks; the fact that he'd made breakfast for me; and even the length of his nearly white hair, which was defiantly longer than the norm in this neighborhood.

Now he led me to the barn's rear wall and up a fifteen-foot concrete ramp running from the hillside to the building's upper loft. This was where Johannes stored his horse-drawn equipment, including the buggy and a hay wagon. The floor here was more like a mezzanine, open on one end and spanning about a third of the barn's length, so I could stand at its edge and look straight down to the hayloft. Øystein explained that as soon as my hay was dry, I'd be driving it up to this floor, then pitching it over the edge to the loft ten feet below.

The gig was a graceful affair, with spoked, metal-rimmed wooden wheels as high as my chest and a flat spindle-back bench with ornately curved armrests. It was so light that we had no problem maneuvering it down the ramp and pulling it around the barn to the farmyard.

My mission this evening was to pick up a new farmhand at the bus stop in Øystese, an American named Robin who had written to the NIU a couple of weeks earlier asking about farm jobs. After a rapid exchange of letters with the NIU and a consultation with Johannes, I received Robin's application along with a photograph of a strapping, bearded, and tanned twenty-six-year-old.

While I fetched Begonia from her forest enclave, Øystein swept dirt, hay, and cobwebs from the vehicle. I liked the way he stood aside after I returned and started grappling with the harness. Instead of taking over, he watched patiently as I positioned and fastened the collar, girth, and various straps around the mare's shoulder, chest, belly, tail, and hindquarters. When I was done, he inspected each union, pointing out those that needed tightening or loosening and explaining the rationale behind his suggestions.

Bella had been keeping a close eye on us throughout this process. She was clearly up to something, but I didn't know what until she took a flying leap onto the buggy's floor and hopped to its bench. There she sat bolt upright, staring straight ahead, sending the clear message that she was not going to be left behind. I climbed up and took my seat beside her.

"You'll need a whip," Øystein said, handing me the lines. "Not for hitting the mare, but to let her know you're in the driver's seat and in control."

He crossed the yard and cut a long shoot from a young willow by the garden. But suddenly, as he turned toward us with shoot in hand, Begonia went crazy. She lurched to one side, quivering and snorting, reared into the air, and began wildly backing up, directly toward the barn's massive rock wall just fifteen feet behind us. I pulled hard on the lines, but that made her wilder still. Panicking, I grabbed onto an armrest, curled head to knees, and braced myself for the collision.

A second later the buggy jerked to a halt. I looked up and there was Øystein gripping Begonia's bridle—he'd managed to stop her just inches from impact.

"There now, there now," he was saying in a deep, calm voice, as he stroked the horse's neck. "Take it easy, girl. Easy now."

My hands were shaking, and I was holding back tears. I drew Bella close—somehow she had kept her seat on the bench—and pressed my face against her soft fur until my heart stopped pounding. The episode had lasted only seconds, but it made me aware, more than ever, of how thin the line was between my inexperience and disaster.

Øystein was shaken up, too. He kept stroking the mare even after she settled down. "The poor creature was terrified," he said, keeping hold of the bridle. "I'm guessing that she's been beaten with a switch, and probably more than once."

At first I didn't understand. But in a flash, a horrible vision of Johannes whipping his gentle mare played in my head. I wanted to think that he couldn't be this cruel, but there was no other explanation for Begonia's frenzy; this was the first time I'd seen her react in fear to anything at all.

"No one should ever whip an animal," Øystein said. "I can't imagine why he'd do such a thing."

Now he went over the incident, reminding me of the strange lip-rolling command I was supposed to use to stop a horse rather than my panic-stricken yank on the lines, and we agreed that it would be foolish to carry anything resembling a whip whenever Begonia was close by. When he finally felt it was safe for me to proceed, he loosened his grip on the bridle and I headed out.

Begonia set off at such a brisk clip that we were soon cruising past Torkel's house. Seated up high on this elegant gig, with my hair streaming in the wind as I tried to hold back my prancing charger, I felt the euphoria of a shield maiden heading to battle.

Rumor had it that Begonia had worked in a circus before Johannes bought her. This was just one of several remarkable stories people had told me that I didn't quite believe, suspecting that either I'd misunderstood or someone was pulling my leg. But by the time we reached town, I began to think that this particular anecdote wasn't a tall tale after all.

From her initial excitement, my charger had reverted to her usual placid pace even before we reached Soldal. After that, she was impervious to all my clucking and rein slapping. But as soon as Øystese came into view at the base of several long switchbacks, a transformation took place. Begonia's pace quickened and her stride grew longer. By the time we hit the town thoroughfare, it was all I could do to hold her to a trot. Prancing and holding her head high, she pricked her ears forward as she looked this way and that, as if to make sure she was the center of attention.

And attention she got. Kids shouted greetings. Others followed on their bikes. Cars slowed and adults stopped to stare. I wanted to project a dignified composure but couldn't completely suppress the huge silly grin that kept trying to spread across my face.

It wasn't that I was the last farmer to drive a horse through town—a scattering of hitching rails attested to that. Rather, it must have been the unexpected elements that prompted so much attention: a strange girl perched on a high seat alongside a dog, driving an almost out-of-control horse down main street.

When we reached the bus stop by the news kiosk, I was thankful that Begonia allowed me to bring her to a halt. I tied her to a rail and waited for Robin.

Seven or eight passengers descended from the bus that evening. I stood a few feet from the door, watching every face. A young man stepped to the pavement just a foot or two in front of me and looked over my head to the right and left. Odd, I thought. Looks like Robin, except he's clean shaven and ignoring me.

When no one else emerged, I went to the side of the bus where the young passenger was collecting his backpack.

"Are you Robin?" I asked in English.

"Yes," he said. "Yes, I am. Who are you?"

I tried to hide my irritation. How could he not know who I was? "I'm Liese. I thought you knew I'd be waiting here for you."

"Oh, I . . . ," he paused and seemed lost for words. "Where's the car?"

"There's no car. The horse is over there. That's how I got here."

"You don't have a car?" He didn't sound pleased.

"No. But we don't need one." It felt strange to be put on the defensive like this. "There's nowhere you need to go that you can't walk to."

He picked up his pack and walked to the buggy in silence.

On the drive home, we asked each other a few questions. He was from the East Coast and had been bumming around the world for seven months, working here and there whenever he needed money. His plan was to spend another year abroad before returning home to figure out what to do in life. We were halfway to Hovland before I asked why he hadn't looked at me when he got off the bus.

"I wasn't expecting a girl," he explained somewhat glumly. "Your name is spelled weird, so how could I know? It never crossed my mind that a girl would be running a farm."

Apparently we were off to a rocky start.

The best thing about Robin was that when he worked, he did a good job. On his first day at the farm, he quickly figured out how to run the cutting machine, and it took him only an hour or two to get the hang of driving *hesje* poles into the ground.

With him covering these two tasks, for the first time I wasn't dependent on outside help to get things done. What bothered me, though, was that our pattern of work now mirrored the divisions found at every farm in the area, where men were setting poles and using machines to mow grass, while women were raking grass and hanging it on *hesjes*.

I found it particularly galling because these women's jobs were monotonous and exhausting, and they went on for hours. Using the cutting machine, in contrast, actually looked like fun and lasted only as long as it took to mow enough grass for the next *hesje*. The other "masculine" task of setting poles was difficult, but it required nothing more than a steady hand and strong arms. And it, too, was a finite operation compared to endless hours of raking and hanging grass. To be relegated to women's work behind a newcomer was a bitter pill to swallow. Even worse, Robin seemed to interpret his ability to mow and set poles as a sign that he was my superior when it came to managing the farm.

Three days after Robin arrived, the weather turned warm and dry. With a forecast for at least seven more days of the same, Torkel advised that we switch tactics. Instead of hanging our grass, he said, we should spread it over the ground to dry, a technique that required us to flip it over every day to keep it well aerated. In this heat, our finer grass would be ready for the hayloft in as little as three days, while coarser patches could take twice that long.

Spreading grass provided a huge relief from the intensive labor of *hesjing*. All went well until day three, when the noon weather report predicted a chance of rain after eleven o'clock that the evening. A "chance" is only a chance, and the weather at that moment was hot, sunny, and humid. So I didn't take this threat seriously—until clouds moved in a few hours later.

I had a huge area of semidry grass lying in the field, a stage that's particularly vulnerable to water damage. The only way to protect it was to rake it into piles—little haycocks actually—and hope that they would shed any rain that might fall. Robin and I spent half an hour making piles before he announced that it was too hot and too late in the day for him to keep working; he was heading to Skårsvatnet to cool off.

"You can't go now," I objected. "We've got to finish raking."

"Then it'll be too late for a swim. But you're so obsessed with this haymaking business that you can't understand that, can you?"

This wasn't the first time he'd criticized me for my focus on the harvest. At first I'd tried to defend my long work hours, until I saw that he wasn't much interested in listening.

"Of course I'm obsessed. Why is it so hard for *you* to understand that this hay is the most important thing on the farm? Look. Look around," I said trying to contain my irritation. "We've got a couple acres of grass that'll be ruined if it rains now. That would be a catastrophe. And besides, think of all the work we've already put into it."

There was so much I wanted to say that I didn't know where to begin. Instead, I just stood and stared. Yet I needed his help—badly enough to beg for it. So I forced myself to calm down and said that of course it was his decision whether to go swimming or not. But could he please help me when he got back?

"Sure," he said, without skipping a beat. "I'll take a swim and come back. No problem."

As I raked grass into piles, I reflected on Robin's question. I regarded caring for the farm as both a job and a responsibility. I'd never given this a second thought. As long as I was living here, I would do whatever was necessary to keep the farm going.

But there was more to it than that. I felt like I was becoming part of this farm and this community, and I couldn't let either of them down. No one here—not Torkel, Inger, Solveig, or Alv—would abandon their farm's hay to go swimming, and neither would I. For centuries, farmers at Hovland had been dependent on their livestock for survival, and their livestock depended on hay. Walking away when rain threatened this vital crop was unthinkable. Were I to leave the grass to rot right now, I'd be drawing a line between my neighbors and me, between the real farmers and the American girl out for a summer lark.

I was still raking at ten o'clock that evening when I watched Robin walk up the road and into the house. When my work was finally done an hour later, I went inside and headed straight upstairs, avoiding the kitchen where the light was on and the radio playing.

In the morning, I went straight to the field. It would be easier to face Robin in the open rather than across a breakfast table. Right away I could see that the clouds had blown away overnight without releasing a single raindrop; all my raking and pleading had been for nothing. I grabbed a pitchfork and started spreading my haycocks back over the hillside.

When Robin appeared an hour later, I let fly.

"Why did you even bother to tell me you'd come back to help? You've told me stuff like that before, stuff that you said you'd do and then didn't. I really don't get it. What are you thinking?"

He shook his head with theatrical disappointment, as if it was obvious to the world that I was clueless.

"Well, you were the one who wanted me to help, weren't you? And *I* knew that *you* knew that I didn't want to. So you should have known that I wasn't going to come back."

"So you're saying you lied to me? You just straight-out lied to my face?" His words were so far removed from my reality that I found them incomprehensible.

"You know, Liese, I discovered a trick a long time ago that's made my life a lot easier. If someone really wants to hear you say something, instead of arguing, you might as well just say it. So yesterday it was a lot easier for me to tell you that I was going to come back instead of explaining everything to you."

He actually sounded proud of this confession, as if he sincerely believed that he'd made a particularly clever discovery years earlier.

"And besides," he continued, "Kari and her sister were at the lake. They invited me to their house for coffee afterward."

Kari was a young schoolteacher who often came to Soldal to visit her parents. I'd been getting to know her family and considered them friends. Learning that Robin had been drinking coffee and eating home-baked treats with them while I'd spent the evening working for naught made me feel more wretched than ever. I turned away and didn't speak to my hired hand for the rest of the day.

Øystein had first shown me how to hitch Begonia to the hay wagon. With its small iron wheels and wooden railings that reached to my shoulders, the cumbersome vehicle reminded me of those old-fashioned wagons that paraded lions and tigers around circus rings.

After my initial lesson with Øystein, for some reason I imagined that I knew how to drive the contraption. On my first unescorted outing, I asked Robin to take the job of pitching hay into the wagon while I stood on its floor guiding Begonia and compacting fodder under my feet as it came flying in. Everything went so well that the following morning

I felt confident enough to work on my own, freeing Robin to focus on mowing.

It was a warm sunny day, the best kind of weather for haying. Families were at work in their fields on every farm at Soldal and Hovland. Driving Begonia and pitching hay in this weather, I was as happy as I'd ever been. Even the chaff filtering its way under my clothes was only a minor irritation—until I worked up a sweat from clambering into and out of the wagon time and again. Then all those little barbs of hay began cementing themselves onto my flesh. As the day grew even warmer, the itching and burning grew so intense that I felt like throwing off every stitch of clothing and jumping into the nearest pond.

By late morning, the only cured hay still in the field was a distant patch of grass I'd spread out to dry a few days earlier: just enough to top off my load. Pulling Begonia into a wide U-turn, I considered for a moment the slope that lay between me and the hay. Might it be just a bit too steep to traverse?

I could circumvent this worrisome stretch by taking a route twice as long but only half as steep. Alternatively, I might be able to drive Begonia straight up the hill to a point where the grade mellowed out, cross over there, and then drive straight down to that little patch of hay.

The first alternative would be a bother. The second, I thought, would be too steep for Begonia and this heavy wagon.

So why not just forge ahead? After all, I was driving a *Norwegian* hay wagon. This country's smart farmers had been working on steep hills for centuries, more than enough time to design an untippable cart. What's more, I figured, if driving across an incline were dangerous, Øystein would have told me so.

High above me, Robin was in full swing with the cutting machine, its engine roaring as he mowed in long strips across a slope far steeper than the one I was studying. If he could mow hay on such an extreme slope, I could certainly drive a wagon across one that was much gentler. Belief in my own perfect logic conquered my instinctive unease. With a smack of the lips and a slap of the lines, I urged Begonia forward.

All went well for a dozen yards as I walked on the wagon's uphill side while guiding the mare. When the slope steepened a tad, I plowed ahead, convinced of the soundness of my reasoning. After another dozen yards, the wagon wobbled slightly, an insignificant motion not worthy of attention. When it happened again, I glanced down to my right and saw that both wheels on this uphill side were suspended an inch or two above the stubble of mown grass. Before I could blink, they dropped back to the ground. Only when they started elevating again a second later did I comprehend. Blurting out the impossible lip-rolling command for "Whoa!" I hauled back on the lines, desperate to reverse my idiotic blunder. But by now, the awful thing that was about to happen had been set in motion.

Begonia had no time to respond to the command before the wheels shot upward and horse and wagon toppled over as one, slamming into the ground with a wrenching thud and a bone-chilling crack. A shrill whinny issued from her throat.

I looked up the hill. Robin was far away, at the end of a long swath.

"Help!" I screamed, drawing the word out at a volume I didn't know I possessed.

He didn't look up; the din of the cutting machine was too great and his hearing protectors too effective.

"Help!" I screamed again, forcing my lungs to carry the word even farther.

I didn't know how much time I had. Flipped almost onto her back, Begonia was locked between the wagon's rigid shafts, flailing her legs in the air. A tangle of straps gripped her head in a sideways curve.

A fall on flat ground would have been bad enough, but on this hillside the arc was longer, the fall harder. And it wasn't just the ground that she hit but the thick shaft that ran from the wagon all the way to her shoulder. If she were not yet injured, she would be soon unless I could free her from the wreckage.

I ran to the downhill side of the pileup, away from those flailing legs. In a second, I unbuckled the bridle and pulled it away. Begonia swung her head upward and nickered softly. The sound filled me with relief; her head and neck, at least, were okay.

Now I went for the most crucial fastener: a pin about the size of my thumb that secured the harness to the left-hand shaft. I pulled on it. Hard. And harder still. But the wreckage was exerting so much force on this union of wood and metal that the pin was jammed in place. Unable to remove it, I had no way of freeing Begonia from the harness binding her to the wagon.

I was frantic. Begonia had to get off her back. She had to get up. If the only way of uncoupling her was to break the wagon apart, so be it. I grabbed the end of the long wooden shaft and heaved myself backward, taking advantage of the downhill slope to amplify the force of my effort.

Nothing happened. No flex. No crack. No give. Nothing.

My last chance was the harness. If I could release some of its buckles, maybe, somehow, the tension on the pin would also be released. Begonia had quieted down. Her head lay on the hill, and now her body was situated more on its side than its back. I couldn't tell whether she'd gone limp because she was calm or injured. But now, at least, I could work on the harness without being struck by a thrashing hoof. I scrambled from one component to the next, releasing her collar, the girth, and every buckle I could find. But when I returned to the pin, it was as unyielding as before.

Suddenly there was Robin, skidding to a stop just above us. He'd caught sight of the wreck, he said, and paused only long enough to turn off the cutting machine. I stepped aside and motioned to the pin. He grabbed it and worked it with all his strength, but still it didn't budge.

Now he straightened up and looked around. He took it all in quickly and almost immediately understood what needed to be done.

"We have to break this off," he said, grabbing hold of the shaft. "It's the only way to get her loose."

I nodded and wrapped my hands around the wood alongside his. None of this seemed real. The horse lying at our feet who might have sustained injuries that would put her out of commission or even put her down. The damage that we were about to inflict on this precious wagon. My guilt. My devastating guilt. And even Robin, demonstrating qualities I hadn't seen in him before.

"On the count of three, okay?" he said. This time, with the two of us heaving ourselves backward, the thick wood cracked apart.

I pulled out the pin. Robin threw the shaft aside. Together we dragged the harness off Begonia and leaped out of the way. With nothing left to hold her down, in one smooth motion she rolled from her right side to her left—swinging all four legs through the air in a great arc to position them downhill—and sprang to her feet.

Every muscle in my body tightened. I was sure this invaluable mare would collapse back to the ground or hobble forward on a broken leg. The fall had been violent. She had landed on a shaft. She'd been twisted into an unnatural position for what seemed like forever. How could she possibly have escaped unscathed from such trauma?

"Steady, girl, steady," I whispered, steeling myself for the worst.

She glanced my way, shook herself all over, snorted, took three or four steps forward, and lowered her head to snatch a mouthful of grass growing up from the stubble.

I started to breathe again, just in time to catch a great "*Hallo!*" that floated up from the barn. There was Øystein, walking our way. He'd heard both my cries for help, he explained upon reaching us, and had come at once.

There was no need to describe the accident. The story lay spread out before him: the overturned wagon, the broken shaft, Begonia grazing free in the field, her harness and bridle strewn over the stubble.

His first concern was for the horse. He ran his hand over her whole body and lifted each leg, checking for injuries.

"She's fine. Just fine," he pronounced. "It takes more than a little accident like this to injure a Norwegian fjord horse. They're as sturdy as can be."

Now he turned his attention to the wagon. It took only a glance to learn that the loud crack I'd heard was the other shaft breaking apart, the one that Begonia had landed on. With this discovery of even greater damage, my eyes grew blurry. I turned aside to wipe away my tears before they could spill out, but Øystein had already seen them.

"Now, now, don't worry," he said reassuringly. "It can be fixed. And if it can't, you can borrow our hay wagon. It won't take more than a minute or two to drive it over here whenever you need it."

He waved his arm toward my wagon lying on its side, its load of hay spilled across the field below. "I'll get Tormod and Arne up here later this afternoon, and we can lift this thing back onto its wheels. With the five of us working together, we should have no trouble pulling it to the barn. We'll come with our wagon and bring all this hay in for you, too."

Rather than stemming the tide of emotions coursing through me, his generosity intensified my feelings. Words of thanks caught in my throat. My attempt at a smile must have looked miserable, because it seemed to cause him distress. He reached his arm around my shoulders and gripped me firmly for just a moment before letting go. As if to make up for this boldness, he gave me two pats on the back.

"It's okay," he said. "Really. We can take care of it."

Later, as I led Begonia back to her forest, I thought about that semi-embrace and how unexpected it had been. Except for uncountable handshakes, this was the first time anyone had touched me since my arrival in Norway. In fact, I couldn't recall that I'd witnessed physical contact other than a handshake between any two people here. Øystein's comforting gesture made me aware that I missed my mother's soothing hugs and the close familiarity of my two sisters. I hadn't had a romantic fling of any kind for a year, and I missed that kind of closeness, too.

I'd enjoyed that attention from Øystein. And for a second or two, I let myself wonder whether he may have enjoyed it, too. As quickly as the question arose, I batted it out of my mind. He was old enough to be my father.

I spent the rest of the day and part of the next consulting with neighbors and calling woodworkers, wagon makers, and carpenters until it was clear that no one could repair the shafts for months. Begonia was alive and unharmed, but the wagon was as good as destroyed. After that, I had to use Torkel's wagon for hay, but only after Øystein gave me a long and thorough driving lesson.

A few days after the accident, just ten days after his arrival, Robin walked to the employment office in town and asked for another job. A day later, he took a ferry across the fjord to harvest fruit on the same farm where I'd been offered work when I first arrived, leaving me to resume my happy life of solitary living.

19

A Temple for the Gods

I was walking home from the mailboxes one evening when a question popped into my mind. If anyone knew the answer, it would be Torkel. So I took a side trip to his barn, where I found him cleaning up.

"What does the word *hov* mean?" I wanted to know.

"That's easier to answer than most of your questions, Liese," he said with a smile. "They say that a *hov* is a heathen temple. And by that they mean that it's a building where the old gods were worshipped. Freya, Thor, Odin, and the others."

"Well, then, why is your farm called Hovland?"

Torkel rubbed his chin and leaned his shovel against the wall.

"I suppose that the best answer comes from those smart university people. They say that if a farm is named Hovland, there was a *hov* on it at some point in time."

His smile broadened to a grin. "So you can write home to your mother that you've joined the heathens at Hovland."

I laughed, but I was more astonished than amused. In junior high school I'd loved reading stories of the old gods. I knew about Thor and his hammer, and one-eyed Odin, and evil Loki, who murdered beloved Baldur. Those Norse myths were the stories that Vikings told each other in a faraway place, a very long time ago.

Now, suddenly, they were not far away at all. If I understood Torkel correctly, these gods had been right here on the farm, worshipped in a temple that his ancestors may have built.

Where was the *hov,* I wanted to know. How old was it? What did it look like? What kinds of ceremonies took place in it?

"Liese, Liese, so many questions!" he cried, throwing up his hands. "I wish I could answer them all. But I can't, and I don't know anyone who can. The one thing I do know is that our old kings started forcing us to convert to Christianity about a thousand years ago. So our *hov* was probably built before then."

"Do you have any idea where it could have been?" I asked, hopefully.

"Maybe. I've always thought that someday traces of it might be found near the burial mound. Of course, the archaeologists would have to dig deep to find anything. A lot of soil has built up over the past thousand years."

"Burial mound?" I asked. I had no idea what he was talking about.

Now he was the one who was surprised. He took me by the elbow and led me outside.

"Up there," he said, pointing to the hill separating his farm from Johannes's. "It's in plain sight from your kitchen window, too."

Of course I had noticed this strange hump. But if I had given it any thought at all, I would have guessed I was looking at a pile of rocks cleared from the field so long ago that soil and grass had now covered it over.

Sensing a new barrage of questions in the offing, Torkel nipped them in the bud by saying he knew nothing more about the mound except that it might be a thousand years old or even more.

"Every site like this is protected," he added. "So unless the state sends a crew to do a proper excavation, we can't know who or what is in there."

I had recently taken to studying a book in Johannes's living room that documented the lineage of all the farms in Øystese Parish. Farm by farm, generation by generation, its pages cataloged names and vital events of every farmer, as well as those of the farmer's spouse and children. It included a wealth of other information, too, like records of livestock and crop production, each generation's accumulated wealth or debt, and positions each farmer had held in the community. Court cases, tragic deaths, a farmer's renown as a fiddle player—numerous items like these added personal details to each brief narrative.

Written in outdated *nynorsk* and full of terms from centuries-old tax tallies, censuses, and church records, the pages were difficult to make sense of at first. But the moment I saw the opening entry for Johannes's farm—"Svein at Hovland, 1603 to 1609"—I was hooked.

Every evening for a week I labored through the eleven-page section on Hovland's three farms until the language started to make sense.

After that, I created a timeline for Johannes's farm of who begat whom from one generation to the next. By the time I reached the last entry—"Marta Hovland, 1887–1951"—I could barely believe my own notes, for Marta was Johannes's mother, and with this final link in the chain, I could see that I was living on a farm that had been in the hands of the same family for at least 352 years.

Johannes and his eleven siblings were the tenth generation to grow up here: the great-great-great-great-great-great-great grandchildren of a man named Brynjulv, who had farmed this land from 1620 to 1643. Brynjulv may have been the grandson of "Svein at Hovland," but the authors did not have enough evidence to prove this. If true, though, Johannes could add two "greats" and forty-two years to his documented pedigree at this place.

Much later, when I was scouring archaeology research papers in a quest to figure out how old the farms at Hovland might be, I would learn that there were *four* grave mounds on the long undulating hill between Torkel's and Johannes's farms. A fifth site had lain just beyond Johannes's woodshed, less than 150 feet from his front door. Sometime in the 1800s, people dug into that pile of rocks and soil to discover a burial chamber made of two large stone slabs set on edge, with a third resting atop them. There was no mention of human remains, but several artifacts were found: a clay pot, a pair of bronze tweezers, and, possibly, various objects made of iron. Supposedly, all were sent to the Bergen Museum. And all have since been lost.

According to some archaeologists, there was a reason that the Norwegian farm landscape had once been studded with conspicuous monuments like this one. In the absence of a written language, burial mounds were a way of documenting ownership and inheritance of farmland. It was not a farm's most stalwart warrior, beloved bard, or cherished child who was immortalized in a tomb. Rather, it was the rightful owner of the land, the person who had inherited it from a predecessor, whose remains lay in a mound just thirty feet away, who had, in turn, inherited it from a guy lying over yonder beneath the big beech tree.

The burial chamber by Johannes's woodshed was thought to be from the Early Iron Age, a period that in Norway stretched from about twenty-five hundred years to fifteen hundred years ago. As old as this burial may be, the farm could be older still. Based on archaeological studies in the region, I wouldn't be surprised to learn that Hovland has sustained more than a hundred generations of farmers, perhaps for as long as three thousand years.

20

"You Know I Did"

I was determined to harvest all the grass I could by whatever means possible. When the weather was good, I dried it on hillsides. In rainy weather, I hung it on *hesjes*. When I realized that a farmer's dignity demanded that his fields be cropped as neatly as a marine's head, I learned how to use a short-handled scythe to "clean up" any stray strands that the cutting machine missed.

The same thing was happening all over western Norway. Along roads and ditches, on little patches of land between people's yards, everyplace there was grass, someone was there with a sickle or scythe to cut it down and turn it into hay. I had reached the conclusion that in this part of the country, few people were more than a generation or two removed from a farm. If a person didn't need the patch of grass growing in her backyard, she would give it to relatives who did. I reckoned that a lot of sheep were being fed by grass harvested with scythes on these random little plots spread far and wide.

Now that it was summer, the sons and daughters of my neighbors were home on long vacations, and many gave me a hand after putting in a day's work on their parents' farms. Hanging out with people who were almost my own age was a pleasure I'd almost forgotten about.

Ingebjørg and Ola, Johannes's sister and brother-in-law, drove up from Øystese to help as often as they could, too. So did Johannes's brother Gunnar. Even Alv, Solveig, and their brother Torgeir lent a hand from time to time when they could get away from their own farmwork. Alfred, a bachelor uncle of Kari's—the schoolteacher who had been serving coffee and cake to Robin while I raked grass late into the night—also came to help sometimes. He was a short, quiet person who lived up to his nickname, *snille* Alfred, nice Alfred.

Edvard, though, was absent during this time. He'd been called away to work on his uncle's farm near the coast for two weeks. I started counting the days on the evening he left, for he promised to visit as soon as he returned. True to his word, he appeared on day fifteen, and from the smile he greeted me with, I imagined that he had been counting, too.

We worked together on a *hesje* for a couple of hours before coming in for supper, then lingered over the kitchen table talking until midnight. For some reason, he waited until then to let me know that he was leaving again.

"My uncle needs me for a few more weeks." He sounded almost apologetic. "Sorry I won't be here to give you a hand."

I tried to hide my dismay as we walked side by side over freshly mown hayfields to the trail that descended into the forest. Standing close as we said our goodbyes, we could hear the quavering call of a tawny owl floating up from the woods below. The affection I could feel in Edvard's voice made my heart race. I searched for words that would keep him with me. When they came, they seemed so simple.

"Did you miss me?"

"You know I did," he said, smiling down into my eyes.

My knees went wobbly. The tawny owl fell silent. I'd been waiting for this moment forever—a moment so brief it barely had time to grow awkward.

"Well, I'd best be going," he said, stepping back. "I'll see you in about three weeks, I imagine."

As Bella and I retraced our path to the house, the words "you know I did" played over and over in my mind. They had been spoken so sweetly, with such certainty. What would have happened just now, I wondered, if I'd brushed my fingers over Edvard's cheek or taken his hand in mine? Oh, what a joke. I was incapable of doing any such thing. Not in a thousand years. Girls never took the first step.

Bella followed me upstairs and stretched out on her rug while I lay awake considering various interpretations of "you know I did." By the morning, I'd convinced myself that Edvard missed me as a friend, not a girlfriend. And that this friendship of ours was more important than my silly infatuation. I would stop daydreaming about him, I told myself. It was a habit I could break, even though it would make me miserable to do so. But what did that matter? My unrequited crush on him was already making me miserable enough.

Late one afternoon, Einar, Kari's father from Soldal, came to tell me that Johannes had hired him to fill the farm's silo. Until then, I'd been trying to ignore the concrete tower behind the farm's venerable barn. It was an ugly Johnny-come-lately with no apparent function.

Einar set me straight by explaining that the modern way to put up grass was to pack it straight into a silo when it was freshly mown. "It's kind of like turning cabbage into sauerkraut or cucumbers into pickles," he said. "If you give your grass the right conditions in the silo, you can sit back and let fermentation do the preserving for you."

But to move heavy green grass around, you needed a tractor and at least four or five helpers. And that's where Einar came in: Johannes had called him because he owned a tractor. He could start work on Friday, he said, which would give me enough time to line up the requisite volunteers.

I'd first met Einar a couple of weeks earlier and had immediately liked him. He was a spare man, not too tall. His thinning, brown hair was slicked straight back, and a stain of chewing tobacco graced his lips. He was funny and practical and one of the few people who seemed genuinely curious about my life in the United States.

Compared to Hovland's farmers, Einar ran a modern operation. His barn was only twenty years old, an imposing concrete structure configured for raising male calves from infancy to slaughter. He owned a tractor—a Swiss-made, four-wheel-drive machine that looked more like a small flatbed truck with an oversized cab than a classic John Deere—and he'd built the area's only sawmill. It was a simple affair, nothing more than a large circular saw and a long carriage protected by a tin roof. But it was good at converting his neighbors' trees into boards, and it saved them the expense of hauling logs to bigger mills down the hill in Øystese.

One time he dropped by just after I'd received a scolding from Solveig, who had caught me using a pitchfork to hang grass on a *hesje*. This was a speedy technique that Torkel had taught me to use but that Solveig considered an abomination, because, according to her, it was a surefire way to end up with a barn full of rotten hay.

"Is she right?" I asked Einar. "Will the grass rot if I do it like this?"

"Ah, Solveig," he sighed. "She doesn't seem to realize that there's more than one way to do anything." He turned his head and spit politely to the side, as if to emphasize his words. "It doesn't help that you learned this from Torkel. She's two years older than he is, and maybe she's always felt that he's just a little kid who doesn't know what he's doing."

He took up a pitchfork and started hanging grass alongside me. With more than five decades of haymaking under his belt, his movements were fluid and quick. Almost before I knew it, a quarter of the *hesje* was filled up. As he turned to leave, I asked one more question.

"Is Solveig older than Johannes, too?"

"Nah. Johannes is the oldest farmer at Hovland. He was born in 1910, a year before me. So he's three years older than Solveig and five years older than Torkel."

He paused for a moment, cocking his head and squinting his eyes, as if reflecting on something that had just entered his mind.

"You know," he said, with a confirming nod, "I'm pretty sure that's why Johannes has always considered himself king of the mountain here."

As he headed back to Soldal, I tried to imagine how growing up side by side on these farms had shaped the way my neighbors related to each other as adults. When Einar talked to Solveig, did he still see a curly-haired flirt who had distracted him during a midsummer's dance years ago? Did Solveig still consider Torkel a snot-nosed pest who might nail her with a spit wad at any moment? As for Johannes, maybe Einar was right. Perhaps some of the problems he had with his neighbors were—after all these years—due to him feeling like a big boy surrounded by a bunch of little kids.

Not for the first time, I marveled at the long, deep, and intimate web of connections that tied my neighbors together. How strange it was that I had fallen into this community by accident, and how grateful I was that it had taken me in without skipping a beat.

21

Pickled Grass

On Friday morning, Einar assembled my four volunteers. He assigned one of them to mow with the cutting machine and another to walk behind the machine and rake the mown grass into windrows. Einar's job was to scoop up these rows with his *silosvans*—a long, forklike piece of equipment mounted on the rear of his tractor—and deliver them to the silo. There my third and fourth recruits used pitchforks to heave the heavy green mass through a small opening in the concrete wall. I was stationed on the floor of this eighteen-foot structure, where I scrambled back and forth untangling and distributing the masses raining down from above and stomping them down with my feet as firmly as I could.

It was nice and cool within the walls at first, but as the day heated up, so did the concrete. With no ventilation, my work chamber became a sauna. I couldn't even wipe away the sweat dribbling into my eyes, because my hands were covered with white residue from the granular substance I was sprinkling over the grass between each tractor load. It was some kind of acidic salt, Einar said, that would promote growth of beneficial bacteria necessary for fermentation.

During our first break, I was astonished to learn that everyone in the neighborhood knew that Johannes's silo was so poorly designed and situated that neither he nor anyone else had ever used it before.

"Sure it's a lot harder to fill than any other silo, but don't let that worry you," Einar said. "We're still going to get a lot more grass into it than you'd ever be able to make into hay."

Everyone nodded in agreement.

"But the poor soul who has to get the silage *out* of it is really going to suffer," he continued. "First he'll have to pitch it back through those tiny openings, which is hard enough. But then what? The barn door is a good thirty yards away. How's he supposed to get it there?"

That evening I sat in the kitchen worrying over the job ahead. It had taken four hours of Einar's tractor work, plus six hours for the rest of us, to amass just two feet of grass. I could probably have gotten by with three helpers rather than four, but even then, I'd need eighty or ninety volunteer hours just to reach the silo's halfway mark. Asking for even a fraction of this aid would be a terrible imposition on my neighbors.

A sudden surge of anger washed over me. How could Johannes expect me to fill his ridiculous concrete beast when he'd never done so himself? Surely he understood that by hiring Einar he was putting me in the position of begging people for help. Maybe it hadn't been too inconvenient for Solveig, Torkel, and others to lend me a hand earlier in the season; at this point, though, it was different. Grass harvest was the busiest time of year. People just didn't have much time to spare right now.

Asking for help had always been difficult for me. I hated being a bother for anybody, much less my hard-working neighbors who had already showered me with a lifetime of favors. But now I had no choice. Over the next month, while I strived to fill the silo and hang grass on my *hesjes*, I had to ask and ask, until the asking wore me down. The kindnesses added up so fast that I knew I'd never be able to even the score. In all its constructions, *takk*, the Norwegian word for "thank you," was becoming the most important part of my vocabulary.

I gave what I could, including my cheerfulness and my ear; I was a new and appreciative audience for my neighbors' stories, old and new, and a well of curiosity about who they were and how they had managed through life. I could nod my head knowingly when Inger grumbled about Solveig, likewise an hour later when Solveig found fault with Inger. And I was a major contributor to the joyful banter of our silo crew—not so much due to my clever wit but because my language missteps and clueless questions provided plenty of fodder for these wags.

The most amazing thing, though, was that my neighbors kept giving without ever making me feel they expected anything in return. Sometimes at the end of a long day I'd sit alone in the kitchen unable to do much of anything except contemplate the generosity of people around me.

It was about this time that my infatuation with doing things the old way began to waver. I couldn't help but notice how much faster the grass got harvested on "big" hayfields in flat areas around town. That's where a few farmers were using forage harvesters: two-wheeled machines coupled to a tractor that cut grass, chopped it into little bits, mixed it with formic acid, and spit it into a wagon driving alongside. With a rig like this plus a grapple or conveyor belt to transfer chopped grass into a silo, farmers were finishing their harvests in less than a week.

If it hadn't been for Johannes's silo, however, I would have missed one of my most satisfying moments of the summer. On a cold and drizzly morning two weeks into the work, I couldn't find anyone to cut grass for Einar, who was scheduled to show up with his tractor right after *middag*. Unless I did the cutting myself, the day would be wasted.

I'd tried running a cutting machine twice before. On the first attempt, I nearly ran Alv's mower into his barn wall. On the second—when Robin was still at the farm—I fought so hard to control the machine that my arms gave out in less than a minute.

But I was stronger now and feeling a little more adventurous. Perhaps it was time to try again, especially because in this weather no one would be dropping by and catching me making a fool of myself. I fired up the Bucher, released its clutch, and held on as the machine surged forward, dragging me with it. But this time I was in full fighting mode. I resisted its pull all the way across the field, wrestling it one way and the other, holding it back, bending it to my will.

When my arms gave out, I kept a grip on the handlebars and picked up my pace. Even if I couldn't control this machine, I was determined to follow it wherever it was taking me. And that was the moment when everything changed. Suddenly, instead of fighting, I was guiding. Left, right, straight ahead, over the hillock. In a flash I realized that I'd been putting all my strength into holding the machine back rather than letting it get on with its work.

When Einar arrived that afternoon, he surveyed the long rows of grass lying on the hillside.

"You cut this?" he asked with a frown that terrified me. What had I done this time? Ruined the cutting machine? Destroyed the crop?

I managed a sickly nod.

He spent a long second looking me up and down, then rubbed his chin and frowned again.

"You're the first girl around here to run one of these machines, I reckon," he drawled. "Looks like you did a fine job."

After that, I was the only one to use Johannes's cutting machine, for mowing became my favorite chore. It was work that went fast and produced instant results, and I loved the challenge of guiding the machine as close as I dared to trees and outcrops in order to get the cleanest shave and highest yield. My strongest motivation, though, was that mowing with the machine—traditionally a man's job—was much easier than the raking and *hesjing* relegated to women and children. And I was ready to wager that men had known this all along.

After three weeks of intermittent work to fill the silo, I called it quits. There was no sense in using up precious manpower and tractor time on the steeper and rockier hills where the grass grew more sparsely and the tractor could not drive in straight lines. With the silo filled two-thirds to the top, it was time to seal it up.

22

Håseter and Hulders

It was my first trip with Øystein to his cabin in the mountains that ignited my passion for the Norwegian *fjell,* those rocky, windswept stretches above timberline that are punctuated by peaks and lakes and strewn with lichens and hardy little plants bearing impossibly delicate blossoms in the summer and vibrantly colored leaves in the fall.

The boys next door, Tormod and Arne, had already told me stories about their uncle's cabin at Håseter when he invited me to join him and these two nephews on an overnight excursion to the *støl.* We set off early Saturday evening after milking, with a promise from Solveig that she would see to the cow's and calf's needs the next morning. Bella came, too, of course, for I rarely went anywhere without her.

The four-mile trail climbed 1,750 feet and took us past Blomseter, Hyrting, and Flyane, the three *stølar* I'd viewed during my first hike into the mountains. We started seeing sheep on surrounding hillsides as soon as we reached Blomseter. Thriving on their mountainous summer range for a full month now, the ewes were looking stronger and more confident. The lambs were definitely stronger, too, and bigger and fatter as well, with luxuriant white coats giving them a roly-poly look.

Even from a distance it was easy to spot Johannes's sheep, not only because I was getting better at recognizing their distinctive earmarks but because they were the only ones that had been sent unshorn into the mountains. Johannes had neglected this important chore in March and April, the only period when it would have been safe for his ewes to have their warm winter coats removed. Now their manure-stained wool hung in long tangled strands hanging from the fluffy-white new growth below.

One of the purposes of our hike was to check on our flocks. Whenever we spotted any of Johannes's or Torkel's animals, we pulled bags of *kraftfôr*—the grain and mineral mix—from our packs and used exaggerated motions to show these wary animals the reward they would receive for letting us come close. Imitating the singsong tones and syllables I'd heard Solveig use while the sheep were still at home, I called the animals to me.

"Sees, sees, sees, sees, koma no seesana, kom no her! Seesana, sees, sees, sees, sees, koma no!" Come here now, lambkins, come now! Ewes lifted their heads and pricked their ears, while their lambs either bounded away or crowded nervously into their mothers. This wasn't just a game. Every farmer with sheep in the mountains saw to them regularly. Our handouts of calorie-rich grain served to remind the animals that domesticity, too, had its benefits.

From the cabins at Flyane, we headed into the alpine expanses I'd gotten a glimpse of on my first exploration above timberline. Our route traversed the flank of a long, high mountain called Manfjell before descending into a dangerously deep and narrow valley awash in bracken ferns, grasses, and wildflowers.

"This valley is called Smørdalen," Øystein told me, as we made a lung-wracking ascent of the canyon's west well, "because it was said that cows grazing here—on all the lush vegetation—gave lots of milk and cream."

It took me a moment to crack this riddle. *Smør* means "butter" and *dalen* means "the valley." So, of course! All that good cream would have been churned into butter.

Less than half an hour later we reached the rim of a small grassy basin, and there ahead of us was Øystein's cabin, perched on the far side of a noisy stream bumping down from heights above. Bella and the boys took off at a run, jumped the creek, and disappeared around the building's uphill side.

"*Ja*, welcome to Håseter," my guide said with a proud smile. "What do you think?"

I was sweating under my backpack and felt ready to drop, but at that moment a cooling breeze swept down from the crags. Ferns and grasses bowed and swirled around us as I surveyed this boulder-strewn landscape and Øystein's austere little cabin. On the mountainside behind us a ewe bawled hoarsely for her little one, who replied with a volley of shrill bleats as he ran to her side.

"Why, it's gorgeous," I murmured. "This place is amazing."

The building sat atop a foundation of hundreds of rectangular-faced rocks ranging in size from shoeboxes to blanket chests, all of them encrusted with a beautiful gray-green lichen that graced every other rock surface in the basin. The downhill end of the building—the side facing us—was high enough to accommodate a full-height door in the foundation. Centered in the cabin's wall above that was a single small window.

"Each time I reach this spot I imagine a *budeie* standing right there," Øystein said, speaking of the milkmaids who spent their summers tending livestock in the mountains. "She's looking out the window at day's end listening to the creek, and she can hear her cows chewing their cud in the barn. I like to think that she loved this place as much as I do, but she must have been awfully tired by the time her work was done."

I stood for a moment taking it all in, overwhelmed by the stark beauty of the place and the image that Øystein had just conjured. Not for the first time my thoughts strayed his way. Since the day we met, I'd been waging a battle against my attraction to him. Now hearing him speak with such deep emotion, my defenses were crumbling.

The cabin was cool and dark inside and smelled not unpleasantly of musty pine walls and old wool blankets. The lower floor was divided into three rooms: a small entry with a door on the right that opened to a narrow bedroom and a second door straight ahead that opened to the main chamber, which served as kitchen, living room, and sleeping room combined. A ladder just inside the front door led to a low-ceilinged loft big enough to sleep four or five people on the floor.

In those precious moments when a *budeie* could relax, she must have enjoyed this snug place and its view of mountains and creek. For me, it went beyond enjoyment. The minute I walked through the door, worries about haymaking, silage harvest, and every other problem facing me on the farm faded away.

My thoughts were interrupted by Øystein, who grabbed a large metal bucket and beckoned me to the creek. As he walked, the pail's handle jangled and squeaked. "This old bucket's been singing Håseter's song for decades," he said. "To my ears, it's the sweetest sound in the world."

We stopped at a small pool just downstream from the cabin.

Øystein dropped to one knee and filled his pail with a single dip. "You need to keep your eyes open here," he said. "Down there, at the edge of the canyon, I once saw a *hulder*."

"A *hulder*? What's that?"

His eyebrows shot up in surprise. "You don't know? They're beautiful women who live inside the mountain. Most of them are quite good at caring for livestock. It's a lucky thing to have one as a friend, because she'll watch out for your animals up here in the summer. She might even visit your barn in the winter and help keep your cows healthy."

I couldn't tell from his expression whether he was kidding or not.

"People say they lure men into marriage," he continued. "They can be good wives or hellions, all depending on how you treat them. But sometimes a *hulder* will take a man into her home in the mountain and keep him there."

"The one you saw, what did she look like?" I asked.

"It was early in the morning and she was standing in the mist, so the only thing I saw for sure was that she had long hair. In the old stories, they have tails that look like a cow's, but I didn't see one."

I'd heard many tales at Hovland of humanlike creatures that inhabit barns, lakes, fjords, and mountains. When I questioned the tellers, they would usually say that they themselves had never seen one but that they knew someone who had. No one seemed willing to dismiss the stories as myth. Here at this magical place called Håseter, it was easy to believe that a real *hulder* had shown herself to Øystein one morning.

"What should I do if I see one?" I asked.

"If you're nice to her, she'll be good to you," he said. "If you're not, be careful, because she could make a lot of mischief. One thing you should never do, though, is follow her, because she might take you someplace you can't get out of."

Back in the cabin we lit a couple of kerosene lanterns in the main room. While the boys set the table with bread, cheese, and other supper fixings, Øystein fired up the woodstove, which provided heat as well as a surface for cooking food and boiling water.

"Do you know how old this cabin is?" I asked after we'd all sat down to eat.

"Not very old at all," Øystein said. "Seventy, maybe eighty, years. But Håseter is supposedly one of the oldest *stølar* in the region. At least that's what I've heard from people who study these things. They say that livestock have been grazing here since 1600 and probably for centuries before that."

"So where was the barn? Was it as old as the cabin?"

Øystein let out a guffaw and Tormod started laughing so hard he almost choked on his food. I looked at them in dismay, wondering how I could have made such an idiot out of myself over such a simple question.

"You're sitting on top of it right now," Øystein said, after he'd pulled himself together. "They squeezed twenty-one cows into the cellar, with a stanchion for each one."

"Twenty-one milk cows!" I exclaimed. It didn't seem possible to house so many animals beneath a building this small. Even more astonishing was that anyone could manage such a herd on her own. Until now, I'd been dreaming about how glorious it must have been to spend summers in this beautiful place surrounded by streams, lakes, and peaks. But tending to a herd larger than any that now existed at Soldal or Hovland without benefit of running water, electricity, or refrigeration would surely leave a person too exhausted to do anything but fall into bed at the end of each day.

"The mountains seem quiet now that they're gone," Øystein said, as if reading my thoughts. "They sang to their cows every evening, calling them in. Each one had her own song. I loved listening to them."

I thought of the book of Norwegian folk songs I enjoyed leafing through in Johannes's living room. Its pages were filled with verses about the pleasures and pitfalls of being a young woman tending livestock in isolated cabins in the country's mountains and forests.

"Are all those songs about *budeier* really true?" I asked. "The ones about their boyfriends sneaking up the trails . . ."

"If only!" Øystein started laughing again. "When I was a boy, I got sent up to Hyrting with one of my brothers a couple of times a week to fetch everything our *budeie* made: butter, cheese, sour milk. She took care of us when we got there, that's for sure. But not like in the songs. She was an old woman, and she stuffed us with porridge. It didn't matter whether we'd had breakfast or not. We had to eat at least two or three bowls before she'd let us leave."

"Why don't farmers send their cows to the mountains anymore?" The question had been on my mind since Torkel had told me that their sister had been Hovland's last *budeie*. "Why are the cabins empty?"

Øystein gazed out the window, giving me an opportunity to study his imposing profile in the flickering light of the kerosene lamps: his broad, high cheekbones, strong jaw, and a handsome jag in his nose.

"There are lots of reasons," he said, turning back to me. "But maybe the simplest of all is that after a dairy was built in Øystese, at some point we had to choose between sending the cows to the mountains for the summer or keeping them at home and sending our milk to town."

"It must have been a lot easier to just send it to the dairy," I ventured.

"No, not at all. It was one of the hardest decisions we ever had to make. The dairy was built before 1900, but my sister spent her last summer at our *støl* fifteen years ago."

"So it took fifty years to make the switch?" I asked. "That sounds crazy."

"It's not so crazy if you knew what we had to accomplish before we could keep the cows home all year and if you knew how hard we struggled to make a living. The grass up here is free," he said, gesturing toward the window. "Before we could stop using it, we had to figure out how to expand our pastures and hayfields at home, and that wasn't easy. In the meantime, we could get more for selling the butter and cheese that a *budeie* made than what the dairy paid us for our raw milk."

"So the *stølar* kept going," I mused, "because of free forage and a *budeie*'s labor."

The statement took him by surprise. "I never thought of it quite like that," he said. "But I guess you could say that was part of it. The other part was that most of us loved these traditions. We were using the resources the mountains provided. Farmers worked together to send their animals up here and bring them home again. Instead of abandoning these mountain farms when they started getting too expensive or impractical, some farmers even teamed up to run them together.

"Finally, though, everything was lined up against us. There were restrictions on selling products straight from the farm. It was hard to find anyone to spend a summer working in the mountains. And if you didn't have children who wanted to fetch the butter and cheese to bring it home, you had to take time to do it yourself. All those things pretty much spelled the end for Håseter, Hyrting, and all the others."

"It sounds like you miss them," I said. "The *budeier,* the *stølar.*"

"You bet I do. They're part of my childhood and a big part of our culture. An important part. They're what kept us from starving for hundreds of years."

He fell silent as he peered out the window again and then turned to me with a thoughtful smile.

"But you know what? The mountains aren't going away. They'll be here if we ever need to use them again."

We woke early the next morning, hurried through breakfast, and started a steep ascent up Skrott, the mountain that Øystein's cabin sat on. As we climbed higher and higher, patches of soil supporting grass, heather, and blueberries gradually gave way to boulders and long sheets of stone. By the time we reached Skrott's forty-three-hundred-foot summit, we were surrounded by nothing but bedrock, the soul of the *fjell.* Our view from this height was a universe of rugged peaks and uplands flecked with snow and etched by dark lakes and tarns. To the south, Hardanger Fjord's shoreline and islands looked like figures on a map. And beyond those, we could see a great expanse of Folgefonna Glacier resting like a white cloud atop the southern mountains.

We clambered down the peak's far side and made our way back toward the cabin along a bedrock plateau. After a quick *middag,* Øystein led us through his departure checklist: dishes washed and put away, every crumb of food secured in canisters or thrown out the door, floors swept, and all blankets and sheets hung over ropes that we strung between screw eyes in the walls. When we were finally ready to leave, he pulled out a key.

"These cabins were never locked before," he said apologetically. "They were here for everyone to use."

It wasn't just a convenience to be able to come inside, he explained. When people got caught in a storm, a cabin could save their life. Twice in the past year, though, he'd arrived to find dishes unwashed, food used up, and sheets and blankets still on the beds, at the mercy of any mice that might have strayed inside. That's when he decided a key was necessary.

Talking little and walking fast, we made good time on the homeward trek. At the marshy area below Hyrting's three cabins, I caught up with Øystein to ask a question that had been on my mind since my first hike above timberline.

"Who owns these mountains?"

"Well, right now we're on land that's jointly owned by the three farms at Hovland," he answered. "And back at Håseter, we were on land that belongs to the Øystese farms."

"Does the state own anything?"

"It sure does. Huge stretches of mountains and forests all over the country. But around here, most mountain land belongs to a farm, or to a group of farms, like Soldal and Hovland."

"Is it okay for us to hike across someone else's land? If they knew we were here, would they be upset?"

I wasn't prepared for Øystein's laugh, long and loud.

"I've heard about all those restrictions your countrymen put on their property and how they fence it off and put up signs warning you away from it," he said, after calming down. "Phew. I wouldn't want to live in a place like that. In Norway everyone has the right to hike and camp wherever they want—in the mountains, in the forest, and even on farms and in town, as long as they respect the privacy of the people who live there and as long as they don't trample crops or do any damage. And all of us have the right to pick wild berries, too, no matter who owns the land."

"So everyone can camp, hike, and pick berries wherever they want, but it's not okay for their sheep to graze on someone else's land, right?"

"Well, of course it's impossible to keep your sheep on your own territory all the time. But a good farmer will do his best to make that happen."

We walked along in silence for another few minutes as I considered everything I'd just heard before opening my mouth again.

"So, does this mean that Johannes isn't the best farmer around here?"

Øystein just smiled and shook his head.

At least once a week, Torkel and Inger invited me for supper: a light meal consisting of cheeses, thinly sliced meats, and other toppings to be eaten with crackers and bread. Now that Tormod and Arne were on summer vacation, they stayed up with us as we talked late into the evening. Sometimes Øystein was there now, too, for he was spending his weekends at the farm to help his brother with haying. At night, instead of making the long hike from Hovland down to his little house on Fyksesund—that narrow branch of the fjord straight down the mountainside from Hovland—he usually slept in Torkel's hayloft to get an early start each morning. There was a bed for him in the house, but he preferred the airy loft, as it was as close as he could get to the night sky without being soaked by dew or rain.

A week after the hike to Håseter, my neighbors and I were seated around their coffee table in the living room when Øystein stood up and handed me a little package. He held himself stiffly and watched closely as I unfolded the paper. Inside was a key tied like a pendant on a loop of string and a topographical map that covered Hovland, Fyksesund, Håseter, and surrounding mountains.

"With this key, you have complete access to Håseter," he said in the formal fashion that he slipped into when he wanted his words to carry weight. "The cabin is yours whenever you wish. May you use this key in good health."

"Thank you. Thank you so much," I mumbled, unable to come up with words to match such a gift. I shook his hand as was proper and felt my face redden. "I'm honored."

He was looking me straight in the eye; if anyone had flicked off the lights, I'm sure my burning cheeks would have lit up the room.

Torkel broke the awkward silence with a smile.

"What did I tell you, Liese? Now that you've got your own cabin, you're almost a real farmer! Next thing we know, you'll be taking over Johannes's farm for good."

"Or you can be a *budeie* at Håseter," Inger chimed in. "I'll send Tormod and Arne to bring home the butter. It's about time we Hovlanders took to using our *stølar* again."

She looked down at our empty glasses and nodded to her husband. "Torkel, more wine! I propose a toast."

Inger paused long enough for our host to dole a shot of his rich blueberry concoction into every glass. As we lifted our drinks she proclaimed, "To Liese and the *fjell*, her newfound love."

We held our goblets high while each of us glanced into the eyes of every other person at the table. Then we took a sip and lifted the glasses again, making a second round of eye contact. I loved this formal way of toasting. Its rules allowed all kinds of intimacy between people. Now, for example, Øystein again held my eyes, making me blush once more.

"But I have to warn you, Liese," Inger said with mock severity. "There's a saying here that once the *fjell* gets in your blood, it's with you forever. So you'd better be careful."

"I think it's too late," Torkel said. "I'd say the girl's already smitten."

Someone proposed another skoal, and as the evening wore on, we drank to mountains, cabins, summertime, and the bond between Norway and America. Sitting with these five people that evening, it dawned on me that I was no longer the person who felt like an outsider in high school, or *gymnasium,* and college. My worries about whether I was liked or accepted had receded. I was sitting in a room with friends and living in a community of neighbors who were walking out the door every morning to make hay or silage, and I was doing the same thing. What I was feeling now was a deep sense of connection to all of this. And that feeling filled me with joy.

Around midnight, when Bella and I headed for the door, Øystein took his leave, too. Together we descended the broad stone stairway. It was a quiet night, disturbed only by the sound of our footsteps treading neither fast nor slow. We reached the road and turned right, the direction leading to both Torkel's barn and Johannes's house. At the barn's portal, Øystein turned and took me in his arms. I must have started, for he released his grip and backed up a step.

He was as old as my father—thirty years my senior. Until recently, if someone had asked me what I thought of men that age, I'd have been hard-pressed to answer. I suppose if I'd bothered to think about them at all, I may have described fifty-year-olds as over the hill. Yet now it was more than Torkel's wine that made me slip forward and pull his brother back into an embrace, for Øystein—powerful, captivating, striking—was just the opposite. I looked into his eyes, and we kissed.

With his arm around my shoulders, we veered from the barn and headed toward my house at a slow pace, keeping our silence. At the door, he loosened his hold and again took a step back, creating a little gap between us. A little space for . . . well . . . for what? Rational thought?

Behind his dark form I could see Bella nosing through the garden, her curled white tail the only object clearly visible in this murky light. I wondered what she was after. A mole, perhaps.

Rational thought? Maybe not. I didn't want to be thinking rationally, because that would mean asking Øystein to return to his brother's hayloft, when right now the only rational thought I wanted to allow into my brain was where I'd tucked away my diaphragm.

Rational thought would be a reminder that local conventions of dating, courtship, and sex were a cultural labyrinth I knew nothing about. In my months in Norway, I had yet to meet an unmarried person who professed to be in a romantic relationship. I didn't even know the words for "boyfriend" or "girlfriend," because they didn't seem to exist. I did know, though, that it wouldn't take an anthropological field study to establish that an affair between a twenty-year-old and a fifty-year-old most likely teetered on the threshold of acceptability in any society.

But that was rational thought. In the end, blueberry wine, months of living alone, and the riveting man at my side joined forces to overcome any number of tut-tutting anthropologists.

I opened the door.

Early the next morning, Øystein stole back to his brother's farm. When he returned to my house late in the afternoon, we walked to a thicket of alders bordering the cow pasture where we could talk without being seen. We sat down together in the grass, and he pulled me into a kiss.

Under the light of day, it felt different. I drew back and looked down, unable to meet his eyes now, after having met them so boldly just hours before.

"I've never known anyone like you," he said. "You're so beautiful. I want to come back to your room tonight. May I?"

I hated myself for having let my desire overcome me, blinding me until now from the sure knowledge that, as much as I liked and admired this man, I did not want a romantic relationship with him.

He sensed my reluctance and sat back.

"This is probably not a good idea," I said, with my head still down. "I'm sorry. It makes me feel bad to say this."

We sat together in silence for a long time, our arms still pressed together.

"Are you sure?" he finally asked.

I nodded, and he edged away.

"You're right," he said. "I'm too old. There's no sense in this."

I could hear in his voice that for him there *was* sense in it, but I was deeply grateful to him for giving me the chance to undo my reckless actions. What was I thinking? I was smart enough to know that my infatuation with Øystein couldn't possibly have gone anywhere, not even for a day. Its chief value lay in the fireball of gossip it could ignite, spicing up otherwise unremarkable exchanges about weather and livestock in living rooms for miles around.

I couldn't put words to any of the thoughts streaming through my head, so we sat there and rambled on about this and that. Livestock and weather, most likely. At length we mumbled our goodbyes. He headed to the trail leading down the hill toward Fyksesund, and I walked back to the house.

23

Johannes Baits the Hook

On August 5, I drove Johannes's elegant gig to town again to pick up a new farmhand. This time, the person waiting at the bus stop was just what the farm needed. Slender and strong, with straight, oat-colored hair that fell below her shoulders, Linda Jolly threw herself into every task and chore and never questioned the long hours. She was smitten by Hovland from day one and within a week had learned enough Norwegian to communicate with neighbors.

Linda and I had met in the spring of 1971 at the University of California Santa Cruz, where I was a freshman and she a sophomore. We were both volunteers in the college's organic garden, an experience that had inspired her to apply for a three-year program in biodynamic agriculture at Emerson College in England. In July, she'd sent me a letter asking if she could come to Hovland to lend a hand before her classes started in September. Johannes had readily agreed, happy to have the extra help. She could stay for as long as she liked, he said, and he would even pay her a small wage.

Late in the afternoon on Linda's first full day at Hovland, Arne came to deliver a message: his parents had received a package for me, and we needed to come get it right away.

When we arrived, Torkel and Inger were standing in front of their barn with big smiles on their faces.

"This way, girls," Inger said, swinging open the wide barn door. "An early Christmas present for you. See how beautifully it's wrapped."

Behind her stood a ragbag of canvas and rope shrouding a bulky form about the size of a small pony.

"We knew you'd gone for a hike, so we told the van driver to leave it with us," Torkel said, patting the wrappings with a proprietary air. "Here's the address label. 'To Miss Liese Greensfelder, Hovland, Øystese. From Johannes Hovland, Voss Hospital.'

"Shall we unwrap it for the ladies, Arne?"

Father and son positioned themselves at either end of the hulking parcel and, with a flourish worthy of artists unveiling a masterpiece, whisked the canvas away. Linda and I both gasped, for there in the gloom of this old barn stood a beautiful little pump organ.

My thoughts were spinning as we examined this marvelous object. As far as I knew, Johannes didn't play the organ or any other instrument. Could it be that his medical crew had recommended he start playing something—perhaps as physical therapy for his arm and hand? Suddenly I remembered that I'd told him that I missed my piano from home. But it didn't seem possible that he'd remembered this, for we'd had that conversation months earlier, and he hadn't even listened to what I'd said.

"Liese, it's bait," Inger said dryly. "The man is fishing for you to stay the winter."

"This is far too precious to be a lure," I murmured, as I ran my hand over the keyboard, counting fourteen stops and four and a half octaves of ivory keys. "It's wonderful."

"We'd better load it up and get it into your living room right away," Torkel warned. "This damp weather's not going to do it any good."

After a quick consultation, we agreed that it would be too risky to hitch Torkel's mare to his wagon, for she spooked so easily she might topple the cart.

"There are enough of us to pull it there ourselves," Arne piped up. "That would work, don't you think?"

Rain was threatening and night falling as three Norwegians and two Americans loaded Johannes's organ into Torkel's cart, secured it there with canvas and rope, and ever so slowly pushed and pulled our way to Johannes's house, where we installed the lovely instrument in the living room next to a window.

A single piece of sheet music—an old Norwegian hymn—had been tucked into the canvas wrappings. I sat down, opened a few stops, fiddled with the foot pumps until I got the hang of them, and started to play. The sound filled this old, dark room and the entire house, almost as if the hymn's Star of Bethlehem was right there on our ceiling, driving away the oppressive gloom.

"I always wanted a piano. Every house needs music. Its own music," Johannes told Linda and me when we visited him in Voss a week later. He was in a different room now, one without all the medical equipment that had surrounded him earlier. Seated in a chair and dressed in a white button-up shirt and loose-fitting slacks, he looked more like a hotel guest than a hospital patient.

"You were the inspiration for this," he said, nodding in my direction. "When you told me that you missed your piano from home, I decided it was time to buy one."

The revelation amazed me, for it meant that not only had Johannes heard me when I mentioned my piano but he'd remembered what I said and acted on it. Perhaps the organ truly was the bait that Inger claimed.

I expressed my gratitude by gushing about how much I was enjoying playing in the evenings after work. I'd bought a book of Norwegian songs, I told him, and Linda and I were now holding our own little concerts for two voices and organ in his living room. I'd soon be receiving a package sent by my mother of my favorite sheet music: a songbook, the score of Handel's *Messiah,* and a volume of easier compositions by various composers.

When I finally stopped talking, Johannes was staring out the window. At length he took a deep breath—not quite a sigh—and gave me news of his own. The doctors were saying that he needed more therapy, he said, so he might not be coming home until after Christmas. And even then, he would need help in the barn—at least until spring.

"So I need to know," he said. "Can you stay at the farm until then?"

The request astonished me. Of course, I hadn't been blind to the fact that Johannes's progress had been painfully slow. As he sat across from us now, his speech was still a bit slurred, his left arm was nearly useless, and he could not rise from a chair or take a step without assistance. For all that, though, he had been telling me at each visit that his doctors were saying he would be released "in a month or two." I knew nothing about strokes and rehabilitation, so I had no reason to question this timeframe, even as it kept getting pushed back. Probably Johannes even believed it, too.

"Wintertime is like a long vacation," he was saying. "I'm never in the barn more than two or three hours a day."

In the back of my mind, I'd always thought that if his condition didn't improve, a friend or relative—someone who actually knew how to run a farm—would step up and take over. I'd heard other scenarios mentioned, too, foremost that Johannes might sell the farm to one of several siblings who wanted it, with the condition that he keep the garden, of course, and that he be allowed to build a small abode right next to it.

I'd long since decided that I wasn't going to leave until I'd herded the farm's flock back home from the mountains. The roundup started around mid-September and could last into October. By then, I assumed, Johannes would be settled in on the farm, and I would be looking for a new job, possibly in Spain or France.

Johannes was frowning. "What are you thinking?" he asked.

"I don't really know," I said haltingly. "I need a few days to think it over. If I do stay, I'd like to take a month off after the sheep come home. Would that be okay?"

My request seemed to take him aback. His answer, though, was straightforward.

"You're free to do as you please," he said gravely. "Of course you are."

Linda was patient with me on our journey home as I debated what to do. The thought of spending a winter living in Johannes's big house scared me. The challenges were huge. Not only would I have to learn how to survive in deep snow and a frigid climate in a house where the only source of heat was four woodstoves, but I would also be responsible for the survival of dozens of animals in a remarkably primitive barn. I'd never lived in an extreme climate before—on the rare occasions in Denmark when snow piled higher than half a foot or so, it usually melted away in a day or two—so I really had no concept of how to cope with snow at all. At Hovland, even in a raging blizzard, I'd have to make my way between four buildings and a silo at least twice a day to care for the animals and bring in firewood. And how would I get to Soldal to pick up the mail?

The memory of my miserable winter in Denmark worried me, too. Surely my depression there had been at least partly due to short days and wretched, cloudy weather that obscured the sun for almost five months. If so, I might be in even more trouble at Hovland. We were three hundred miles closer to the North Pole here, which would make the days shorter still.

And then there was Johannes. I didn't know how long I could live

Johannes's farm and snow-covered Klyvenuten. Fyksesund, a long, narrow branch of Hardanger Fjord, lies between the hills in the foreground and the white peaks beyond. January 1973. Courtesy of the author.

Torkel and Inger's storage shed and barn. Solveig, Alv, and Torgeir's farmstead with its yellow house is down the road. Early January 1973. Courtesy of the author.

Tormod, Torkel, Inger, and Arne Hovland on the hill between their farm and Johannes's. Solveig and Alv's barn can be seen behind Arne. August 1972. Courtesy of the author.

Torgeir, Alv, and Solveig Hovland in front of one of their outbuildings. July 1977. Photograph by Bob Erickson.

Johannes and others bringing in the hay. The woman holding a rake is Hildur Hovland, Gunnar's wife and Svein's mother. Circa 1962. Photograph by Gunnar Hovland. Courtesy of Svein Hovland.

Begonia, Johannes's purebred *fjordhest* (Norwegian fjord horse). January 17, 1973. Photograph by Per Arne Carlsen. Courtesy of the author.

A *hesje* that Linda and I loaded with green grass. Depending on weather conditions, it usually takes one to two weeks for grass on a *hesje* to dry into hay. August 1972. Courtesy of the author.

Johannes's *troskytje*, a shed for storage of *hesje* poles. September 8, 1972. Photograph by Linda Jolly.

Øystein and I taking a rest at this peaceful spot in the mountains above Hyrting known as *grøne brekkene,* "the green steep hills." August 1972. Photograph by Linda Jolly.

Sheep graze in the mountains above Hyrting. September 2022. Photograph by Marian Bolstad.

Hyrting. September 2022. Photograph by Marian Bolstad.

Sheep at Skårsete, a *støl* about half a mile east of Hyrting. July 2023. Photograph by Marian Bolstad.

A belled sheep and her lamb grazing on lush vegetation that obscures the treacherous, boulder-strewn walls of Smørdalen, "Butter Valley." The only sheep outfitted with bells when I lived at Hovland were one or two of Solveig's flock. Early summer 1989. Photograph by Bob Erickson.

When autumn's first snow turned peaks white, Linda and I rushed into the mountains with visions of snowball fights dancing in our heads. Here Bella and I sit just below Blomseter, taking in the view of Fyksesund and Hardanger Fjord. September 8, 1972. Photograph by Linda Jolly.

Fyksesund. Summer 1977. Photograph by Bob Erickson.

Bella at my side as I play the organ in Johannes's living room. November 30, 1972. Photograph by Erik Berglund. Courtesy of *Bergens Tidende.*

Johannes's woodshed: for seven months I did battle every day with gnarly oak, alder, and birch to keep the kitchen warm enough for human survival. November 30, 1972. Photograph by Erik Berglund. Courtesy of *Bergens Tidende.*

Loading the sledge to haul away rotten silage and hay stems so coarse that even Begonia won't eat them. November 30, 1972. Photograph by Erik Berglund. Courtesy of *Bergens Tidende*.

A reporter and photographer working on a magazine story asked Inger Hovland and me to pose in Johannes's living room. In reality, no self-respecting Norwegian would wear her formal *bunad* while doing common work like spinning. January 17, 1973. Photograph by Aage Storløkken for *Aktuell*. Courtesy NTB.

With nothing to hold on to for support, my biggest challenge when driving the sledge was keeping my balance. November 30, 1972. Photograph by Erik Berglund. Courtesy of *Bergens Tidende*.

Bribing the sheep with handfuls of grain. November 30, 1972. Photograph by Erik Berglund. Courtesy of *Bergens Tidende*.

Håseter, Øystein's cabin in the mountains. Easter week 1973. Photograph by Linda Jolly.

Øystein and Edvard at Håseter. Circa 1975. Photograph by Tormod Hovland. Courtesy of Arne Hovland.

Linda and Bella at Hyrting. Easter week 1973. Courtesy of the author.

My little black and white calf, just three weeks old. Circa May 1, 1973. Photograph by Erik Berglund.

Håseter. From left to right: Arne Hovland; Vigdis Tangen; my husband, Bob Erickson; me; Øyvind Flatabø; Tormod Hovland sitting with his wife, Anne Maritha Mo, and their son, Tommy; Bob's nephew, Andrew; and Bob's and my 10-year-old son, Tor. Summer 1989. Courtesy of Bob Erickson.

At Blomseter with Tor. Summer 1989. Photograph by Bob Erickson.

Driving the manure cart as winter's sun casts long shadows. Snow-bedecked Fagraseteggi juts into the sky behind us. January 19, 1973. Photograph by Steiner Døsvik.

under the same roof with a man who misinterpreted almost everything I said and whose temper could boil over at any minute. Linda brought up yet another issue. If he and I lived together, who would do the cooking and cleaning? I knew for sure that I didn't want to take on barn work *and* housework for him.

On the positive side, Tormod and Arne had promised that they would teach me how to ski if I was still their neighbor when the snow came. And Inger had offered to give me lessons on the spinning wheels in Johannes's living room. Spending a winter here would give me a chance to get to know more of my neighbors and to have a few hours every day to read and to play the organ. If what Johannes said was true—that he never worked more than two or three hours a day in the winter—there would be time for all these things and more.

Linda's patience finally ran out.

"Enough already!" she pleaded. "Why are you doing this? You know you're going to stay. Could you please just say so?"

"What makes you think that?" I asked in surprise.

"Because every day since I got here you've told me how much you love the farm and all your neighbors. So why aren't you jumping for joy right now? Johannes just asked you to spend the next six months here."

She was right, of course. And as we walked up the hill from Øystese, we made plans for Linda to come back at Christmas and learn to ski with me.

The next morning we were hanging grass on a *hesje* when I spotted a familiar figure walking our way from the cows' pasture and forest trail.

Edvard hadn't visited for weeks. During this time my campaign to stop thinking about him had been only moderately successful. Now it suffered a setback when he drew up to Linda and me with his off-kilter smile and shining eyes. I introduced my friends to each other and called for a break.

"Look here," Edvard said, after we were settled in the kitchen with coffee in our cups and a plate of home-baked sugar cookies on the table. He pulled a letter from his knapsack and unfolded it for me to read.

"I'm glad I got this," he said in mock earnestness. "I was beginning to feel left out, because everyone else already has one. Look. He writes that he 'won't tolerate' me coming to the farm again."

Johannes's unmistakable script filled the page. My eyes darted to a scattering of words underscored by lines so dark they nearly rent the paper: *forbidden, deceptive, never again.*

I was dumbfounded. What in the world was wrong with this man that he would send such a message to a friend? Not just any friend, but one who had spent hours working on his farm for no pay.

"Maybe he's jealous that you have so many friends and he doesn't," Edvard suggested, only half in jest. "So he wants to get rid of us. Really, though, it's hard to understand him sometimes."

This scribbling stopped me cold, reminding me of how angry I'd been back in June when Johannes declared that he didn't want Edvard or other men to visit me at the farm. He had never returned to this issue—not even when he and I had talked face-to-face just twenty-four hours earlier—so I'd foolishly grown to believe that he'd come to respect me as an adult who could make her own choices about visitors.

This letter changed everything. It was cruel, furtive, and controlling all at the same time. If this was the kind of man Johannes was, there was no way I could keep working for him.

Edvard must have read my thoughts, because before I said a word, he jumped to the farmer's defense.

"You can't let this get to you, Liese," he said, waving his cookie in the air for emphasis. "I'm sure even Johannes doesn't understand why he does things like this. Sometimes I think that once a crazy thought gets into his head, he has no way of stopping himself from acting on it. Like he's living with a demon that just keeps stirring him up."

"But how can I keep working for him when he treats you like this?" I objected. "It's not right. You know it's not, and I'm sure he knows it, too."

"What do you mean by that . . . 'how can I keep working for him?'" Edvard asked. "For one thing, there's no one besides you who's going to keep the farm running. He needs you. And the *farm* needs you. But, of course, you know that, right?"

I nodded my head morosely.

"Maybe you don't want to work for Johannes Hovland. But what about Bella and Begonia? And the sheep? What would they do without you this winter?"

If I'd learned anything over the summer, it was that the survival of the farm was hanging by a thread. Now Edvard was expressing the same thing. And the fact that he was trying to convince me to stay after receiving these cruel lines from Johannes lent weight to his words.

"You know that I want to stay," I said softly. The mere thought of leaving saddened me. "But when Johannes comes home, I just don't see how I can live here with him."

"You won't have to," Edvard said earnestly. "Once he's here, it will be easier for him to get on the phone and find someone else to help. Or he'll make a deal with Alv or some other neighbor to rent the farm for a few years."

He and Linda and I talked at length about what the winter might bring, until finally I let them convince me. I would stay at least until Johannes came home, whether that happened soon or sometime next summer. "But what about you?" I asked my friend. "He doesn't want you to come here anymore."

A smile lit Edvard's face.

"If he wants to kick me off his place, he's going to have to catch me first. And I don't think the old geezer can run very fast right now."

"Hey, Linda, how does this sound?"

It was a Monday night, late in August. Linda and I were sitting at the kitchen table writing letters to our families in California. Outside it was cold, dark, and raining.

"Dear family," I read aloud. "Yesterday the heifer suddenly broke into a gallop when I was leading her to pasture. The problem was that I had to run with her, because my arm was all tangled up in her lead chain, so I would have been dragged under her feet if I fell. Then when she headed right toward a thicket of trees, I was pretty sure she was going to smash me into them. Just before she did, I somehow managed to break loose. Boy, was that lucky for me."

I'd actually spared my family from the worst of it, for I hadn't described how my only thought in the seconds before the imminent collision was that this crazed animal was going to either break my bones or outright kill me.

Johannes's black heifer was a troublesome beast. A week or two after I released her from the barn in June, she'd learned that the farm's rickety fences were no match for her brawn. At least every other day, she broke out of her pasture and ambled through the hayfields, trampling the precious crop. On several of these jaunts, she ended up peering creepily through the window at my front door. I think she liked me, in an odd bovine way, so she would wander around until she found me. Mean tempered as a bull, she sometimes put up a fight when I tried to lead her back to pasture. Of course, as soon as I closed the gate, I'd have to inspect the long fence line to find where she'd broken out and repair the breach. The best thing I could say about her was that she had not gone into heat again after being inseminated. So I assumed that she was pregnant.

Now Linda looked up and rolled her eyes. "If I were your mom, I'd wring your neck just so I wouldn't have to worry about you anymore."

"So you don't think I should tell her about the heifer," I asked, "or how I almost killed you with the hay wagon on the barn bridge?"

We'd had a number of accidents and close calls in the past few weeks, and neither of us exercised much discretion in describing these scary events to our families. In fact, we amused ourselves by imagining how each mishap could have been far worse. These morbid fantasies would end with one of us narrating a mock letter to the mother of the other: "Dear Mrs. Jolly, I regret to inform you that . . ." or "Dear Mrs. Greensfelder, it is with great sadness that I send you these words . . ."

"Well, I do think we have to start being more careful with what we write," Linda replied. "I'm sure our parents are worried to death about us."

She sat silent for a moment, staring past me at nothing in particular. When she started up again, her voice was hesitant.

"There's something else that's been on my mind. I wasn't going to bring it up, but now I think I have to." She twisted around in her chair, grabbed a piece of firewood, and added it to the stove. "What I've been wondering is what you write to your family about Øystein."

I pushed the letter aside and tightened my grip on the pen.

"Well, what do you think?" I said, a little too defensively. "I'm telling them about our hikes to Håseter and how much work he does around here."

She rolled her eyes for a second time that evening. "What about that kiss he gave you last night?"

"You saw that?" I asked in surprise.

"Yeah, I did. You were right below the window, after all."

"Okay, so what?" I felt my face reddening. "It was no big deal. Just on the cheek."

To balance the ten to eleven hours Linda and I had been putting in six days a week during the past month, every Sunday we took long hikes into the mountains. Arne and Tormod sometimes accompanied us, and their uncle Øystein almost always did. This Sunday Øystein had stayed for supper after our return. When he got up to leave, I walked him to the road, where, just as I said goodbye, he snatched my shoulders and kissed me on the cheek. Barely a peck.

Although I'd told Linda that the kiss was no big deal, it actually worried me terribly. Until that moment, in spite of numerous hints to the contrary that I'd done my best to ignore, I could maintain an optimistic belief that Øystein felt nothing other than friendship toward me.

"Okay, so it was just on the cheek," Linda said. "But I haven't seen anyone else get kissed on the cheek around here. And think of how much time he spends with us."

"A lot of people spend time with us." I listed off four or five names.

"If you think any of them are here as much as Øystein, you're off your rocker. He's here every Friday night, he works with us all day Saturday, and he spends all day in the mountains with us on Sunday. Don't you think that's strange? Think about it. No guy hangs around a girl that much just because he's her friend. He's got to be in love with you. In fact, I'm sure he is."

I'd never told Linda about my night with Øystein, for no matter how often I tried to reassure myself that making love was a natural, normal, and delightful part of life, the memory filled me with shame, embarrassment, and guilt. More than that, I was terrified that word of our night together might seep out to the neighborhood, starting with my closest neighbors and best friends: Øystein's brother and his family. It would take a more self-assured person than me to walk down the road to Øystese knowing that this shocking piece of gossip would be on the minds of every soul who saw me. If word leaked out, I was sure that staying at Hovland would be impossible.

Øystein was a remarkable man, and my admiration for him hadn't died after our night together. At first, everything had seemed fine between us. I enjoyed spending time with him, and he did nothing to make me think that he was still hoping for a romantic relationship. What I hadn't yet told Linda was that now his long weekend visits were making me tense. I was beginning to feel hemmed in, watched over. Linda and I worked hard, with little time off; on weekends we both needed a chance to just hang out and do nothing. I'd already been trying to get up the courage to ask Øystein to let us hike into the mountains on our own some Sunday, but I just couldn't think of a way to frame such a request without hurting his feelings.

Linda and I finished up our letters and left the warm kitchen for the cold bedrooms upstairs.

"You said I should smile less at him," I mused, as we climbed the stairs. "Well, in case you haven't noticed, I haven't been smiling very much at him recently. I'm sure he knows I'm not in love with him, and I can't think of any reason to hurt him even more by asking him to stay away."

"There are two reasons I can think of," she said soberly. "I know you'd be happier if he stopped spending so much time here. And after I leave, it will just be you and him alone."

The wild berries ripened while Linda was still at Hovland. What a glorious riot of flavor and color! By mid-July the first strawberries had already turned red and sweet. Then came raspberries, growing along roads and trails, offering their voluptuous fruits to every passerby. A few weeks later, the mountains began to yield their bounty. Lingonberries—*tyttebœr*—like miniature cranberries, red and hard. And crowberries—*krekling*—small, black, and sour, growing in tight clusters on ankle-high plants. Tormod taught us to slake our thirst while we hiked by grabbing a cluster or two and crunching them between our teeth to release their abundant juice. Occasionally we came across cloudberries, *molter*. These soft, salmon-colored fruits had a sweet, musty flavor a little like apricots. Queen of the *fjell*'s wild harvest, they were easy to spot, for they sat on stems that rose an inch or so above low-growing plants that thrived in peat bogs.

Best of all were the endless acres of shin-high blueberry plants festooned with midnight-blue fruits that grew bigger, sweeter, and juicier week after week. During the height of blueberry season, just about everyone in the region hiked into the mountains to harvest this wild treasure. Linda and I gathered them with little wooden harvesting boxes that someone at Hovland had made a generation earlier. These ingenious tools were outfitted with a wooden handle and a row of metal fingers. When we combed them through blueberry foliage, almost every berry would pop off and roll into the box. In a single day, the two of us picked enough fruit to make twenty-three quarts of jam.

In the week before Linda left, chilly nights painted the farm's aspens, maples, ashes, and oaks in a palette of autumn colors. Apples, pears, and plums on Johannes's fruit trees were growing larger every day. Nestled in dark, fertile beds on the farms of Hovland and Soldal, the potato crop was finally ready for harvest. Alv redeployed his mare, Stella, from retirement to drag his potato plow up and down the rows of their hillside plot. While Torgeir guided her, Alv kept a firm grip on the plow's two handles, keeping it in line with each row and maintaining the share at proper depth. Linda and I gave Solveig and the two brothers a hand one afternoon. After only an hour bent double combing our hands through the loosened soil to retrieve every one of the farm's precious fruits, our backs were screaming to be released from this torture.

Colder, damper weather and shorter days were also thwarting our haymaking efforts. On the few *hesjes* still standing, grass was hanging heavy and limp. When we noticed a moldy odor emanating from one of these wire-and-pole structures, we realized it was time to call it quits. Linda and I drove our last few loads of cured grass into the barn and started dismantling the drying racks, stringing wires back onto spools and pulling stakes from the ground. Two and a half months of haymaking had come to an end.

In mid-September we bid each other farewell on a pier in Bergen. Linda boarded a ferry bound for Newcastle and sailed away to start her new life at college. Back home at Hovland that night, my life felt much lonelier as I sat in the kitchen listening to rain pouring down outside.

24

Stuck on a Ledge

Øystein showed up earlier than usual the next week and announced that he was taking a fortnight of sick leave due to a problem with his hands. "So I'll be here to round up Hovland's sheep," he said with a smile. "Torkel's are easy. They stay pretty close to Blomseter and Hyrting. Yours are so scattered it might take weeks to find them all."

I couldn't see anything wrong with his hands, so it struck me as suspicious that his sick leave should coincide so well with the annual roundup. Linda had known and I had learned—and by now probably everyone in the neighborhood suspected—that Øystein was crazy about me. My face still reddened every time I thought about how I'd allowed this to happen. Right now, though, the only thing I felt was gratitude that he was willing to help me bring in the sheep, a task I couldn't possibly accomplish on my own.

On a cold and rainy Friday afternoon two days later, he and I set off for Håseter with Bella in the lead. As we climbed above timberline, the sun came out just long enough to light up fall's brilliant hues: scarlet carpets of dwarf willow, copper waves of bracken ferns, and pink swaths of flowering heather. Blueberries were at their peak right now, plump, juicy, sweet, and so densely loaded on their low-growing plants that we barely broke stride to grab them by the handful.

"It's a good day for the hunt!" Øystein called out when he heard me stirring the next morning. "We need to eat quickly and get going."

I pulled on my clothes and tottered to the cozy little cabin's main room, where I found a fire roaring in the stove, breakfast fixings on the table, and a pot of coffee ready to pour. Øystein started strategizing as soon as I sat down.

"We'll hike up Smørdalen first. My guess is we'll find about ten sheep there, maybe a dozen. Then we'll turn around and start driving them home. If we're lucky, any sheep we find at Hyrting will jump in with the crowd."

He took a sip of coffee, fixed his gaze on the floor somewhere to the right of my feet, and added, "I'm not sure I mentioned this, but a couple of friends are hiking up for a visit this afternoon. So after we get to Hyrting, I'll be coming back here with them."

His words left me speechless. Memories flooded back of the evening in spring when Johannes's elusive flock turned a calm group of friends and neighbors into sweating lunatics.

He laughed awkwardly and told me not to worry, because once the flock got moving, they'd be just as happy whether one person or an entire company followed them. And even if I did lose a few at Hyrting, those that strayed would be more than halfway home and would surely wander back to the farm on their own.

This was all shaky logic, at best. My sheep were freethinkers, disinclined to flock together. It would be hard enough for the two of us to drive them down the hill, I thought. But alone? Surely that was impossible.

The more he said, the more upset I got. He was simply inventing excuses for not telling me earlier. If he had, I'd never have made the long trip to Håseter with him. I wondered whether he was doing this by design, in retribution for having been spurned, or perhaps to demonstrate that I was dependent on him. At this point, though, I could only sulk. Which I proceeded to do, admirably well, until we finished breakfast and were out the door.

Bella trotted ahead as we made our way to an outcrop high on the rim of Smørdalen, "Butter Valley," the treacherous ravine named for its udder-engorging blanket of grasses and ferns. Clouds had disappeared overnight, and the air was crystal clear in this chilly sunlight, making it easier to distinguish distant clusters of sheep from flecks of snow or patches of rock.

From our vantage point, we quickly spotted eight animals in three widely scattered groups. And then something else: a trio of whitish smudges on the steep and rocky south face of Håstabben, a stubby peak sandwiched between its two higher neighbors, Skrott and Manfjell.

"Are those sheep, do you think?" I asked.

Øystein pulled an old pair of binoculars from his pack and studied the cliffs.

"Yeah, a ewe . . . and two lambs." He steadied his back against a boulder to get a better read on the trio. "And it looks like they're *skorfaste.* If I'm right, it's going to be quite a job getting them out of there."

The concept of being trapped in the mountains extends so deeply into the Norwegian psyche that when a Norwegian finds herself in a bind of any sort, she's likely to say, "I'm stuck on a mountain ledge." Not just any ledge, but one from which she can't escape without help. Once a person has gotten herself into such a predicament, she is *skorfast,* where *skor* means "mountain ledge" and *fast* means "stuck."

I'd been told that every summer a few sheep from Hovland and Soldal found themselves in just such a jam. Thanks to an abundance of sharp-eyed hikers, however, most of these hapless creatures were discovered before succumbing to hunger or thirst.

Hikers who spot a *skorfast* sheep are usually quick to report the news. An animal's owner then works even more quickly to assemble a crew and head to the hills. Rounding up volunteers is rarely a problem, for rescue expeditions afford participants an unparalleled opportunity to do a good deed while at the same time demonstrating the full range of their strength, skill, and ingenuity.

Some expeditions promise a greater prize than drama alone. An especially gripping rescue can bestow honor—nay, *immortality*—on all who participate. In my neighborhood, even the youngsters could provide details of a decades-old rescue party that freed three sheep from a cliff above Fyksesund.

The hardest part of any expedition is the showdown between humans and sheep on a cramped mountain ledge; any wrong move could send an animal, or even a person, over the edge. Rescuers must first capture unwilling ewes and lambs, securely bind them, and sometimes even wrestle them into a sack. Other team members are then needed to hoist or belay the animals to safer ground.

Only when every effort to capture a sheep fails does an expedition resort to its rifle. No one wants to leave an animal to starve to death.

With a clean shot and deft field dressing, rescuers can at least return home bearing a fleece and a sack of meat.

It took us nearly two hours to reach the head of a steep cleft, which was surely where the three sheep who were eyeing us from about one hundred feet below had taken a wrong turn, for now we could see that they were indeed *skorfaste*. To free them, we would have to help them climb back up to this spot. We used one of our ropes to secure Bella to a rock, and then, with boots sliding over dirt and scree, we devised a rescue plan as we made our nerve-racking descent to join the trio on their tiny perch.

As we approached, I could see that I knew this ewe. She and her lambs had spent half the summer near Hyrting, where she'd grown accustomed to my visits and handouts. As soon as we landed, she dashed to my outstretched palm and snapped greedily at an offering of grain, while her two young cowered together as far from us as possible. Without a doubt these sheep had been *skorfaste* for days, for the ground beneath them was thick with sheep pellets and every bit of herbage had been gnawed to the quick.

Øystein immediately took his position and stood like a statue with his back to the rocky wall just behind me, while I sank to my knees and continued to dole out feed. For our plan to succeed, I needed to lure this ewe into exactly the right position: standing broadside right in front of me. We would get only one chance.

She followed my fist as I waved it slowly back and forth, releasing a bit of grain every so often. After four or five passes, she began to calm down. And suddenly she was right there! I lunged forward and clamped my arms around her chest and rear. She lurched violently, and we both fell backward. My head hit a rock. Something sharp tore at my wrist. Øystein was with us in a flash, binding his rope into a harness around the ewe's neck and trunk as I held onto her like a bulldog. Meanwhile, two anxious lambs remained huddled together at the very brink of this small ledge.

"This should hold her fine," Øystein said when he was done with the knots. "Now we've just got to get her out of here."

With him tugging in the lead and me pushing from below, we forged our way up the perilous cleft. Supported between us, the ewe showed no fear in making an ascent she hadn't dared face earlier. When we reached Bella at the head of the cleft, all three of us turned to look back.

"They're going to kill themselves!" I cried. Far below, the frenzied lambs were a hair's breadth from disaster, hurtling back and forth from one end of the ledge to the other.

Øystein ripped the lashings from our captive. "Get going, girl!" he exhorted, shoving her away from the cleft. "Show them you're okay!" She took the hint and tore down the steep hillside rather than revisiting the perilous trail we had just ascended. Seconds later she skidded to a halt on the slope opposite her young. Seeing her so close, the twins froze. For a moment they even seemed calm—until they realized that some twenty feet of thin air separated them from their dam. All three animals let out plaintive bleats.

Øystein and I stood dead still. Even Bella didn't move. This was not the outcome we were expecting. We'd figured that the lambs would follow at a distance as we made our way up the cleft. Now there didn't seem to be any way to retrieve them.

The ewe, however, thought otherwise. As we humans stood helplessly by, a clarion call resounded through the valley. A call like no other from mother to young. A tremendous "baaaa!" that echoed off surrounding mountains, summoning the twins to action.

And act they did. First the smaller lamb, then her larger brother hurtled across their prison's rocky floor and launched themselves into space. I held back a scream as the duo flew through the air and thudded to earth beside their mother on the mountainside they had left days earlier. All three touched noses, glanced back at us, and took off running down the valley.

"Well, I'll be damned," Øystein breathed in quietly.

Finally, we could start our slow march home, with Øystein sweeping Smørdalen's west face and Bella and me the east. My little companion wanted to help, but lacking any training she immediately started to herd a group of sheep in the wrong direction. The second time this happened, I shouted at her to keep behind me, which she seemed to understand. By the time we reached Hyrting two hours later, a flock of fourteen sheep trotted in loose formation ahead of us. We corralled another eleven animals into our herd just below Hyrting's three cabins, then started down the steep trail toward Blomseter. Five minutes later Øystein called out a farewell. "Just keep them moving! Don't give them a chance to do anything except stay ahead of you." With that, he turned and headed back to Håseter.

His optimism immediately proved to be overblown. Within minutes, the flock's left flank registered his absence and galloped away in tight formation. Ten sheep lost and the rest of them conspiring to follow suit. Not if I can help it, I swore. And I started running.

Somewhere in Norway there must be a flock of sheep that pitter-patter their way down the mountain ahead of a solitary shepherdess. Apparently Øystein had once herded sheep like this. But Johannes's animals were too much like their master to stick together. Over and over, small groups peeled away ahead of me to make a dash for freedom. I couldn't chase after them because that would simply spook them farther afield. Instead, I had to run in a wide circle to get ahead of the wayward animals and turn them back toward the main group. In the excitement Bella kept charging ahead but always pulled back at my commands.

Each time I left my position in the rear to nab a runaway covey, another band would pull away. My homeward course traced a drunken zigzag over the terrain. I ran and ran and ran. I tore uphill and downhill and jumped over rocks and creeks. I fell and rolled back to my feet. I didn't notice the bruises on my legs or the fire in my lungs. I ran through bushes and branches and didn't see anything except the sheep I was chasing and didn't think about anything other than getting them home. At some point, my brain stopped working and my body took over. How strange that my legs kept going even when I turned and headed uphill. When the ground leveled out, my feet sprouted wings to rocket me over mosses and creeping willows, and I felt like I was flying down the mountain. My body wouldn't let me stop, not even for a second, because it understood that if it did, I wouldn't be able to start again.

All the while, I knew that my biggest obstacle lay ahead: I needed to drive the flock through Hovland's gate. And the gate was closed. If I could just settle the animals to a halt, maybe I could glide around them and open this entryway to the farm without causing alarm. Then I could circle back to nudge them slowly, ever so slowly, through the terrifying portal to their home pasture. Not a perfect plan, perhaps, but the only one I had.

By the time we slowed to a stop some seventy feet from Hovland's upper fence line, my flock of twenty-five had dwindled to eight. And I knew from their earmarks that three of these animals weren't even my own. Circling wide and walking slow, Bella and I reached the gate without causing a disturbance. But as I cautiously pulled it open, four animals tore into a copse of birch trees on our right, while the remainder turned tail to disappear back up the trail.

My tears erupted without warning. Sobs racked my lungs. Overwhelmed by anger and completely worn down, I collapsed to the ground. I cupped my face in my hands and felt my chest sink into the mud. I blamed Øystein for putting me through this torturous day, then dynamiting any hope I had of bringing in my sheep. I couldn't understand why he'd waited until there was no turning back to tell me he was going to abandon me at Hyrting.

Then there was Johannes, that haughty and irresponsible farmer who'd created this flock that scattered to the wind instead of surging home like Solveig's sheep. Where were the helpers he kept promising to send? Didn't he care enough about his farm to make sure all of his animals made it back home? Here I was with only an untrained dog for backup. Why did he think this was a task I could accomplish on my own?

What's more, now that I had stopped running, I could no longer ignore the pain from the wounds I'd suffered during my wrestling match with the *skorfaste* ewe. Really and truly, this wasn't fair. *Nothing* was fair. Everything was *so* unfair that even after my tears let up, I couldn't bring myself to rise from the soggy ground.

Bella sat miserably at my side, her worried eyes trained on the trail behind us. At length something caught her attention and she stood up. I followed her gaze and saw the final group of eight sheep standing in a knot just fifty yards away. Their ears were pricked forward and their eyes were on Bella and me. Were they feeling sorry for us—or had the approach to Hovland's pastures sparked old memories of the long grass and easy life within?

I let myself wallow in self-pity a while longer, then rose and started after them once again. Calmer now, the ewes were more willing to let me circle to their rear and start moving them forward. Just half an hour later Bella and I drove the last of them home.

25

Pork Chops for Johannes

Johannes's phone in the anteroom did not ring very often, and I rarely made calls myself because charges were so high, even between neighbors. So when my boss had called just before Øystein and I set off to the mountains in search of sheep, the news was important: Sunnaas Hospital near Oslo, the best rehabilitation facility in Norway, had accepted him as a patient. He would be transferred there by month's end. But before that, he was coming home for a visit—his first since an ambulance had carried him away four months earlier.

It was good to hear Johannes sounding hopeful again. The last time we'd spoken, he had little to report in the way of progress. Now he was making plans for the future. Come spring, he said, he was going to build a big new water lily pond just below the house.

After we hung up, I felt sick with apprehension. Right now my top priorities were bringing the sheep home and getting the barn cleaned and repaired for winter. Where would I find time to spruce up the garden? The house needed attention, too. Not that it was messy or dirty. It was just, well, *mine.* Did I have time to undo the changes I'd made to it?

At length, I put these worries aside and started scribbling a list of everything that needed to be done. Then I grabbed a broom and started sweeping.

On the first Sunday of autumn the sun climbed into a cloudless sky. I arose early to do more cleaning and still have time to make *middag* and bake treats for the guests I was expecting. These were no labors of love. I yearned to be outside in this extraordinary weather and felt a twinge of resentment both toward Johannes for visiting on such a fine day and against Norwegians in general because their culture demanded a table laden with good food on an occasion like this.

Not for the first time I fumed over the life of a girl farmer. A bachelor could get away with serving old stew, stale cookies, and boiled coffee. As long as he did a good job of farming, no one would flinch at piles of dishes teetering in his sink or dog hair and dirty socks blanketing his floor. But when people came to my kitchen, I was sure they judged me on how well I kept house. And when they entered the barn, I imagined they took my measure by the quantity of hay in the loft and depth of manure in the pens.

A glance at the kitchen made it pretty clear that I wasn't going to win any good-housekeeping ribbons. When I'd raced around the rooms at ground level to expunge any suggestion of encroachment on Johannes's personal life, I was horrified to find that the only mark I'd made on the place was a substitution of his piles of books and papers with heaps of my own. As to decor, it hadn't improved in the least since my arrival: the kitchen showpiece was still Johannes's calendar with its photos of mountains and cities.

Rutabagas and potatoes were boiling and pork chops sizzling when Gunnar drove into the farmyard. I watched from a window as he helped his older brother exit the car. Johannes straightened up and stood on his garden's rim as if transfixed, scanning his beloved terraces and ponds for such a long time that Gunnar finally pulled him away.

When they turned in my direction, I could see their faces for the first time and was reminded of their striking similarity. If you gentled the angles of Johannes's stern features, bleached his hair and eyebrows to the color of straw, and transformed his gray eyes to blue, he would be Gunnar's twin.

I took a deep breath and went to the door.

Bella froze when she saw him. Johannes was leaning heavily on his brother's arm, eyes trained on the uneven footing as he made his way up the path. I reached down to give my little friend a reassuring pat and felt her quivering.

Johannes saw her the moment he looked up.

"Bella!" he called. "My Bella!"

In a heartbeat the dog bounded to her master. She leaped into the air three times, spun tight circles around his legs, and leaped into the air once more. He bent down and stroked her from head to tail, over and over, turning his head aside to hide the tears coursing down both cheeks.

Middag did not provide the pleasant interlude I'd hoped for. After expressing his disapproval over the state of the garden, Johannes claimed that he could have finished weeding in a couple of days.

When I asked what he wanted me to do with the cow and calf, his answer, though not unexpected, filled me with sadness. Both animals were to be sent to the slaughterhouse, he declared. The cow was a poor milker who wasn't worth another winter of hay. She wouldn't be missed, he claimed, because the heifer would provide us with plenty of milk after she calved in March.

I'd known all along that the red calf was destined for slaughter; only the very finest male calves ever got a chance to live to adulthood. Yet I'd held out hope for my dear cow. Yes, her teats were problematic and her udder was on the small side, but she was still young and could provide many more calves and enough milk for the household, plus a bit for sale.

In addition to every male lamb, Johannes continued, several other animals were to be slaughtered, as well. With his good hand, he wrote descriptions of his four oldest ewes. These sheep had served him well over the years, he said, but now they would be too feeble to nurture another round of lambs. I recognized all four from his notes about torn ears and other damage and also because these were the most haggard members of the flock—and the most placid.

When he told me that he'd decided to expand his flock to fifty ewes for the winter, I finally couldn't keep quiet.

"Fifty!" I exclaimed. "That's five more than you had last year! There won't be enough hay—you know the *hå* never got cut."

Hå was the grass that grew up after a season's first crop of hay had been harvested. At lower elevations with longer growing seasons, farmers could bring in one cutting of hay and one or even two of *hå*. At Hovland, though, only the best plots could support a second harvest. With so much bad weather this summer, and with no manure to serve as fertilizer, even Johannes's deep-soiled meadow below the house couldn't eke out more than one cutting.

"Don't worry about the *hå*; it's still there in the fields for the animals to graze on. So you won't have to bring the sheep in until Christmas," Johannes said. "They'll do just fine outside, even with a little snow on the ground."

Now I really did feel sick. Torkel, Solveig, and her brothers had all assessed my summer's harvest. After checking both the hayloft and silo, they agreed I had barely enough fodder to sustain Johannes's regular stable of forty-five ewes through the winter. Johannes was now telling me to keep a larger flock than he'd overwintered in more than a decade, and he hadn't even set foot in the loft. I tried again to object, yet he dismissed my arguments out of hand.

After dinner, Gunnar went for a walk while Johannes rested on his lumpy sofa beneath the kitchen windows. As I washed the dishes, I kept trying to glean information from him. I desperately needed his guidance. What were his instructions for shearing? Should I find someone to slaughter the lambs at home, or did he want them sent live to the slaughterhouse? Who could I hire to shear? Who to slaughter? How would I sell the meat? Had he made any arrangements for taking care of the place during the four weeks I planned to take off in October?

He'd already found someone to do the shearing, he told me, and had contacted Sigurd Nesheim, a professional butcher who lived near Skårsvatnet, to do the slaughtering. Gunnar had earlier explained to me that Johannes always sold some of his lambs directly to a few people in town. As I understood it, this provided more income (or perhaps lower taxes) than selling them to the slaughterhouse. Now Johannes told me that Ola and Gunnar knew most of these private customers, so they would be helping him procure orders. As soon as they had a final tally, he would let me know and I could coordinate a slaughter date with Sigurd.

When I finally couldn't delay evening milking any longer, Gunnar loaded his brother into the car and drove off. By then, my head was throbbing. I hadn't had a break for days. And between now and when I planned to leave on vacation in two or three weeks, I was facing far more work than I could possibly accomplish on my own.

My most important job was to bring the rest of Johannes's flock home from the mountains. Each search expedition would require at least one extra hand, preferably two or three. On days when I couldn't find anyone to help, I would tackle the other most pressing tasks: dismantling all the remaining *hesjes* and mucking out sheep pens I hadn't gotten to in the spring.

Those were chores I actually knew how to do. The others, the ones that Johannes spoke so reassuringly about, I knew nothing about: shearing, slaughtering, contacting buyers, and making sales. He would firm up all these arrangements later in the week, he said, and would send details as soon as he got to Oslo.

A pang of apprehension ran through me as those words sank in; Johannes had already been telling me for weeks that he was lining everything up. This new pronouncement left me thinking that he'd been doing no such thing. But there was nothing I could do about any of this except get on with my work.

26

Little Bo-Peep

On the day of Johannes's visit, Solveig's brother Torgeir had herded home thirty of my sheep. The ewes in this group were the farm's wise old ladies of the peaks. Knowing that winter was on its way, they'd gathered up their lambs and headed for the lowlands all by themselves. Those thirty, plus the eight that I'd already brought home, left seventy-six animals still at large.

In the week following Johannes's visit, I spent five days searching for them. Alv, Gunnar, Øystein, and Ola joined me when they could. We scoured the slopes beyond Håseter, zigzagged across both faces of the long mountain called Manfjell, and pushed through treacherous alder thickets crowding high cliffs that dropped into Fyksesund.

Edvard reappeared for a short time too. Busy with his last year of maritime school, he'd been away for weeks. No matter when, or how sporadically, he turned up, I was always overjoyed to see him. By now I knew that our relationship would not be blooming into a romance. Instead, I enjoyed the friendship we'd developed, one that allowed us to work and hang out together like old partners, comfortable whether we were talking or just sitting in silence. Even so, try as I might, I'd never been able to completely subdue the lingering fantasy that he would someday take me in his arms.

We wandered through the mountains together that day, finding no sheep but making discoveries: an eagle feather fluttering down from the open sky and a ptarmigan that nearly gave me a heart attack when it whirred up from the ground almost at my feet; not long after, my heart missed another several beats when I trotted over to see what Bella was so interested in—and found her nose to nose with a coiled adder. I jumped back and called her to me. As we watched it from afar, Edvard pointed out that in this cold weather the snake was too torpid to slither away, much less strike.

Numbers were everything during those weeks of autumn roundup. Conversations with neighboring farmers invariably started with a precise tally of the sheep each of us had brought home, and how many were still at large. Then we'd speculate about where our missing animals might be, and where we knew they were not. If a hiker or herder had recently returned from the mountains with a sheep sighting, we dissected the news as if it were the neighborhood's juiciest gossip.

One of my contributions to this daily grist was the occasional foreign ewe with lambs that I herded back from the mountains along with my own. I'd make a sketch of their earmarks to show any neighbors I happened to meet. Without fail, my drawings elicited heated discussions, bolstering my conviction that earmark identification was one of the region's more popular competitive sports. Once an ID was confirmed, I immediately contacted the owners, who generally showed up within hours to retrieve their animals. This always left me feeling good. Like any other farmer, I was pitching in where I could.

In June we'd driven 114 sheep into *utmarka*, the vast territory beyond Hovland's fences. When I finally gave up searching, only ninety-nine had come home. Over the summer, I'd found the bodies of two of my lambs, one in the woods, one above timberline. Both were swarming with blowfly larvae. These infestations, as well as parasitic worms and accidents, were among the most common killers of sheep in the area. Hikers reported finding three more dead lambs of mine over the summer, but in each case, these carcasses were too far gone to provide any clues as to how the animals may have perished.

This disappearance of fifteen sheep from a flock of 114 was huge: three times higher than what a farmer in the area could expect to lose in a season. Not knowing why the losses had climbed so high or what had become of the missing animals tormented me. I held out hope until November, when a snowfall blanketed the mountains, that at least a few of the five ewes and five lambs that had vanished would make their own way home.

A week after Johannes's visit, his youngest sister and her husband, Ingebjørg and Ola, along with their two young daughters dropped by to give me some welcome news. Ingebjørg had made up her mind that she and the girls would stay at Johannes's house, her childhood home, during the month I was planning to take off. Ola, who had a long commute to work, would remain in Øystese with their three boys, coming to the farm on weekends to help however he could.

For the first time in weeks, I felt myself relaxing; I could take my vacation knowing that the farm would be well cared for.

At Ola's suggestion, we spent the afternoon hunting (in vain) for my missing sheep above the horrifyingly steep cliffs that dropped into Fyksesund. As we clawed our way through thickets of scrubby birch and alder, he mentioned that Gunnar and he were making plans to come to the farm the next evening. It was time for me to separate my sheep into two groups, he explained: those to be slaughtered and those to be kept. To do this, the entire flock would have to be driven into the barn. And, of course, I'd need a posse of helpers to get the job done.

My volunteers from Øystese and Hovland made their appearance right after supper: seven adults and five children.

I'd been curious to learn how we might convince ninety-nine semi-wild animals to promenade into the farmyard and then enter Johannes's claustrophobic barn through an ominously dark and narrow passageway. The answer revealed itself almost immediately, when Gunnar ordered us to chase down the ewes one by one and drag them in. We broke into teams of three: two whose job was to catch ewes and do the dragging, one to persuade their lambs to follow along.

As our captives started filling the barn, its stale air was replaced with the scent of fresh meadows and evening breezes, fragrances infused into thick wool coats of sheep just returned from a summer in the mountains. But by the time we hauled our last fugitive through the doorway, this sweet aroma was overshadowed by a humid mixture of urine, manure, and anxiety. The barn was now a sea of wool, the sheep crowding every pen and walkway, with no room for them to lie down and no place for me to set a bucket of water that wouldn't instantly be knocked over.

"You're going to have to work fast, Liese," Gunnar warned, in a tone even more serious than usual. “The animals can’t stay crowded like this for long.”

I wouldn’t have been quite so bothered by this self-evident advice if Gunnar hadn’t provided it until after all my neighbors had gone home and just after he’d announced that today was his fifty-first birthday, so he and the others from Øystese were rushing to town for his party—leaving me alone to do a hands-on assessment of ninety-nine sheep. I didn’t even know what that entailed. And even if I had, I wasn’t physically capable of winning ninety-nine consecutive grappling matches with animals that were at least as strong as I was.

“Ask Torkel to help,” Ola offered as he stepped into his car. “I’m sure he’d be happy to.”

It had been impossible to keep lambs and mothers together while we were strong-arming them into the barn. All through the night, the cries of these distressed animals—separated for the first time—pierced my bedroom window. I spent those dark hours worried sick that my poor sheep might die of thirst or suffocation before daybreak and wondering how I could possibly ask Torkel for help yet again. He had a mountain of his own farmwork that needed attention, and he and his family had just spent an evening bringing my sheep into the barn.

Walking up my neighbors’ steps just after sunrise that morning was the most excruciating moment of all my months at Hovland. Yet for what seemed like the millionth time, Torkel made it easy for me when I asked, answering with a smile and saying he’d be over right after breakfast.

Male lambs were the unluckiest creatures on Hovland’s farms. Because each farm required only one ram to service all of its ewes, every lamb in a flock was either a half or full sibling to every other lamb in its flock. Thus a ram lamb couldn’t stand as stud on the farm where it was born. So Torkel and I first had to push our way through a sea of sheep to pluck out each of my thirty young rams and pack them into four pens allocated to animals bound for slaughter.

The fate of my forty ewes came next. I grabbed the one closest to me and held her for Torkel’s examination. He pried open her mouth to check for missing or loose teeth, inspected each of her hooves, examined her udder, and worked his hands through the quaking animal's dense wool to check for any problem that might worsen during a long winter in the depths of a barn. She passed this nerve-wracking evaluation with flying colors, and I led her into the field to enjoy a few more weeks of freedom before winter's confinement.

Torkel took extra care when examining the flock's four oldest ewes. Johannes's written descriptions made it easy to identify these elders. When presented with the first one, my neighbor nodded in agreement. "See here, she's missing a molar," he said. "And the others are worn to a nub." He grabbed an incisor and wiggled it back and forth. "With a mouth like this, the other ewes will eat her rations out from under her. Even if she manages to survive until spring, she'll be skin and bones."

Escorting this matriarch into the pen of boisterous young rams was almost more than I could bear. She was a dignified soul who'd spent the summer tending her twin offspring high up on Manfjell. I'd enjoyed our encounters whenever a hike took me her way, and she always seemed grateful for the feed I left on nearby rocks.

Torkel had no argument with the next two entries on Johannes's list, either. But after poking and prodding the fourth old animal, we found that her teeth, udder, legs, and joints were still sound. If I wanted to keep her, Torkel said, there was no reason not to. I jumped at this reprieve and escorted the ewe outside to join her younger companions.

At noon, Torkel went home for *middag* and I went to the kitchen to fix myself a few slices of bread with cheese and jam. When we reconvened in the barn, I had some bad news.

"Johannes called," I told him. "Now he wants me to keep sixty ewes this winter, not fifty."

My neighbor's jaw dropped. "You can't pack that many animals in here. This barn wasn't built for that. There's no ventilation at all, and I know for a fact that water flows into some of your pens during big storms. The more animals you have in here, the worse it will be for all of them."

"And there's not enough hay or silage," I moaned.

"Don't worry about that," Torkel scoffed. "Johannes can just stop putting money into his garden and buy the hay he needs. But there's nothing he can do about the barn."

“So what should I do?” I asked. “You know it’s impossible to make him change his mind. When he doesn’t like what I say, he just doesn’t listen.”

“Yes, but remember, Liese, he gave you full authority.” Torkel’s expression was dead serious. “This wouldn’t be a bad time to use it.”

His counsel was so unexpected that I didn’t know how to respond. Flouting Johannes’s orders by having a drink with friends in the farmyard was one thing. Overriding his desire to fill the barn with sheep was quite another.

If what Torkel was saying about the barn was true—and I was sure it was—crowding the pens would be detrimental to me as well as the animals. After all, I was the one who would be caring for them all through the winter. As their guardian, I shouldn’t let anything endanger their welfare, not even their owner. But Johannes was irrational and volatile, and the thought of disobeying him scared me. Even with Torkel’s backing, I couldn’t find the courage to completely disregard my boss’s iron will.

“We’ll keep fifty-five,” I said at length. A cowardly decision but better than none at all. Torkel nodded his assent. And we started counting.

Three of my forty ewes were headed to the slaughterhouse. That left me with thirty-seven overwintering ewes. To raise that number to fifty-five, we needed to select eighteen of the twenty-nine ewe lambs that were now cowering in a huddle as far from us as possible.

By the time our work was done, eighteen happy young ewes had been reunited with their dams on Hovland’s yellowing fields, while three aging ewes and forty-one lambs, all destined for slaughter, remained penned up inside.

When I’d learned in the spring that I was headed to a sheep farm, I’d harbored the vague notion that sheep were raised for wool. Oh sure, lamb chops and leg of lamb had to come from somewhere. But my mother had served them to us so infrequently that I assumed lamb was a rare commodity. Wool, on the other hand, was ubiquitous. So by this logic, it didn’t cross my mind that sheep farmers might be in the business of slaughtering their animals for meat.

No single event or snippet of information disabused me of the notion that Johannes was a wool farmer. Instead, the hints began adding up soon after I arrived at Hovland. Within a few weeks, I understood that the farm's true product was meat, that is, lamb. Still, I had no difficulty in accepting the reality that at least half of the impossibly cute creatures scampering across the farm's hillsides would not live to their first winter. I'd been put in charge of a farm that raised sheep, and I took my mantle of "full authority" seriously. The flock would be sent to the mountains for the summer, and lambs would be slaughtered in the fall. 'Twas ever thus here at Hovland. And I was on board with it.

I was also a meat eater. Not an unquestioning one, though. I often contemplated the morality of eating the flesh of animals, and for half of my eighteenth year, I'd completely abstained. Yet in my contemplations, I generally arrived at the same conclusion: humans had evolved as omnivores; thus, meat was a natural part of our diet. So I felt no guilt in continuing the tradition, as long as the meat I was eating came from animals that had been treated humanely.

Nowhere in this calculus, though, had I been faced with the morality of slaughtering a calf who I'd come to love, an old ewe who I admired for her mothering skills, or a companionable cow who I'd milked a couple hundred times with my body pressed against hers in an intimate tangle of warmth and tranquility.

I had no way of dealing with the pain I was experiencing whenever I caught sight of my dear cow and calf in their pasture or walked past my three old ewes penned up in the barn. My pride wouldn't let me talk to neighbors about my sorrow, either. After all, they'd spent their entire lives surrounded by animals destined for slaughter. Surely they'd become so inured to this inescapable aspect of farm life that they couldn't possibly make sense of my city-girl sentiments.

Johannes never did make the promised arrangements for shearing or slaughtering. Instead, he sent a letter from Sunnaas Hospital saying that he would be sending me complete instructions in another day or two. But when I found no information at all in the letter that arrived a few days later, I felt my brain explode; my boss had led me right into the middle of shearing and slaughtering season with no guidance, information, or help.

I threw the useless letter into the air and ran to Sigurd Nesheim's house at the south end of Skårsvatnet. The butcher's wife answered my knock and confirmed my suspicion that Johannes had never contacted her husband. Unfortunately, he was awfully busy now, she said, but he might be able to squeeze me in next week sometime, depending on how many animals I had for him to slaughter. And, of course, I would need to hire an assistant for him as well. She and Sigurd did not own a phone, so she advised me to come to their house every day to report on my progress.

Thus started my frantic search to find a shearer and an assistant slaughterer for hire. For three days I made calls to people who had phones, ran to Soldal and beyond to talk to those who did not, came home and waited in the kitchen for return calls, and ran down the hill to leave messages for Sigurd.

Through all of this, I made it a point of not asking either Torkel or Alv for help. Like every other farmer in the area, they were facing the biggest workload of the year, and I didn't want to put them in a position of having to turn me down. Yet when I still hadn't found a shearer after all my searching, out of utter desperation I headed down the road to pay Alv a visit.

On my walk back home an hour later, I should have been ecstatic, because not just Alv but Solveig, too, had agreed to start shearing in the morning. Instead, I felt rotten, for I'd also just learned that I'd badly hurt Alv's feelings by spending the past week trying to hire every shearer in the region but him.

27

Blood and Wool

Viking shepherds would have recognized the sheep shears Solveig was carrying when she and her brother arrived the next day; a nearly identical pair accompanied two women into the afterworld aboard the Oseberg Ship, which had been buried in a mound of soil near Oslo in the year 834.

Forged from a single piece of metal—Vikings used iron, Solveig's were made of spring steel—the clippers were folded over like tongs and had cutting surfaces that resembled razor-edged chef's knives sharpened to wicked points. To make a cut, you squeezed the blades past each other; when you released your grip, tension in the metal propelled them back open.

Shearers spend hours doubled over their woolly charges while using their arms, elbows, knees, and feet to manipulate the animals into an array of awkward positions. On the farms around Øystese, this brutal job had been women's work until the first electric shearing machines started showing up in the early 1960s. After that, men took over: an odd turn of events, given that these newfangled overgrown electric razors made the job faster and easier than the traditional Viking style shears that women had been using.

Expert shearers claim that a novice needs to clip a thousand sheep before getting good at the job. Solveig with her hand shears and Alv with his electric clippers had both shorn far more. Under my neighbors' even temper, firm grip, and steady hands, the animals remained calm, allowing themselves to be turned, tugged, and rolled this way and that. I watched in awe as some of the older ewes even slumped against Solveig's legs with eyes half-shut as if in a salon for a cut and massage.

Brother and sister worked with confident strokes, peeling back fleece after fleece glistening with golden lanolin. As crimped inner fibers were cut, the wool billowed out like a flower unfolding from the bud. I was amazed to see that each fleece hung together to form a blanket of plush that grew larger with every sweep of the blade. My job was to separate out trimmings from legs and around the tail, then roll up each fleece like a sleeping bag before tucking it into an emptied *kraftfôr* sack.

Every lamb that I pulled out of a pen looked like a shaggy little bulldozer. When I dragged them back in after their shave, they looked like badly drawn cartoon figures with scrawny bodies, stick legs, and bony, outsized heads fringed with tufts of wool that gave me a new perspective on the term "muttonchop sideburns." This metamorphosis was so complete that even the sheep didn't recognize one another. Each ram that I led back into a pen was set upon by his companions for a hearty round of headbutting until the proper pecking order had been reestablished to every animal's satisfaction.

On Monday, October 9, a box truck pulled to a stop at the farm's gate several hundred feet away. I spotted it from the kitchen, where I was eating a late lunch following a fruitless hike into the mountains in search of my missing sheep. It was the slaughterhouse van, I knew, and it was here for three old ewes, nineteen lambs, and my cow and calf.

I'd called for the pickup on Friday. By then, Alv and Solveig had sheared all forty-four sheep in the barn, the butcher Sigurd Nesheim had confirmed he could spend a day working for Johannes sometime in the coming week, and Ola and Gunnar were making strides in finding buyers for our farm-slaughtered lambs. As of this morning, they had secured a total of twenty-one orders—plus one more. In a surprising act of generosity—or contrition—Johannes had told Gunnar to reserve one lamb for me. This was an incredible gift that I was thrilled to receive. Because meat was extremely expensive and I was forever mindful that Johannes was paying for my weekly groceries, I never ordered it except in the form of cheap sausages, canned liver pâté, and ultra-thin-sliced lunch meats. I understood this lamb from Johannes as an acknowledgment of the work I'd done on his farm. And I knew I deserved it.

My Hovland neighbors had seen the vehicle as it wound its way past their farms. Knowing that a small crew would be needed to load so many animals, Solveig, Alv, Øystein, and Arne showed up within minutes to lend a hand. The task should have been easy, but this was

Johannes's farm, where the word "easy" existed only as a delusion. The van had stopped at Johannes's gate hundreds of feet away for a reason: the gateway opening was too narrow for it to pass.

I wondered what the driver was thinking as he watched our motley group debate what to do. Here was tall and imposing Øystein declaring that each of us could lead two lambs at a time from the barn to the truck, while stout and stern Solveig in her sneakers and blue work dress argued that this would take too long. An American girl speaking in local dialect was suggesting that she fetch her mare and hitch up a hay wagon, at which a young boy with long blond hair piped up that it would be quicker if he were to run home and harness his horse instead.

Standing apart from the others, a lean man with a shy smile made the decision. "You still have Torkel's hay wagon in the barn, don't you?" Alv asked me. "Why don't you just go get Begonia and we'll load the lambs. That will be easier than anything else."

I ran back to the barn and grabbed a halter.

It took me less than fifteen minutes to find Begonia and lead her back to the yard. But by the time I got there, I was stunned to see that, far down the road, my cow and calf were already being coaxed into the slaughterhouse truck. I threw Begonia's lead rope to Øystein, who had just emerged from the barn with the horse's harness. Without thinking, I snatched up some grain and raced down the road to bid farewell to my beloved bovines.

But I was too late. By the time I got there, cow and calf were already cramped into two small compartments behind a firmly locked door. Alv, Solveig, and Arne were headed toward the barn to help Øystein load up the sheep, while the driver, irritated by this long delay, was standing off by himself smoking a cigarette. All of them would think it was silly of me to want to say goodbye to some animals. After all, fall slaughter was a normal part of life here, like getting up in the morning or inviting friends for coffee and cookies. So in the end—because I couldn't bring myself to ask for something that would make me look foolish—I lost the chance to wrap my arms around my companions' necks, scratch their muzzles, feel their wet noses, and smell their meadow-scented breath one last time.

All I could do was peer at the two prisoners through gaps in the compartment's plank siding. It was a relief to see that the calf didn't seem frightened. Actually, I'd never seen him alarmed by anything in his short life. When presented with something new or unusual, he always responded with curiosity or annoyance. Now he was looking around and nosing the unfamiliar surroundings—with irritation, mostly, but also with a good dose of interest. The cow was fidgeting some, and I spoke to her quietly as I tried not to cry. I closed my eyes and thought back to the hours spent leaning into her warm, undulating flank listening to the rhythmic sound of her milk coursing into a pail. I pictured my calf flying across the pasture, cavorting with Bella, burbling with pleasure as he gulped down his milk.

After all the sheep were loaded and secured, the driver handed me a form to sign. And that was that. I stood with my friends and watched until the vehicle disappeared over the hill beyond Solveig and Alv's farmyard. My head was aching and my chest was tight. Solveig was chattering away, trying to make me feel better, I think. So I pretended to listen to her saying something about a pudding she had on the stove—until I finally couldn't hold back any longer. I turned from my neighbors without even thanking them and walked home sobbing so hard I could barely breathe.

Solveig came over that evening, the first time she'd ever paid a visit after supper.

"How are you?" she asked, in an uncharacteristically gentle voice.

"Okay, I guess," I lied.

"It's hard, I know," she said, in this surprising new tone. "We take care of these animals, they become our friends . . . and then we have to slaughter them. I've never gotten used to it, and I'm sure I never will."

Her revelation stunned me. How could I have been so self-centered to think that I alone among my neighbors could grow attached to animals under my care? My mind flew back to those first weeks at Hovland when our flocks were still on home pasture. I'd stood by as Solveig showered affection not just on her own ewes but on mine, as well. She'd shown me how to be gentle with the cow as I milked her and had never failed to say a few kind words to Begonia whenever they met. Of course she loved her animals. And of course my other neighbors did, too. I'd heard it in their voices and seen it in their eyes.

Now I took solace in her words. Knowing that I was not alone, I could grieve without feeling ashamed of doing so.

"Thank you," I said. "And thank you for your help today. I'm sorry I walked away. It was so hard not having a chance to say goodbye to the cow and calf."

"Why didn't you just go into them, then?" she asked.

Seeing my puzzled expression, she explained that there was an unlocked door on the passenger side of the truck that led to the compartments. So there had been nothing hindering a final farewell.

After she left, I went upstairs to my room and started crying all over again.

Sigurd Nesheim drove into the yard at nine o'clock the next morning.

My neighbor from Skårsvatnet was about fifty years old, with short hair turning white at the temples. He had a round face that reddened in a friendly way when he laughed and blue eyes that lit up with his pursed-lip smile, a fleeting half grin that lent him a mischievous air. He was not one to chat unnecessarily. Yet he was quick to find humor in a situation. And as the day wore on, I found that I enjoyed his company very much.

He greeted me with a distracted look, holding our handshake for an extra beat as he glanced around.

"Who's coming to help?" he asked.

The question caught me off guard. "I . . . thought I told you I couldn't find anyone."

I was sure I'd explained this standing on his doorstep making arrangements. He must not have understood. "I asked a lot of people," I said by way of apology. "But everyone was too busy." A frown crossed his face before I quickly added, "So I'm going to be your helper."

Actually, it had been a relief when I finally gave up looking for an assistant for Sigurd, because it forced me to step in. All through the fall my neighbors had insisted that slaughtering was definitely no job for a girl. They were the experts and I was their pupil, so I accepted what they told me. Yet I couldn't stop thinking that nothing at Hovland was more significant than these two days of slaughter: the grim final step in animal husbandry's annual cycle. It didn't seem right to sit inside while hired folks executed such a consequential task without me.

Sigurd took a deep breath and blew it out through pursed lips. When I dared glance up, it was a relief to see his blue eyes dancing.

"I can't complain about a pretty assistant like you," he said. "If you don't mind getting splashed with a little blood every now and then, let's get to work."

A thin layer of ice blanketed the garden's ponds on this cold gray day. I couldn't help wondering whether our hands would stay warm from the heat of the animals we would soon be slaughtering. Now Sigurd started unpacking his tools, handling each with care: an axe, a bone saw that looked much like a hacksaw, a case of knives with a sharpening stone, a gambrel made of iron and wood for hanging carcasses, and a small tubular metal device that he said was a slaughterer's pistol that he wasn't going to use.

The only animals I'd ever killed were fish. I was not yet ten the first time I smacked one over the head after catching it from a pier on San Francisco Bay. I'd killed dozens more since then without much compunction. Today was going to be different. Instead of cold, small-brained, vacant-eyed animals, we would be killing warm-blooded creatures with eyes that express happiness, fear, and pain. I didn't know if I could get through the day, so I reminded myself that I had to do whatever I could to help Sigurd, because he and his instruments of death were here to keep the farm alive.

My first job was to help him set up a makeshift table in the middle of the yard between barn and garden. The second was to fetch one of the warm-blooded creatures from its pen while Sigurd hung the gambrel in a portal in the barn's stone wall.

Having spent all but the first and last weeks of their lives running free on home pasture or high in the mountains, the lambs had been skittish during their weeklong confinement. But today when I approached with rope in hand, they were absolutely terrified, tearing away from me and bunching into a corner of the pen, the ones at the fringes madly trying to pry themselves into the huddle by jumping onto the haunches of those crushed together. When I finally got a rope around the neck of one of the smallest rams, he jumped and kicked and dragged his legs all the way to the yard—as if he knew that his life depended on it.

"You're going to have to hold him still," Sigurd said matter-of-factly. "Here, get your legs around his back and hold his neck like this. And be sure to keep your own head back, because it's the lamb I want to hit, not you."

I knew what was going to happen next because people had been providing me with details for weeks. Straddling the animal as directed, I grabbed its neck and held tight. When the axe rose, I turned my head and squeezed my eyes shut. One heartbeat, then two, and the full force of the instrument's blunt end crashed onto the lamb's skull. The little animal's muscles went limp under my legs, and it sagged to the ground.

My hands shook as Sigurd took hold of the unconscious animal's forefeet and told me to grab its hind legs. Together we lifted it onto the table, leaving its head dangling over the side.

"Keep hold of those legs for me now," Sigurd said, pulling a long, thin knife from his stock. "The blow doesn't kill the animal, just knocks it senseless. Even so, it might start kicking again. Only a reflex, that's all."

He lifted the slack head and stuck the knife's sharp tip into the neck just below the jaw. With a sure, quick motion, he cut through the neck and its arteries. At least that's what I learned later, because I shut my eyes again the moment the knife neared its target. I felt the ram kick a few times—muscle spasms, I told myself—and then its legs quivered under my hands for a second or two before falling still for good. When I opened my eyes, a thick red stream was draining from the open slash into a bucket at Sigurd's feet.

"Pretty windy this morning," the butcher said. "Something get caught in your eye?"

I forced a smile as the stream slowed to a trickle.

"I'm going to slaughter four animals before we start flaying," he said as he picked up one of his larger knives and severed the lamb's head. "So just keep bringing them out to me."

The second and third blows were as bad as the first. With each, I felt as if a thick band were being ratcheted tighter around my skull. The fourth blow tightened it even further, but at least now I was able to keep my eyes open. The one thing I could not get used to was the feeling of a struggling lamb going limp between my knees.

None of these lambs had ever grown accustomed to humans. On my summer visits to their haunts above timberline, they behaved just like wild animals, fleeing in fear when anyone approached. Even as I lured their mothers to me with grain, the young ones kept their distance, watching nervously from afar. As much as I loved my ewes and admired them as the canny, attentive parents that they were, I had no emotional attachment to their untamed offspring.

Yet it devastated me that these young creatures' last minutes were filled with terror and that Sigurd and I were the source of it. So we both worked as fast and efficiently as possible to keep those dreadful minutes to a minimum, and I consoled myself with the knowledge that the lambs had lived happy and free for most of their short lives. At one point, as I straddled one of the ram lambs, I imagined my calf standing under the axe instead. The image was so horrifying that I forced it out of my mind and banished it forever.

Flaying proved to be far less bloody than our initial tasks. I was surprised to discover how white the inside of a hide was and that a carcass—sheathed in protective layers of fascia and milky-colored patches of fat—was a pinkish color and rather pretty.

Sigurd used his knife sparingly, working it around bony joints and other places where the skin was stuck to flesh and connective tissue. Elsewhere, he worked his fist between the hide and the body to separate the two. When the job was finished, he held up the hide for inspection: it was as intact as a new wetsuit straight from the package.

Now he picked up a saw and had me steady the carcass as he cut through its breastbone from top to bottom to expose the chest cavity. Finally, he severed all four feet and cut a slit between the hock and a thick tendon on each hind leg. Moments later, he and I worked together to hang the carcass by holding it aloft and slipping a hook of the gambrel through each of the slits.

With one long, careful slice down the belly's midline, Sigurd exposed what until then I'd only seen in textbook illustrations or in bits and pieces neatly displayed in a butcher case: smooth lobes of liver; a dark-red heart; spongy pink lungs; bulging masses of compound stomach; and endless serpentine intestines. With two or three flicks of his knife, the butcher removed liver and heart and handed them to me to immerse in a bucket of cold water. Warm and heavy, the liver still felt alive. And the heart, with its thick arteries and crosshatched muscles, was all but pulsing as it lay cupped in my palm.

Now all it took was a few tugs to the remaining guts to slosh them to the ground. Only two bulbous kidneys embedded in white fat remained in the long cavity, tucked against the backbone at the loin.

"If you know what to look for, kidneys can tell you if the animal was healthy when it was alive and how long it's been dead," Sigurd explained. "Most butchers remove them nowadays, but I think it's more honest to leave them in."

I stared at the naked headless, footless, gutless carcass hanging above the pile of offal at our feet and couldn't put this together with the fluffy, kicking animal I'd dragged from the barn less than an hour earlier. Sigurd was staring at the carcass, too. Something seemed to be troubling him.

"Your job," his face reddened as he spoke, "I mean, the *assistant's* job, is to weigh each carcass. But it's not girl's work. You might not be able to get them onto the scales. So if you don't want to do it, I will."

It gave me a thrill to prove that I was as good as any other assistant. I nodded a yes, and together we lifted the lamb from the gambrel and loaded it into a wheelbarrow.

Johannes's scales hung from the ceiling of his cellar alongside an array of meat hooks. The small carcass was easy to lift onto the instrument's hook, which dangled just below eye level. I took its weight to the nearest tenth of a kilo and made my first careful entry in a grammar school essay book I'd bought in town for just this purpose.

The meat hooks, however, were nearly a foot above my head. Trying to work one of these hooks through the hock slits with my right hand while clasping the carcass to my chest with my left arm was far more difficult. By the time I brought the wheelbarrow back to Sigurd, he'd skinned the second lamb and hung it on the gambrel himself. He looked at me in surprise.

"Did you get it onto the hook?" he asked.

"Yup, no problem," I answered, less than honestly.

He raised his eyebrows. "Not bad. I was sure you would need help."

Actually, I was just barely strong enough to lift the largest carcass of the day, a monster fifty-three-pounder. It felt strange to wrestle with this warm, lifeless thing: wrapping my arms around its stripped flesh, turning it this way and that as I tried again and again to hold it high enough to maneuver a single hook through both hock slits. When I finally got back to the slaughtering table, Sigurd gave me an amused look.

"I was just about to join you. Figured you and the ram were drinking coffee without me."

Inger showed up at noon, carrying a big basket filled with a hot dinner. She'd cooked her own plums into a pudding for dessert and had even made a cake for our afternoon coffee. A few days earlier when she told me of her plan, I tried to object. But she cut me off.

"Don't be silly, girl," she snapped. "There's not a farmer in the county who doesn't get *middag* served to him on slaughtering day. And we can't start making exceptions just because you ask for one."

I felt a rush of pride. She'd called me a farmer. A Hovland farmer, for here I was with Sigurd doing the farm's real work.

There's something fascinating about gore. So maybe it wasn't odd that as the day wore on, I grew less and less squeamish and more and more engaged in the work. Who would guess, though, that humans aren't the only animals that take a fancy to entrails and severed arteries?

The heifer couldn't take her eyes off us the whole day. She stood craning her neck over the fence a couple dozen paces from where we were working, grunting occasionally to attract our attention. As the hours passed, I recounted for Sigurd all the troubles and near-death experiences she'd put me through. By summer's end, she'd been regularly breaking through every fence on the farm, even trotting up to Torkel's house one afternoon. In the last week alone she'd been crashing into Johannes's garden at least once a day.

"An animal like that doesn't usually change," Sigurd said. "Maybe she'll settle down a little after she calves, but I wouldn't count on it. And she'll never stop breaking through fences now that she knows she can just push her way through. She's always going to be impossible."

Until then, most people had only chuckled when I described the animal's antics, and I'd laughed along uneasily, figuring that she was no different than any other bovine teenager. Now Sigurd was confirming my worst fears: I had a big problem on my hands.

True to form, the burly black brute plowed her way through the fence right after *middag* and charged toward us, tossing her head in the air like a bull facing a matador. She skidded to a stop and thrust herself between Sigurd and me to sniff the half-flayed sheep we were working on. Before I could grab a rope and beat her back, she nosed the bucket of blood below the table and nearly knocked it over.

"Stupid animal! Get away!" I shouted as I lashed her toward the flattened fence. She ambled ahead of me in a lazy way as if my shouts and blows didn't concern her a bit.

"You wanted to see how the slaughtering pistol worked," Sigurd reminded me when I came back half an hour later after repairing the fence. "We could tell Johannes that she broke her leg and we had to put her down. Think about it."

Although he was speaking only half in jest, I do believe that had I assented, he'd have done the deed. A day earlier I'd been shattered by the loss of my cow and calf. Now I realized with a start that if Johannes would give me the go-ahead, I'd slaughter the heifer in an instant. My months at Hovland, combined with this day of slaughtering, had transitioned me from a novice to a realist. The beast was dangerous and destructive and, as far as I was concerned, not worth the hay it would cost to feed her through the winter.

The buyers started arriving just before supper on the second day, a few hours after Sigurd had finished his work. When placing their orders, all had specified a weight range for the lambs they wanted. With twenty-one orders and only twenty-two lambs, it was impossible to satisfy everyone, which caused a few people to grumble. Each sale required that I weigh the carcass in front of its buyer by hanging it onto the cellar's scales, calculate the price at either 11.85 or 12.25 kroner per kilo by doing longhand multiplication in my essay book, take cash, make change, write a receipt, and make a duplicate ledger entry of the transaction for Johannes's records. And I had to do all this with constant interruptions from these good citizens of Øystese, all but one of them men. Impatient buyers were lining up, I was the seller, the responsible party, and no one was being particularly helpful.

There was only one bright spot in the midst of all this: my discovery while assisting Sigurd that Johannes actually had a working tool on the farm. His scales were providing consistent and reliable readings of every carcass.

After two hellish weeks without a break, topped by two long days of butchering, I'd been a mess even before the evening started. Under the strain of juggling every aspect of each sale while dealing with so many people I didn't know, in a language I didn't completely understand, the band around my head clenched ever tighter until my hand started shaking when I made entries in the ledger. I desperately needed to run far away, to a place where I could let my tears burst out and relieve this overwhelming pressure. Just when I thought I couldn't hold out any longer, Ola showed up to lend a hand. I was never so happy to see him.

The last person to arrive that evening was a butcher from Øystese. After he drove off with all twenty-two lamb skins and most of the livers and hearts, the only thing I wanted was a chance to lie down and fall into oblivion. But there was still more to be done. With his usual generosity, Ola volunteered for the job I'd been dreading: disposing of the enormous pile of entrails. And once again, Øystein, too, showed up to help. While he and Ola pitched guts into the manure cart and hauled them to a far corner of the farm, I hosed down buckets and tools and cleaned scraps of hide, flesh, and blood from the yard.

Even then, our work was not finished; twenty-two lamb heads stacked in the barn were calling out to us. Months earlier when Tormod and Arne first mentioned that sheep heads were one of their favorite dishes, I was sure they were joking. Since then I'd learned that after being salted, smoked, and cured, these heads were a revered regional delicacy. If we didn't get them salted down that evening, they'd be spoiled by morning.

Our work started at the stone hearth in Johannes's *eldhus,* an ancient outbuilding sandwiched between house and barn, where generations of Hovland's women had done their baking and washing. We built a fire in the old brick oven and waited for big chunks of wood to burn down to coals. Meanwhile, I cut several shoots from ash trees and whittled them into skewers, while Øystein and Ola picked up head after head, using their sharp knives to lop off a bit more than half of each ear.

The *eldhus* had never been wired for electricity, and on this cloudy night there was no moon to provide even a glimmer of light. So it was by the ghostly glow of a bed of embers that I watched Øystein pick up the first head and work a skewer deep into its nostril. He handed me this gruesome trophy and skewered another snout for himself.

For an hour, all three of us crouched at the hearth, tending and turning skewered heads over the coals, taking care to singe hair from skin without scorching the flesh. Blackness held our voices to whispers. I glanced sidelong at the shadowed faces of my companions and saw two cave dwellers roasting their day's hunt over a fire. With every piece of tissue that dropped from a ragged neck or dripped from a nostril, the fire hissed and popped, filling our senses with an acrid smell of burning muscle, wool, and bone.

When the final head was charred, Ola headed home to Øystese, leaving Øystein and me to complete the job. We lugged our blackened heads outside, where a dim bulb above the barn door provided just enough light for us to work by. There Øystein used an axe to cleave each head in half lengthwise, taking care to not damage the tongue. My jobs were to sever those tongues from their muscled attachments and to remove battered brains from cloven craniums, scooping them out like yolks from soft-boiled eggs. Finally, we rinsed our forty-four split heads under a hose and packed them into buckets along with generous handfuls of salt from Johannes's pantry.

By now I was so tired I could barely stand. When I tried to thank Øystein, my voice was shaking.

"*Takk, Øystein, tusen takk,*" I mumbled. "A thousand thanks."

Needing more than feeble words to express my gratitude, I grabbed the bucket I'd filled with lamb tongues and pushed it into his hands. These tongues, I knew, were considered a great delicacy. He objected, but I insisted. In the end, he gave me a great smile and turned down the road toward his brother's house, bucket swinging in hand.

28

Freedom!

I awoke in the morning to an empty barn and a song in my head. Free! I was free! The animals that weren't dead could take care of themselves for a spell, and after five months of unceasing responsibilities for cows, calf, sheep, dog, harvest, shearing, slaughtering, garden, fences, house, and farm, I could take a four-week break.

That same day I hopped on a bus to Bergen to meet my seventeen-year-old brother, Ben. Just a few weeks earlier he'd sent me a query: now that he'd graduated from high school, could he visit the farm and tag along on my journey through Europe? We made the arrangements through a quick exchange of letters and a phone call, and I postponed my vacation for five days so he could come to Hovland and meet my friends.

Those extra days were just what I needed to tend to all the business that had gone undone while I'd focused on searching, shearing, and slaughtering. Ben was there to help with all of it. We drove the horse and cart to Soldal to pick up a ninety-pound sack of potatoes Johannes bought from a neighbor to see me through the winter. In a cold and drenching rain, we harvested the fruits still hanging on Johannes's trees scattered across the farm. We packed apples and pears into bins in the cellar and cooked plums into almost three gallons of jam, replenishing Johannes's big buckets of preserves that I'd been eating all year.

Gunnar helped me partition the lamb Johannes had given me and showed me how to make a salt solution to preserve the meat. Torkel promised to retrieve legs and ribs from the brine in a week or two and process them in his smokehouse along with his own meat. Solveig took the long, lean flank steaks to make *rullepølser*: salted and smoked rolls of meat that were one of my favorite sandwich fixings.

Two nights before Ben arrived, autumn's first brutal storm stripped every gold, scarlet, and purple leaf from every tree in Hardanger. The weather my brother stepped into at Hovland was dismal, wet, and raw.

"Norway looks like a big rock with a little bit of soil sprinkled on it," he commented about his view from the plane.

It was a good time for a break.

Taking advantage of the best-ever train fare package for young people, Ben and I traveled to Denmark, Paris, Grenoble, Zaragoza, Pamplona, Oxford, London, Sussex, and York, staying with friends everywhere except Paris and Spain. We visited the Louvre, Notre Dame, the Basílica del Pilar, Westminster Abbey, the Tate Gallery, York Minster, and other architectural wonders.

Some days we got along fine, delighting and finding humor in any number of unusual experiences. But we also endured a number of miserable days in each other's company. That was probably my fault. I was the controlling big sister who still considered him my little brother rather than the tall, handsome, and intelligent seventeen-year-old he was. In France I directed our decisions because I spoke French. The friends we stayed with in Denmark, Grenoble, and England were my friends. In Spain, I outdid him in Spanish. Pleading my own case, I submit that he was at least as critical of me as I was of him. And he drove me batty by regularly sleeping three or four hours longer than I did.

On the day of our departure, no sooner had a bus whisked us away from Øystese than I felt my spirit lighten. Since Johannes's visit to the farm more than four weeks earlier, I'd been consumed by work, anxiety, and, not least, anger against my boss. Now as each stage of our journey put more distance between Hovland and me, this wonderful feeling of lightness grew stronger and stronger. The farm was in Ingebjørg's capable hands. The barn was empty. Ola had told me that there might be just enough forage on Hovland's fields to sustain Begonia, the heifer, and all the sheep during my absence. And should anything go wrong, Ola and Gunnar were both standing by to jump to the rescue. With nothing to worry about, I put the farm and Johannes behind and focused on our adventures ahead.

As Ben and I traveled hundreds of miles across six different countries, one thought kept coming back to haunt me: by the time I'd staggered into bed late at night after packing forty-four cloven lambs heads into buckets, my plan to spend another couple of years working on various farms around the world had lost some of its allure.

Over the next couple of weeks, as I spent hours on end staring from train windows at mostly bare fields, I had plenty of time to consider the future. As I did, it seemed more and more clear that doing manual labor on farms couldn't provide the fundamental knowledge about animal husbandry and crop cultivation I'd need in order to problem-solve across the diversity of cultures and agricultural systems I was hoping to work with.

By the time Ben and I reached England, the last country on our itinerary, I'd decided against wandering south in the spring to Spain or Africa, with the hazy idea of finding work on another farm. Instead, I planned to start investigating agricultural programs at universities in the United States and Norway.

Two weeks later, by the time we stepped aboard the steamship *Leda* in Newcastle, bound for Bergen, I was so tired of traveling and so homesick for Bella, Begonia, my sheep, and all my Hovland neighbors that I couldn't wait to see them and get back to work.

29

Metamorphosis

Thanks to the tilt of Earth's axis while it orbits the sun, from winter solstice to the first day of summer six months later, each day is a little longer than the last. The farther north or south of the equator, the more extreme the change. At Hardanger Fjord, on the globe's sixtieth parallel, the sun spends nearly nineteen hours above the horizon on the longest day of the year.

Summer nights at this latitude are a time of playfulness and laughter; of trysts awash in magic luminosity; of long walks with no concern for losing your way; and of seeing owls, foxes, and hedgehogs going about their nocturnal business stripped of the cover of darkness.

Vi skal ikkje sova bort sumarnatta, Norwegians say to each other; we mustn't sleep away the summer night. It's far too precious. Those foolish enough to lie down for a nighttime snooze find themselves fighting against light that pours through windows, filters through blinds, and squeezes beneath closed eyelids.

Yet the wheels and gears of the solar system spin like clockwork, driving the months forward, and for each season there is an equal and opposite. Even during the most seductive weeks of June and July, no one forgets that the longer the days are in summer, the shorter, darker, and drearier they will be six months later.

Ingebjørg, her two daughters, and Arvid, one of her sons, were snowed in at the farm beneath a foot and a half of powder when Ben and I returned from our trip on a Friday night in the middle of November. The taxi we took from Øystese couldn't get any farther than Soldal, because that was as far as municipal snowplows ever went. If it hadn't been for Arne and Arvid, who hitched Begonia to Torkel's homemade snowplow to clear a narrow strip in the middle of the road from Soldal to Johannes's house, Ben and I wouldn't have made it home. Exiting the cab, we shouldered our backpacks and took the last stretch on foot by moonlight.

That night my brother and I froze in our unheated bedroom under the roof as the temperature dipped to nearly 0 degrees Fahrenheit. Too cold to venture from bed to find additional blankets, I lay awake for more than an hour watching the moon's bright light sparkle through ice crystals spreading over the inside surface of our single-pane windows.

At six thirty in the morning, it was dark. Oppressively, gloomily, creepily dark. I could hear Ingebjørg working in the kitchen downstairs, and my inclination was to join her. But the gloom was so heavy it crushed me against the mattress and back into oblivion. An hour later, I again opened my eyes and this time detected a hint of gray tingeing the blackness.

By eight o'clock, I could no longer ignore the pressure on my bladder. In a race against hypothermia, I threw on my icy clothes, ran downstairs, and sailed out the door. Maybe a skater or skier could have kept her balance skidding across that packed snow, but I was neither, so I ended up like every other beginner on a ski slope—on my rear end.

Being forced to retire my slippery black clogs—the ones I'd worn to the barn all summer because they were so easy to pull on and kick off—was the first shock. The second came just moments later, at the end of the snow-packed trail to the shed that doubled as an outhouse. Previously, my visits there had been solitary. Now when I burst through the door, eighteen sheep in four pens turned and pricked their ears my way, welcoming me home with a chorus of baas.

Sitting on the makeshift commode with my back to the animals, I could feel every eye turned toward me. A few bold ewes thrust their noses through the slats to nibble my sweater. In this cold, murky place, I took comfort in their nudges, and for the first time, it hit me just how close the flock and I would be this winter. I'd first met my ewes in the spring as they ranged over the hills of Hovland. Through the summer, our encounters took place high in the boundless *fjell*. Now in these confined quarters, I could see that our relationship was going to become much more intimate. Starting from this moment, these animals would be dependent on me for their well-being throughout the winter and far into spring. Although I didn't realize it at the time, I would be dependent on them, too, not just for their nudges, nibbles, and other gentle attentions but by the very fact that, in looking to me as their keeper—the only person they had to watch over them—they would give me a guiding purpose through those dark months when I often felt that I was losing my way.

Night loosened its grip around half an hour later. Peering around in that dim first light, I couldn't see any sign of the verdant Hovland I once knew. Where Johannes's crazy quilt of terraces, ponds, bushes, and vines once stood, there was only tranquil whiteness, indistinguishable from anything else in the snow-shrouded landscape.

The cold front that froze us in our beds overnight had also frozen pipes that supplied the house and barn. So our first order of the day, Ingebjørg instructed, was to heat enough snow on the stove to defrost two sections of exposed pipe we discovered in dry ground under the roof overhang. That technique worked on the kitchen sink but not on an uninsulated standpipe just inside the barn door, which was the sole source of water for both the barn and the shed. I wouldn't get that defrosted until I redoubled my effort two days later after the thermometer inched up a bit.

Ingebjørg and I were walking to the barn at nine thirty when a glint of sunlight first appeared above the mountains in the south. As we watched, this radiant segment hugged the ridgeline in its westward crawl, gaining elevation so gradually that it seemed tethered to the peaks.

I held my breath in wonder when the full orb finally broke free. The low angle of its light combined with the clarity of its illumination was unlike anything I'd experienced before. This winter sun, distant and wan, was casting strange new shadows, bathing our surroundings in a glow as gentle as it was sharp. The effect was beautiful and exhilarating. Yet it also awoke a bewildering sense of sadness in me, like a grieving over a lost memory or a forgotten way of seeing the world. Or perhaps these pale rays were kindling a primal remembrance that such light and shadow are immutably tied to a dark and difficult winter.

This was the coldest it had been since she arrived, Ingebjørg told us. While Ben and I were away, she and the girls had been besieged by one storm after another. It had rained and sleeted, but snow had only begun falling three days earlier. As soon as the clouds had cleared the previous afternoon, the temperature plummeted.

Fortunately, just before this big storm hit, Ola, Gunnar, and their boys had driven up from Øystese to herd Johannes's livestock into the barn. The ewes proved surprisingly tractable, worn down, it seems, by the miserable weather and the damage it had inflicted on their forage. Every last one of them, Ingebjørg said, shambled into its winter abode with nary a look back. Since then, Arvid had stayed at Hovland to help his mother with morning and evening chores.

Ola arrived again that afternoon—this time on foot from Soldal, where he had parked his car—to fetch his wife and children. I carried one of their bags back to Soldal with them and returned to Hovland at three o'clock, just in time to watch a gibbous moon rise above the mountains across the fjord. Half an hour later, the sun disappeared behind that distant range. At its zenith, it hadn't provided a hint of warmth, not even when I closed my eyes and faced it full on.

My brother kept me company for four days while I started making the difficult adjustment to winter. One of the first things I noticed about this new Hovland was how closely it held you in its clutches. Until I could find a pair of skis and figure out how to use them, my walking was going to be limited to two tracks: a T-shaped path that Ingebjørg had shoveled between the house and outbuildings and the lane that Arne and Arvid had plowed down the middle of the road to Soldal.

Even within the house we felt confined, for the only room that stayed above freezing was the kitchen, where we kept a fire going all day. The simple act of getting our food and putting it away required that we don a jacket to make a foray to the pantry, two doors removed from the kitchen. After our first bone-chilling night, we knew enough to store our pajamas in a kitchen cupboard so we wouldn't have to change into them in the frigid upstairs bedrooms.

Ingebjørg didn't have the heart to break the worst news to me. Instead, I learned of it the day after our homecoming, when I braved the long, slippery walk to Soldal to mail a letter. From her living room, Solveig had a view of my progress after I reached Torkel and Inger's place. As usual, she timed her exit into the yard just as I approached, making it appear like a complete coincidence that we had bumped into each other.

"So there you are, girl!" she greeted me. "You've been missed."

Now both her brothers emerged from the barn beyond their yellow house to join us: Alv with his kind eyes and gentle smile, Torgeir with his exaggerated grin. The two rarely left their work for a neighborly chat; to be welcomed home like this felt good, as if I were part of the family.

"What places in the world did you get to?" Alv asked.

I mentioned Pamplona in Spain, named a hike in the mountains near Grenoble, and was halfway through the word "London," when Solveig caught me cold.

"That's really a shame about those sheep of yours," she said, shaking her head.

"What sheep?" I asked in alarm. "They all seem fine to me."

"Didn't anyone tell you?" Her eyebrows shot up. "Two of your ewes disappeared while you were gone. They both just vanished."

The words struck like a blow to the chin.

No one knew when, she said, because it wasn't until Ola tallied the animals in the barn that he realized they were missing.

Two more sheep lost, on top of all the rest. Thinking of the weeks I'd spent searching for my flock in the mountains, I felt sick to my stomach. Home was where the animals were supposed to be safe. Not where they died. And certainly not where they disappeared. Yet my dismay was tempered by knowing that with two fewer mouths to feed, my haymow in the loft now had a greater chance of lasting till spring.

My heart sank again the very next day when I inspected the silo for the first time since summer and found a black mat of rotting grass beneath the plastic sheet we'd used as a seal. Alv waded up our snowbound road that afternoon in response to my appeal for help. We slid through a portal into the big vat and used five-pronged silage forks to grapple with the matted fodder beneath our feet.

"Looks awful and smells just as bad," Alv said. "Let's hope we find something better farther down."

In August, I'd helped Einar—my Soldal neighbor who'd used his tractor to fill the silo—to lay down the plastic seal atop the twelve feet of grass we'd dumped into it. We'd pulled up the edges of this sturdy plastic sheet to create a basin, which we then filled with water. The idea was to have this tremendous weight compact the grass beneath it, forcing out moisture and air to give fermentation an edge over decay.

Now Alv and I were discovering that the weight had been all too successful, compacting snarled stems into a dense block that was almost impossible to dig out. We pried our forks into it again and again, attempting to fish out big clumps of the interwoven grasses. More often than not, all we came up with were a few strands dangling from the tines.

Finally, after we managed to dig eight inches into the dark mass, a yellowish-green layer with a good tangy odor appeared.

"Well, Liese, here you have your silage. But it's not going to be much fun messing around with it all winter." Alv gave me a sympathetic shrug. "And I'm pretty sure this black stuff on top won't be your only rotten layer."

It didn't take long to grasp the full impact of his words. Between prying up a wheelbarrow load of my fermented fodder, pushing it through snow for one hundred feet to the barn door, then carting away untouched rotten globs from every manger, by week's end I understood that working with silage was adding an extra two hours to daily chores.

Despite ravaging storms and the disappearance of two sheep while I was gone, most of the animals had fared well outside. The bigger problem was the barn itself, which was in complete shambles. For all my good intentions, I'd only cleared the thick, compacted masses of manure from three of the nine pens now inhabited by sheep. On top of this, Johannes's rickety pens and mangers had taken a beating in October when we jammed every ewe and lamb into the barn for a night. Wood-slatted enclosures were cracked and falling apart, mangers were broken, gates were falling off their hinges, and sheep manure littered every aisle.

I spent much of my time between morning and evening chores straightening Johannes's supply of bent nails and using them to reinforce all these broken parts. My amateur repairs usually held up during the day. At night, however, a dozen or more ewes would break down my handiwork and range throughout the barn, making an even bigger mess.

Once again it was my neighbors who came to the rescue. Especially Alv, Torkel, Øystein, and Kari's nice uncle, *snille* Alfred, showed up over and over to help. I loved watching these accomplished craftsmen at work. Like chess players planning a set of moves, they always started with a frown and a moment of deliberation. Then they would take up whatever tools or random pieces of lumber were available and implement their plan. Under their skilled hands, even baling wire could be twisted and turned into a thing of beauty to serve its intended purpose for years to come.

30

Misery

At home in California it was a couple of days after Thanksgiving, and at Hovland I was miserable. A fire was burning in the kitchen's woodstove, and an extra fire was throwing off heat in the living room, where I was sitting in a chair feeling sorry for myself, with my feet propped against the wall to get me as close to the hot metal as possible. If only I could warm up, I might start feeling better. So far, nothing was working. I'd even lifted Bella to my lap for the first time ever. She and I both knew she was no lapdog. With imploring eyes, she begged for release from this ignoble service.

I'd been back for less than two weeks. Ben was long gone. And I was sitting here in clothes that reeked of the barn. I was not just cold but hungry, unwashed, exhausted, and lonely. My clothes smelled because I hadn't had time to wash them in the kitchen sink. I was cold because I owned no boots or socks that could keep my feet from freezing. Dirty because it had been too cold all week to strip naked in the kitchen for a sponge bath. Exhausted because every day my work was getting harder. And hungry because I was too tired to fix a meal.

Probably none of these things would have been so bad if only I hadn't been feeling so lonely. For months I'd been yearning for a real boyfriend, someone to lie close to who would keep me warm and happy. Someone I could talk to about everything that mattered and all the little things that didn't. Over the past half year, I'd met a dozen worthy young men and spent hours daydreaming about many of them. But if any were interested in me, they hadn't let on. Living alone at the farm felt like being stranded on a tiny island surrounded by an ocean of masculinity—and not knowing how to swim.

Now I was settling on a theory that in this culture there was no such thing as a fling or a casual relationship—that the friendly romances

Californians dabbled in were not part of the social fabric here. Unless a man had marriage in mind, he wasn't going to flirt with a pretty young woman across the room. In fact, I'd come to understand that even after a relationship had been established, a couple would go to great pains to conceal it from the outside world. I felt I was living in a Dickens novel, where every courtship was either suppressed, hidden, or squelched.

It was a maddening cultural mismatch. From my early teens, reckless infatuations had been a bad habit. I was a California girl who didn't know much about taking one's time, and I was definitely not interested in settling down. Considered in this light, I told myself, it was probably a good thing to remain single, given that any relationship would most likely end in disaster.

But these dark days at Hovland were making everything worse. Having reached the conclusion that a courtship or even a flirtation on this farm at the end of a long road in the Norwegian mountains was unattainable, I felt lonelier still. Especially after a horrible week that had laid bare just how difficult this winter was going to be.

The weather was terrible. The sun had not shown its face for what seemed like forever. It had been raining for four days straight, and the downpour had turned the snow into a dirty, slushy mess.

What else went wrong that week? Oh, not much, except that winter gales broke holes in the barn roof and I had to move a mountain of hay to keep it from getting wet. And then, when the snow that had piled onto the silo's roof began to melt, it poured through the haphazardly placed sheets of corrugated roofing onto my precious fodder below. To remedy this, I had to take a shovel into the barn's upper level and walk over a lattice of sticks that Johannes had placed across exposed joists. At the far end of this "floor," a little port in the wall opened onto the silo's roof. I have a well-developed fear of heights, so shoveling snow off the slippery metal sheets eighteen feet above ground level, then rearranging these sheets and the rocks that held them in place, was one of the most terrifying tasks I'd been confronted with all year.

And what about the fear and indecision that tormented me every time I fed the barn's inhabitants? Actually, this was just about the very worst part of my work. I really didn't know how much hay and silage, or what combination of the two, to feed the various animals. If the silage looked just a little spoiled, should I throw it out or feed it to the sheep? How much of it could a ewe tolerate without getting sick? If the animals in a pen didn't touch half of the hay I dished out to them, was that because I'd given them too much, or was the hay moldy or too coarse? I knew that if I overfed the sheep, they would ignore the coarser hay, and I'd have to throw it out after it had sat for a day or two in their manger. Yet if I discarded any hay at all, I'd end up running out of fodder even sooner in the spring. On the other hand, I'd been told that well-fed ewes were more likely to bear twins than singles. And their newborn lambs would be bigger and healthier, too. So providing the "optimal" rations was a key component of my work.

Yet how was I to know how much was "optimal" when each pen held a different number of sheep, the quality of the hay and the silage varied wildly, and I had only Solveig's vague instructions about how many armloads of hay and forkfuls of silage to throw into each manger? These uncertainties kept me eternally anxious.

This was not the winter I'd envisioned: a quiet time when I could relax and putter around, finish little projects I hadn't gotten to in the summer, spend time with friends, get to know more distant neighbors, read books, and play the organ. Instead I was working nine to ten hours every day, feeling anxious, scared, exhausted, and lonely.

31

Magnar's Ram

A couple of days before I'd clambered onto the silo roof to clear it of snow, Magnar had huffed his way to my barn with a young ram in tow.

"Here's a fine dala sire for Johannes's ewes," the corpulent farmer with bleary eyes pronounced. "Your boss called me this week and asked for the best of my stock. This is the one: a year and a half old, just reaching his prime."

I hadn't grown any fonder of Magnar since we met at the bus stop on my first day in Øystese. I found him to be boastful and, like Johannes, disparaging of his neighbors—while they, in turn, held their distance from him.

The few times he'd visited, I had the uncomfortable feeling he was looking for something, anything, that might benefit him, whether it be gossip to hand off to Johannes or more tangible assets, like the time in July when he showed up with a lead rope, mumbling about sausage and my calf. I don't know what would have happened if Torkel and Solveig hadn't spotted him as he walked past their places with his rope in hand. Suspicious and curious, they hurried over and confronted him in the barn. Words flew fast and furious until Magnar steamed off empty-handed. "He wanted to get Johannes to sell him the calf," Torkel explained. "For cheap, I'm sure."

Now I examined the ram standing at Magnar's side. Something didn't seem right. For one thing, the animal wasn't shorn, which was strange, because every other sheep in the region was. And its coat seemed oddly thin. I thought back to Johannes's ram, the one penned up in the barn when I first arrived. Now, there was a prize animal, with his big broad head, keen eyes, tightly curled fleece, and powerful body. Magnar's ram was gaunt—only a trifle larger than my ewes. And he was curiously disinterested in his surroundings.

"He seems a little small," I ventured.

"Small? He's not yet full grown! He's a fine specimen, big for his age. Come. You'll see what he can do when we get him into a pen with your girls."

Keeping hold of the rope, Magnar opened the gate of a nearby pen and pushed his ram into the enclosure. Only a couple of ewes expressed interest in the newcomer, challenging him with lowered heads. When nothing more happened, Magnar pulled his charge to an adjacent pen. Here one of the ewes pricked her ears and scrutinized this potential mate before approaching. He returned the attention, sniffing her nose and tail before throwing his head back and curling his upper lip, exposing pink gums and yellow teeth. Holding this grimace while swinging his head back and forth, he looked to be in terrible pain. (Later I would learn that this behavior helps a ram sense whether a ewe is in the fertile phase of her reproductive cycle.)

"There now, you see," Magnar chuckled, "he'll mount her soon."

But this skinny beast just kept bobbling his head in the air and squinching his snout, even as the ewe rubbed her head against his flank and backed her tail into his face.

Magnar brushed this off. It was possible the ewe was just coming into estrus, he said, in which case the ram would take care of her within a day or two. Or perhaps estrus was just over and her hormones were on the wane. No problem. She'd come into heat again in another twenty days.

"Your job for the next few weeks will be to lead this fellow around to every pen twice a day, morning and evening," he instructed. "And his job is to breed with any ewe who's interested."

I led the placid creature to the stall where Johannes's old ram had stood. Now that Magnar was gone, I took a closer look at my new ward. Was his wool finer than what I was used to, or was the problem that his fleece was thinning? I worked my hands down his back and felt a spine that protruded like a rocky ridge and ribs that stuck out like a washboard. Either he was starving, wormy, or horribly ill.

———

"Alv and Torkel say it's strange that the ram isn't shorn," I told Magnar when he came by a few days later to look in on his animal.

"That just goes to show how little they know," he countered. "The big farmers in eastern Norway only shear their rams in the spring. They stopped shearing in the fall years ago."

What I wanted to tell him was that both men had been startled by the ram's condition. Scandalized to find that the animal was unshorn, they were convinced that Magnar was trying to conceal the scrawny carcass they could feel beneath its fleece.

"The farmers around here just don't know any better," Magnar continued. "If you shear a ram, it gets cold, and that can affect its performance."

"Well, he seems awfully skinny to me."

"Of course he's skinny! He's supposed to be! If you fatten him up, he's going to forget all about your ewes." Magnar sounded exasperated. "Then the only thing he'll be interested in is the food in his manger."

I felt bad that I couldn't mount a better defense against Magnar's attack on my friends. But I had no way of confronting this aggressive and self-righteous farmer with my conviction that the others were right and that he was taking advantage of both Johannes and me. I didn't know much about rams, but I did know that this one wasn't interested in my ewes *or* the food in his manger. Every morning and evening since his first sluggish performance, I'd taken him on his rounds and waited an eternity for him to get on with his work. I couldn't let him leave a pen until he'd nosed under the tail of each ewe, which was the only way I could be sure that he wasn't bypassing an animal in heat. Even when one was clearly receptive, he would stand pawing the ground for as long as five or even ten minutes before mounting her. And then, after doing the deed with just one or two ewes, he lost all interest in the flock.

My poor sheep! The ones in heat pushed their way through the crowd to reach him. They brushed their heads against his body and wiggled their tails at his nose while he all but ignored them.

Pulling him around to all these females took nearly an hour every morning and another hour every evening after supper, when it was so dark and cold outside that all I wanted was to be sitting inside by a warm stove.

Every day I was angrier with Magnar for bringing this animal to the farm and with Johannes for allowing him to do so. When Torkel had offered to sell his big, beautiful ram to Johannes earlier in the fall, my boss had declined in favor of cutting a deal with Magnar. Now Torkel's ram was wrapped up in packets of ribs and roasts and tucked away in a freezer somewhere, while I was here dealing with Magnar's unresponsive beast.

Our neighbor wasn't doing Johannes a favor, either. This was strictly a business arrangement between two farmers: for each ewe his ram impregnated, Magnar would receive three kroner. Right from the start Johannes was on the losing end of the deal because Magnar had brought his animal to the farm a week later than he should have. Come spring, this lapse would delay lambing by a week. What's more, if the listless ram didn't impregnate every ewe in this first go-around, I'd have to give him a second chance two to three weeks later when the ewes came into heat again. If that were to happen, some sheep would be lambing almost a month late, which meant keeping them in the barn for an extra month while feeding them hay that I didn't have. Even worse, their younger, smaller lambs would fetch a lower price from the slaughterhouse in the fall.

The ram was a time bomb, and I had no voice. The few times I'd tried to stand up to Magnar, he'd brushed me off. Unless the ewes started coming into heat again, I had no proof that anything was wrong with the ram, and by then it would be too late. So I was stuck in the middle, frustrated, angry, and worried all at the same time.

I'd been instructed by Johannes—as well as every other farmer in the neighborhood—to take careful notes on each ewe's estrus cycle and her experiences with the ram. According to my logbook, by his eleventh day of service, Magnar's ram had managed to mount half of my ewes. During his rounds that morning, he wore himself out with just two copulations, completely ignoring another four or five ewes desperate for his attention.

When Alv dropped by a short while later, I let loose with every grievance I held against this miserable creature.

"Our ram had a pretty quiet morning. I'm sure he'd be happy to pay your flock a visit," my neighbor offered in his soft-spoken manner.

An hour later, Alv's older brother, Torgeir, came walking up the road leading a robust dala ram. By now, the sexual shortcomings of Magnar's animal had become a matter of community concern, so when Torkel caught sight of his next-door neighbor passing by with a ram in tow, he immediately fell in with him.

As all three of us entered the dark and gloomy barn, the ram bolted ahead so suddenly that he nearly jerked Torgeir off his feet. The doubts I'd had about the health of Magnar's ram were confirmed the moment this new stud burst into a pen and went about his work with unstoppable force.

"Attaboy," Torkel murmured, when the ram reared into position for his second copulation.

Torgeir nodded his head and spoke softly. "He's a fine one, he is."

Beside me at the railing, Torkel and Torgeir were keeping a close eye on the ram's performance. My eyes were glued straight ahead, too—and not because I was watching the action. Rather, with a frenetic animal performing one sexual act after another right in front of us, I was struggling so hard to hide my embarrassment that I was frozen stiff even as my face was burning red.

Gunnar and I both sent letters to the convalescent ward at Sunnaas Hospital sounding an alarm. Apparently, we captured Johannes's attention, because soon after, he made a rare phone call to his brother. Johannes was furious, Gunnar reported, and had entreated him to find a replacement right away.

Two weeks to the day after Magnar had walked his ram to the barn, Gunnar arrived with a new stud all bundled up in the back seat of his car. Without much effort, he lifted this strange package to the ground and removed the ropes and blankets securing it. My first sight of the farm's new ram made my eyes grow big.

"He's different, you see," Gunnar said.

An understatement, at best. Here was the oddest sheep I'd ever seen. He was tiny—no bigger than my smallest ewe—with short, delicate ears, a slender head, and a small dark nose. His stubby tail was nothing like the long sturdy appendages that graced Hovland's sheep. And instead of the fine curly wool that our flocks sported, his coat stuck out like a feather duster. Strangest of all, he wasn't white but mottled black and gray. Fidgeting nervously at the end of his lead, he looked more goat than sheep.

"It wasn't easy finding a ram this time of year," Gunnar offered by way of explanation. "Most went to the slaughterhouse in October. The ones that are left are awfully busy just now."

The ram was only seven months old, the same age as my ewe lambs, Gunnar told me. He was not a dala, Cheviot, or Rygja—the most common breeds in the area—but a purebred spæl sheep, closely related to the Old Norwegian breed kept by Vikings. Unlike more common breeds, these sheep had not been bred and cross-bred over the centuries, so they were remarkably similar to their wild forebears in looks, behavior, and hardiness. Spæl sheep were nearly as tough and agile as goats, Gunnar went on. Ewes had little trouble lambing and were fiercely protective mothers. They could survive in rugged terrain and rotten weather, subsisting on coarse grasses, heather, and other woody plants that Johannes's dala sheep would simply reject.

"If they're so great, why don't more farmers keep them?" I wanted to know.

"*Ja,* that's a good question." Tugging the new ram toward the barn, Gunnar seemed absorbed in thought, oblivious to the little animal that kept turning to butt him in the leg.

"It must be because every farmer loves his own sheep," he finally said. "He inherits a breed or he chooses one, and that's what he knows best and is most comfortable with. Then he spends his life improving his flock by deciding which rams to use and which ewe lambs to keep. After that it would be a huge decision to switch breeds. He'd have to start from the beginning again."

This description of a farmer's love for his own breed gave me pause. "But, isn't using a spæl ram kind of a way of switching breeds?" I asked. "Will Johannes be upset when he finds out his lambs aren't pure dala sheep?"

"Like I said, it wasn't easy rounding up a capable animal so late in the season," Gunnar said tersely. "My brother's lucky to have any ram at all right now."

We entered the barn and were enveloped by its pungent smells of acrid manure, meadow-sweet hay, briny silage, and the mustiness of dank rock walls. The ram captured yet another odor, one that humans couldn't perceive. He butted Gunnar once more, pulled on his lead rope, and steered us toward a pen brimming with ewes. Now I was glad he was so small, because he was going to be a lot easier to lead around than Alv's brawny stud.

It had been less than an hour since the young animal had been torn away from his flock and thrown into a car for the first time in his life. Despite his eagerness, we needed to let him settle into his new abode before introducing him to the harem. There were no free pens in the crowded barn, so we turned him in with Magnar's ram in a small pen out of sight of the ewes. The older animal made a weak show of defending his turf, lowering his head in a lackluster display that didn't impress anyone. The spæl ram feinted a couple of charges at this ostensible rival but settled down when no counterattack was forthcoming.

I went to the barn early that evening and hurried through chores. My new ram was on edge, pushing his head between the slats of his enclosure each time I passed his way. When I finally secured his lead rope, he pulled me to the nearest pen and rushed inside the second I opened the gate. Fleeing in terror, my ewes packed themselves into a far corner. Undeterred, the little ram leaped into the throng, hoping perhaps to land atop a panicked ewe in just the right position. When they scattered again, he chased them madly around and around until their flanks were heaving.

Now he paused, raised his head, curled his upper lip, and absorbed the waves of ovine hormones that were buffeting him like a dinghy on a stormy sea. This gave my ewes just enough time to calm down before he lunged at them again, mounting one then another from the side, rear, and head—wherever his desperate vaults landed him. From my morning rounds, I knew that one of these ewes was in heat, so I steered him toward her, and, finally, he managed to do the deed right.

32

A Social Whirl

Even my oldest neighbors, with scores of Christmases under their belts, seemed excited about the upcoming holiday. My own preparations had begun in October when I scoured markets in Spain and France for gifts for everyone in the neighborhood.

By mid-December, the good women of Hovland were conducting Christmas baking in earnest. Ingebjørg explained that it was a host's grave responsibility to offer a platter laden with treats to anyone crossing her threshold during the holidays. If she failed to do so, or, God forbid, a guest refused to sample her offerings, local lore had it that upon departing, the guest would take Christmas away with him.

On nights when I finished chores early, I turned on the oven and started creaming butter with sugar. I had no hope of matching my neighbors' baking prowess, for tradition required them to produce no fewer than ten varieties of cookies. I would have rankled at such an obligation, but as far as I could tell, the neighborhood's women delighted in it. What my output lacked in variety and volume, I made up for in novelty. Surely no one else in Hardanger had the recipe for my mother's almond and anise biscotti or her special date bars or my grandmother Grace's ginger cookies.

A week before Christmas, Alv and Torgeir split a mountain of birch firewood into kindling-sized sticks. That evening we three women of Hovland put big pots of potatoes on our stoves to boil. Solveig and Inger instructed me to cool my spuds overnight and bring them to Solveig's baking room—in her cellar—the next morning.

When I arrived, smoke filled the air, Inger was standing at a massive table peeling boiled tubers, and Solveig was pressing them through her ancient ricer, a kitchen tool that looked like an oversized meat grinder carved out of wood. Alv and Torgeir were there, too, trying to stay out of the cooks' way while tending the fire beneath Solveig's big *bakstehelle*, a heavy iron plate used for cooking flatbread, lefse, *krotekaker*, and all the other thin round breads that had been a mainstay of the Norwegian diet for centuries.

Today our task was to make Hardanger's version of *potetkaker*, potato cakes, a soft, thin, round treat similar to lefse but consisting of nothing more than our own homegrown, red-skinned, sweet-fleshed potatoes plus a little flour and salt.

It was a rare sight to see Inger and Solveig working together. My two closest neighbors had lived within sight of each other since late in World War II, when Inger—like eight thousand other children in Bergen—had been evacuated to the countryside to decrease her chances of being killed by a bomb while increasing her chances of having enough food to sustain her.

Inger, the newcomer, was giggly and sharp-tongued, ever ready to turn a conversation on its head with a quip or an unorthodox observation. Round-faced and spirited, she couldn't have been less like Solveig, whose roots in farming most likely branched down through every generation of *Homo sapiens* that had occupied these western fjords. She and her two brothers who were helping us had been born in this house and lived their entire lives here. Ten years Inger's elder, Solveig was stocky, serious, deliberate, and easily scandalized. Except when she traded gossip in a conspiratorial whisper, almost everything she said boomed out of her.

So here we were, the three of us, working as a team for the first time, with Alv and Torgeir darting nervously in and out whenever we called for help or for more of their perfectly split sticks of quick-burning wood.

When all of our potatoes were peeled and riced, Solveig sprinkled them with flour to create a dough that we mixed with our hands. I was relegated to forming globs of this soft mass into round balls, while they used long rolling pins, another dusting of flour, and quick, sure strokes to flatten each ball into wafer-thin rounds nearly eighteen inches in diameter.

To move these fragile creations onto the *bakstehelle*, each woman used her own *bakstefløyg*, a two-foot-long wooden spatula the width of a schoolchild's ruler. It was a sight to see how skillfully my baking companions could wrap one of our huge thin disks around a *fløyg* and unroll it atop the hot metal plate without making a single tear in the delicate dough.

"Ladies, it's time to sample our wares," Inger announced when the first *potetkake* had cooled. Solveig cut it into pieces and ordered Torgeir to fetch butter, sugar, and cinnamon. The first piece I tried was spread only with butter. Delightfully soft and chewy, it tasted nothing like a potato, or, rather, it seemed to have condensed the mild flavor of a potato into something much richer. With the addition of cinnamon and sugar to my second piece, I wondered why I would ever again buy one of those expensive little confections that line a baker's shelves when this simple *potetkake* was so good that it satisfied every craving I had for a treat.

After they cooled, we folded each *kake* in half, and in half again, to form a triangle. These we packed together by the half dozen for freezing. I was given three fresh rounds, and Solveig put my name on two packages that went into her freezer, ready for the holidays whenever I needed them.

Walking home that afternoon, my thoughts wandered to provisions I had on hand for the winter. In my pantry were a couple hundred homemade cookies waiting for guests, buckets of jam from the farm's plums, and more than a dozen liters of wild blueberry jam. On a separate shelf were several rounds of *rullepølse,* the delicious cured sausage that Solveig had made from the flanks of my slaughtered lamb. In the cellar I had a large sack of potatoes from a farm in Soldal and boxes of apples and pears harvested by Ben and me in October. Curing on hooks hanging from the ceiling were four salted chunks of meat from the lamb Johannes had given me: two legs for *spekekjøt* and two racks of lamb, meat I was holding in reserve for the most special occasions. Solveig had my potato cakes in her freezer; Inger had my salted and smoked lambs' heads in hers; and down in Gunnar's freezer in Øystese was the rest of my lamb, wrapped up in a couple dozen packages.

No, not I nor anyone who came for a visit this winter would go hungry.

A few days before Christmas, Linda crossed the North Sea from Newcastle to Bergen through a ferocious storm. My California friend had just wrapped up her first semester at Emerson College and was returning to Norway for three weeks to help with farmwork and celebrate the holidays with me.

Her first view of Hovland in winter was far different than mine. Weeks of wind-driven sleet, hail, and rain had wiped away the foot and a half of snow that had fallen in December, along with the snow that had greeted Ben and me in November. Then, just a week before her arrival, the temperature soared to 50 degrees. So now she was met with a stark landscape of bare trees and old yellow stubble.

We spent our first full day together, *vetle julafta,* "Little Christmas Eve," cleaning house, wrapping presents, cutting a big bushy fir tree in Johannes's forest, and making paper decorations to hang on it.

The next morning, Christmas Eve, we awoke to a small miracle. In spite of a forecast that had called for rain, the fields of Hovland were buried beneath a foot of snow. We ran downstairs shouting and laughing, hardly believing that our dreams of a white Christmas—the first for both of us—had come true.

Our plan was to hurry through chores and breakfast, then tour the neighborhood, distributing a big sack of gifts to all our friends. But they beat us to it. For five hours, starting right after breakfast, a stream of people showed up at the door bearing boxes and bags to put under our tree. Each person or group stayed just long enough for a cup of coffee and a few cookies before heading home for their own Yuletide celebrations.

Early in the morning, I'd fired up the living room's stove for only the second time during my many months on the farm. Now instead of directing visitors to the kitchen, Linda and I ushered them into that venerable room next door. I'd never felt at ease there. During summer's long, light days, it was dark, cold, and imbued with a forlorn aura emanating from dusty spinning wheels and other old objects.

On this day, though, everything changed. Now the darkness was outside. Inside, we had a Christmas tree, our friends, and a warm fire breathing light and life into these old wooden walls and Johannes's displays of his farm's rich heritage. The room could not have felt more comforting and intimate.

Like most of our neighbors, Linda and I were going to have *pinnekjøt,* cured and smoked lamb ribs, for Christmas Eve dinner: the year's most sumptuous holiday meal. When I took her into the pantry to show off the two racks of lamb hanging there, I could barely contain my pride, for I'd had a hand in raising and slaughtering the animal they came from and in partitioning, salting, and curing its meat.

Inger had given me instructions on how to prepare this delicacy. We were to soak a slab of ribs in water for twenty-four hours before cutting it into two-rib portions. These would then be steamed for two hours over a lattice of birch sticks. We'd harvested thin birch branches on *vetle julafta,* whittled away their bark, and sawed them into more than a dozen pieces just long enough to fit crosswise in our largest pot.

We started the steaming process before evening chores. Two hours later, Linda and I sat down to our very own Christmas dinner that included smoked lamb that was so succulent it was falling off the bone: the best ribs we'd ever had.

Only when all our day's work was behind us did we go to the living room to light the candles on our tree and take our first long look at the presents piled beneath it. Handel's *Messiah* was just starting on BBC radio, and we listened in silence through the tenor's tender recitative "Comfort Ye, My People." Finally, we bent down and plucked up matching boxes: one for Linda, one for me.

As we opened package after package, I drew closer and closer to tears. Here were linen table runners stitched with intricate Hardanger embroidery, a wall hanging woven from local wools, hand-knit mittens and socks, a box spilling over with special Hardanger cookies and cakes that Solveig had made. Tears finally did spill over when I opened the present from Torkel and Inger's daughter and son-in-law, Solveig and Nils: a narrow burlap wall hanging festooned with handmade decorations of woven hearts, Christmas elves, little snow-covered trees, and the inscription *Til Liese—Jul 1972.*

After Handel's oratorio ended at midnight, Linda and I sat for another hour by the light of our candles. We talked about our experiences at Hovland and traced the series of events that had brought us to celebrate this Christmas together in a hundred-year-old farmhouse in the mountains of Hardanger. We marveled over our neighbors, who had been such steady and welcoming teachers and friends. And we agreed that in the short time we'd been here, this place had left an indelible mark on our hearts.

At length, Linda went upstairs to bed, but I stayed by the tree a while longer. My thoughts turned to how lucky I was to have become a part of this community of such big-hearted people; their acceptance of me was the greatest treasure I'd ever received. And I reflected on how difficult it would be to pull myself away when the time came to leave.

Bella sprang to her feet when I stood up, then ran ahead through the dark as I walked to the barn. I went to the pregnant black heifer first and gave her a handful of grain and a good head rub. In Begonia's stall, I leaned into the mare's soft muzzle and felt moist air from her nostrils warm my face. When the little black ram caught sight of me, he started prancing in his enclosure, hoping, I'm sure, for another visit to his ewes. But like the heifer, he was content with a handful of grain and a head rub.

Finally, I headed to the sheep pens to check on my charges. A few ewes were on their feet drowsily chewing their cud; others were lying down with legs tucked under their chests as they kept track of me with half-closed eyes. The flock's smallest ewe lamb squeezed out of her pen to greet Bella. The two were longtime pals who enjoyed romping up and down the walkways together. I returned the little one to her fold before bidding goodnight to all my good friends in the barn. Then Bella and I walked through the snow to the warm house; I tossed a log into each stove. And we went upstairs to bed.

December 25 is merely the first day of Christmas in Norway and the most subdued. Presents have already been opened, so on this day families spend their time eating, walking, eating some more, resting—and then eating more and more and more. Visits and parties commence on December 26 and continue to Epiphany, the twelfth day of Christmas. On every one of those days, Linda and I hosted visitors, many of them young people I'd gotten to know over the summer who were home for the holidays from their jobs and schools.

On all but one of those days, we were also visitors ourselves, sallying forth to coffees and parties at homes in Øystese and all the small clusters of farms lying between Hovland and Fyksesund, the narrow branch of Hardanger Fjord far below us. For good measure, we threw a party or two of our own. And, of course, we always offered cookies and coffee to anyone who dropped by.

The neighborhood, too, put on a big bash: a dance in the community hall down the hill by Skårsvatnet. Nearly every woman came dressed in a stunning Hardanger *bunad*, the region's traditional costume, which transformed the dance floor to a kaleidoscope of red, black, green, and white. Two accordion players and a guitarist banged out Rhinelanders, waltzes, mazurkas, and Hamborgars. As dancers spun to the music, the women let their heavy pleated skirts fly outward, encircling them in undulating waves of black. Hans Skåre, a young father of six boys and a baby girl, taught me the Rhinelander and didn't seem to mind when I stepped on his toes. I was giddy with the music and aching for a *bunad* of my own.

It was the darkest time of the year, but everyone was in high spirits. At Torkel and Inger's one day, Ola Mæland and Gunnar Hovland lifted me by my hands and feet and swung me back and forth while I laughed so hard I could hardly breathe.

Night after night we went to bed in the early hours of the morning, tipsy from the fellowship of friends and the myriad delicacies and homebrews our hosts had crafted especially for Christmas.

On one such evening, when I left a party at a neighbor's house, another guest followed me out, a young man from the area who now held a good job in a distant city. He was handsome, athletic, and smart and had helped me with haying several times over the summer; I'd been attracted to him since the day we met. That morning, he'd paid Linda and me a visit, and when we told him that we were having a hard time learning to ski, he said he'd give us a lesson the next day.

He and I stood outside in the dark and made small talk. When I turned to leave, he offered to walk me home. Halfway there, he put his arm around me. It was warm and comforting, and I responded in kind. Once we started to kiss, there was no stopping.

Linda had not been feeling well and had headed back to the house hours earlier. So we sneaked upstairs to my bedroom, which was separated from Linda's by an empty chamber. Later in the coal-black winter morning, it was easy for him to slip out the front door and down the road, unnoticed by neighbors.

He didn't show up for our skiing lesson that day. Or the next day or the next. My heart wasn't broken. After all, a crush is only a crush. But this was the first man who'd touched me since the night with Øystein. And I was sad that I wouldn't have another night with him or another kiss.

A couple weeks later he sent a letter, addressed to both Linda and me, saying that he'd had a wonderful time with us at Christmas and was looking forward to seeing us again. To top it off, he asked us to please write to him. While this went a long way toward his redemption in my eyes, it only heightened my confusion over local cultural norms. My bewilderment deepened even further at our next meeting, many weeks later, when he was as cordial as he'd always been. And that was the problem: he displayed not a trace of embarrassment, or intimacy, or any other sign that we'd spent a night together or that he'd missed our ski lesson the next day. It was as if all of this had been completely blotted from his memory. Where did *that* fit in with the social fabric I was working so hard to make sense of?

Two weeks of Christmas festivities made no difference in the barn. Linda and I fed and watered the sheep, heifer, horse, and black ram twice a day. We continued shoveling away the remains of feed that issued forth from our charges as manure. Forking up silage was just as impossible and frustrating as ever, rotten floorboards in the hayloft just as terrifying. Between morning and evening chores, we had outbuildings to repair, firewood to chop, the house to keep clean, meals to make, and clothes to wash in the sink. One day, at Johannes's direction, we gave worming medicine to all the sheep. I caught each animal and held it tight while Linda dropped fifteen milliliters of the liquid down its gullet.

How we managed to squeeze skiing into our lives through so much working and partying is hard to figure. But ski we did. Every day that weather allowed, we lugged poles and skis up bare hillsides to get to snow higher up. Like me, Linda was a complete novice. Careening down hills and through stands of trees with limited ability to turn or stop, we fell time and again, got beaten and bruised, tangled in trees, and continually risked death or permanent brain damage. But, oh, was it fun.

Of course, we were still leading the ram to my ewes morning and evening. After arriving, it had taken the little black stud a couple of days to settle down. Meanwhile, Magnar waited more than a week to retrieve his sickly ram, forcing me to expend hay and time on an animal that contributed nothing to the farm. Yet now that I was no longer wasting hours each day prodding this frail creature into doing his job, I began to feel sorry for him, especially since I figured he was bound to end up in a freezer sooner rather than later.

By the time his little rival took over, Magnar's ram had mounted thirty-two ewes in heat. Five days after his dismissal, I was aghast as I watched his very first mate nuzzle up to the flock's new consort, who was more than happy to accommodate her. Over the next couple of days, ewes number two, three, four, and five did the same. By early January, the little black ram had mated with fifteen of the thirty-two, leaving Magnar's ram with an overall score of seventeen fruitful pairings versus fifteen barren. Thanks to Johannes's friend and his ram, lambing was now doomed to start a week late and extend two to three weeks longer than usual.

33

Suddenly a Celebrity

Just after New Year, in the midst of our holiday partying, four people from NRK, Norway's national broadcasting service, arrived from Oslo to spend two days filming footage of Johannes's farm, his garden, and me. The crew included a producer and a cinematographer, Johnny Bergh and Arild Nybakken, who were so well known that everyone in the neighborhood recognized their names. They were also hysterically funny. As they wandered about setting up scenes and shooting their footage, they kept up a running dialogue, singing little ditties and telling slapstick jokes that made me burst out laughing every time they pointed the camera my way.

Six weeks earlier, a stranger had appeared at my door, introducing himself as Sverre Djønne, an acquaintance of Johannes's. He'd come to tell me about a letter he'd just mailed to a man named Erik Bye, who, he said, was NRK's greatest celebrity. Every year, he explained, Bye produced a handful of wildly popular television programs highlighting entertainers as well as ordinary people with unusual skills, occupations, or compelling life stories.

In his letter, Sverre said, he'd told Bye about a farmer with a marvelous botanical garden and an American girl who had taken over when he fell ill. He was sure that Bye would be interested.

And, sure enough, he was. A few days later, an associate of this famous man showed up at the farm to check things out. Bergljot Engeset was a beautiful woman with dazzling blue eyes accented by long, dark lashes and coal-black hair that fell in a thick, wavy frame around her face. A formally trained stage actress, she was now hosting a television program for children, which Arne regularly watched. Most likely just about every other kid in Norway who lived in a house with a TV watched it, too, because NRK's single channel was the one and only television channel in the entire country.

From the moment we met to her departure the next morning, Bergljot and I stopped talking only long enough to catch a few hours' sleep. She spent the afternoon working alongside me, and she helped with evening barn chores, too. Over supper, we talked about farming, California, her stage career, and Erik Bye, whom she described as a man larger than life. As a child, she told me, he'd toured internationally with his opera singer father, and as a teenager during World War II, he'd joined the Norwegian Resistance against Nazi occupiers. Her boss was a journalist, poet, composer, folksinger, and, quite possibly, she said, the second most beloved man in Norway, eclipsed only by the country's reigning monarch, King Olav V.

Soon after returning to Oslo, she called to say that Bye had been so enthusiastic about her report from Hovland that he'd gone to Sunnaas Hospital himself to interview Johannes. He'd returned just minutes earlier and had directed her to invite Johannes and me to take part in his mid-January broadcast. If I agreed, a film crew would show up at the farm in a few weeks to shoot background footage.

Inger immediately volunteered to make *middag* for the crew. She and I had no problem agreeing on a menu, for we both wanted to treat these Oslo folk to a table heaped with traditional Hardanger fare. And for this, nothing would be more appropriate than the lambs' heads I'd packed into buckets in October and the second slab of *pinnekjøt* hanging in my pantry.

Now, some might consider a lamb's head an indelicate choice: there's always a chance that a person who hasn't grown up with such a dish might not enjoy it at all. Yet I was filled with excitement over the bragging rights that my very own smoked and cured heads would afford. What better way to show these television people how thoroughly immersed I was in my life as a Hovland farmer than by exhibiting nerves of steel as I dug into a boiled cranium served under the light of day?

A humid and smoky aroma of cured meats that had been cooking since early morning hung in the air when Torkel opened his door and ushered the NRK crew, Linda, and me to his big family table in the kitchen.

"Welcome to our home," he said with a flourish. "Please be seated."

Our chorus of thanks was followed by a round of oohs and aahs as Arne and Tormod, with great ceremony, delivered two large platters of *pinnekjøt* to the table. Moments later, when Inger presented a third platter, this one laden with lambs' heads, two guests gasped in delight.

"Sheep heads! Such a treat!" one cried.

"I haven't had them since I was a kid!" the other said.

Both of our happy diners, we learned, had grown up in western Norway. Our other two guests (who did not look nearly as pleased) were from regions where smoked and boiled heads were most likely considered an abomination.

Inger and I had agreed that the only way to serve this dish was for her to circle the table, heavy platter in hand, giving each guest an opportunity to demur. After making her round, however, a neatly cloven half head lay on each visitor's plate, eye side up. Only then did it occur to me that no matter how unappetizing a dish might be, no guest would be so rude as to turn it down.

Since that dark night in October on the heels of two long days of slaughtering, this was my first close look at the waxen objects now resting before us. All our singeing, salting, smoking, soaking, and boiling had done nothing to hide the grim reality that these were severed heads of lambs, albeit with inch-long stumps for ears and the ghastly complexion of exhumed corpses. Each head's lips were turned up in a faint smile, revealing four little milk teeth on the lower jaw. Every eye was closed—yet this only made me conjure up horrible images of what those sealed lids might be hiding.

All these intimate features shattered my conceit: no nerves of steel here. Instead, I was a shepherdess who couldn't look her food in the eye, much less force it down her gullet. Not that I didn't try. Inger showed me how to peel back the tough skin to access tender slivers of meat tucked into sinuses honeycombing the long snout. They tasted fine. Delicious, in fact. But they were infused with a sticky substance that glued my fingers together, and this was enough for me. As other connoisseurs scooped eyeballs out of sockets, savoring them like oysters on the half shell, the two city slickers from Oslo and I sat quietly, enjoying the succulent *pinnekjøt,* keeping our eyes fixed on our plates, gazing neither left nor right.

Bergljot, Johnny Bergh, and an NRK car and driver were waiting for Linda and me when we landed at Oslo's airport on Wednesday afternoon a week later. Johnny had come to say hello, and Bergljot was there as our designated escort in the big city. She and her husband, Per, would be serving us dinner, she told us, as she directed the driver to her house in Asker, a suburb of Oslo.

Our first meal in eastern Norway could not have been more different than the potatoes and smoked meat we were used to at Hovland. Our hosts spread the table with cheeses and fresh crab and shrimp and filled our glasses with chilled white wine. Deep into this unexpected and delightful repast, we were interrupted by a loud knock. Per opened the door, and into the room strode a strapping man with a voice to match his six-foot-six frame.

"So here is the girl who rescued Hovland!" Erik Bye proclaimed, enveloping my hand in both of his and giving it a strong shake. "I've been looking forward to meeting you for quite a while."

At first it was hard to imagine this bear of a man as a celebrity. His attire was unremarkable except for his pants, which rode up to his ankles and were a little too tight at the waist and too baggy below the knee. He hadn't put much thought into his hair, either. Combed back from a high widow's peak, it shot out in a few unruly brown plumes before ending in an upward flip over his neck. He was not handsome in a movie star way, but his large face was complex terrain, and I found myself mapping its rectangular outline and diverse features. When he smiled, the contours changed. Furrows became laugh lines, his eyes lit up, and the thin stroke of his mouth transfixed me with its charm. His manner was contagious. He was interested in everyone's stories and had quite a few good ones of his own to tell. Before we knew it, the room was a flurry of conversation and laughter.

An hour or two before midnight, Bye suggested we move the party to his house, saying he'd like us to meet his wife, a well-known politician and community activist. We all piled into his car for the short drive. Tove Bye greeted us at her front door, and with barely a pause for introductions, the conversation took off again, continuing without a lull until two o'clock in the morning, when Erik called a cab to take Linda and me to our hotel in the heart of Oslo.

For weeks leading up to the television show I'd been growing more and more anxious. The thought of speaking Norwegian in front of a roomful of strangers was nerve-wracking. What if I couldn't think of anything to say, or, even worse, what if I said something stupid? I was determined to speak my dialect, but eastern Norwegians had a notoriously dead ear when it came to understanding the language of their western countrymen. Probably they would think I was just speaking garbled Norwegian, a thought that worried me more than anything.

By the time Linda and I arrived at the studio on Friday afternoon, I was so nervous I wanted to sink into the floor. But the first familiar face we saw distracted me from my worries. It had been four months since I'd seen Johannes Hovland on that September day just before he left for Oslo. Now here he was leaning on a cane talking with Erik Bye at the foot of the stage in this modest auditorium. To my surprise, it felt good to see him now.

"So here you are, Liese," Johannes announced. "And here we both are with Erik Bye!"

I'd never seen him so animated. Instead of shaking my outstretched hand, he embraced me with his one good arm. Now I was surprised again, for hugging, of course, was not something people did in Norway.

Johannes seemed healthier and stronger. Yet he still couldn't walk without support, and his left arm still hung limp at his side. He was in a fine and talkative mood, and there was a lot of farm business that needed our attention, but we barely got started before I was called away by Bye's assistant with a few last-minute questions. After that, it was time for the makeup artist to fuss over Linda and me. Then there were microphones to get used to. And so it went until the audience started to file in, and Linda and I were led to our seats in the auditorium's front row. Behind us sat Sverre Djønne dressed in the man's version of the Hardanger *bunad,* with its black wool jacket and knickers, long wool socks, and something like one hundred silver buttons. Next to him was another man from Øystese and three of my friends from Soldal, including Ågot Soldal, a woman in her fifties, wearing her own regal Hardanger *bunad.*

Linda and I spent an hour turned around in our seats talking with these neighbors until Bye finally took the stage. The long wait had calmed me down; I was with friends from Øystese, not an audience of strangers.

About half an hour into the show, I knew my turn had come when the renowned host started telling a story about a farmer from Hardanger who had fallen ill and a girl from America who had taken over for him. His story went on for a while until finally I was called to the stage. For the next twenty minutes Erik and I sat side by side on a wooden bench talking about my experiences on the farm and my life back home in Mill Valley.

I should have known that I'd be in good hands with this famously charming interviewer. He put me at ease as he moved from serious question to humor and back again. The longer we talked, the more I relaxed, and soon I was reveling in my ability to speak the deep dialect of Øystese and Hovland, pausing occasionally to translate a particularly arcane term into what I knew from my Danish would be considered "good" Norwegian by this *bokmål*-speaking Oslo audience.

Magnar's ram and all of its shortcomings were thrown into the national spotlight that night. And at some point the conversation turned to *møkk*, manure, that is. I expressed my opinion that without it, Norwegian farmers would have gone bankrupt centuries earlier.

"In fact, I'm going to be spreading manure at Hovland next week," I said to Erik. "Why don't you come for a visit and help for a day or two?"

"No, I don't think so," he said, shaking his head. "I've already done enough of that."

He paused for a beat, struggling to keep a straight face. "Why . . . I've been spreading manure around NRK for years now!"

He barely got the words out of his mouth before bursting into laughter. The audience roared along with him, and for one scary moment I was sure his huge frame was going to tip the bench backward, sending us both to the floor.

When Johannes was called to the stage, Erik kept me at his side while the two of them talked. The farmer read a long poem about ferns and recounted a story about a Christmas Eve he had spent alone at Hovland.

Finally it was time for me to return to my seat. But wait, Erik said. There's one more thing.

At that moment, Sverre, Ågot, and Linda appeared from backstage, each of them bearing pieces of a Hardanger *bunad:* a wool dress with a bright red bodice and black skirt with yards of pleating; a hand-laced apron and blouse; a beaded breast cloth; a woven belt; an embroidered apron sash; black shoes with silver buckles; and a king's ransom in jewelry to go with them.

"This is for you, Liese," Ågot said as the trio displayed their armloads of finery to the audience and cameras. "A gift from the people of Øystese."

And what a gift! Ågot was presenting me with the exquisitely hand-wrought clothes that had been worn for special occasions by generations of women in Hardanger, a region with one of the longest and strongest unbroken practices of making and wearing this traditional attire. There were no words that could express my astonishment and gratitude. This *bunad* represented the essence of everything I had fallen in love with in Norway. When Ågot draped the surprisingly heavy dress over my arms, I felt its weight as a tangible link to the age-old traditions and culture of Hovland, Soldal, and beyond.

While the audience cheered, Ågot shepherded me to a dressing room backstage where she helped me don the complex outfit. This was a borrowed *bunad*, she explained. When I got back to Øystese, I'd be measured for one that would be tailor-made for me.

After we got everything on and adjusted to Ågot's satisfaction, she handed me two pairs of shoes.

"We knew you had big feet," she explained apologetically, "but we didn't know the exact size. So we got two pairs to be sure one would fit."

Two pairs: one big, the other bigger. But neither big enough.

It was a crisis of the highest order. A *bunad*'s roots run deep; the black clogs I was wearing would be an affront to tradition. Bergljot commandeered every available crew member to scour every studio and prop room in the building as well as to scrutinize the shoes of any woman they chanced upon. Surely they could find a pair of black shoes big enough for me. They had ten minutes, no more. When the searchers returned out of breath and empty-handed, Ågot held a quick conference with Bye's people to weigh the alternatives: clogs or barefoot?

The show was coming to an end. Sent backstage to fetch me, Simon the violinist struck up a western Norwegian tune. "Follow me!" he ordered. Ågot gave me a little push, and I swung out behind the fiddler in stocking feet. Under the lights of the stage, I swirled in great circles with the *bunad* billowing around me in full glory.

34

The Shepherdess's Lamb

Tuesday should have been a day of celebration. When I'd led the black ram from pen to pen on Monday evening, not a single ewe had paid him the slightest heed. Truth be told, they'd been ignoring him like this for nearly three weeks now. The fact that none of them had come into heat during this period meant that every ewe was now pregnant; the little stud had successfully inseminated all of them on his first try, unwittingly putting himself out of his favorite job. As for me, after serving seven weeks as an ovine go-between every morning and evening, I could finally hang up the ram's lead rope for good.

But instead of rejoicing, I was worried sick by a lamb hunched up in her pen with head hanging low. It was going to be a busy day, and I didn't know what to do about the animal except keep an eye on her.

At midmorning, reporters from two newspapers showed up, and a third arrived unannounced at noon. Each came with a photographer. For most of the day, all six followed me everywhere, observing, asking questions, snapping photos, and traipsing into the barn every hour or so as I checked on the lamb, who seemed worse at each visit.

Bergljot had warned me in December that some of Erik Bye's guests had become the focus of regional and even national attention. Yet I was completely unprepared for the flood of reporters, both announced and unannounced, who started streaming to the farm after the show aired.

When Harald Johan Nilsen, a reporter for *Norsk Ukeblad,* one of the country's largest magazines, followed me into the barn on Wednesday afternoon, the lamb could barely stand. Having grown up on a farm in Norway's far north, Nilsen insisted that we search out Torkel for advice.

As always, my neighbor put down his own work without a grumble to help with mine. In the barn, he took one look at the animal and said something I never expected to hear. All year I'd been watching him and my other neighbors devise their own solutions to every problem they faced, whether dealing with buildings, machinery, crops, or livestock. Now he was telling me to call the veterinarian. Right away.

The vet arrived early in the evening and made a quick diagnosis. He was an ill-natured man and—I was pretty sure—drunk. But he seemed confident that the lamb was suffering from bacterial meningitis. Most likely she would die, he said. Antibiotics would give her only a small chance. Yet he gave her an injection and wrote a prescription that I could get filled in town if I chose to do so. Most importantly, he told me to isolate the animal from my other sheep because the disease was contagious. That's when I understood the urgency of Torkel's counsel. Suspecting meningitis, he feared not so much for the lamb but for the entire flock. Now I was terrified.

Nilsen helped me hammer together a small enclosure next to Begonia's stall. We put down a bed of straw and laid the little creature onto it. It was the reporter, too, who told me that the lamb was most likely dehydrated and needed milk. I ran to the house and returned with a baby bottle filled with store-bought milk—every sheep farmer keeps bottles for feeding lambs—and Nilsen helped me get it down the little one's throat.

In the morning, my poor sweet lamb was lying down and trembling. Her head was thrown back, her legs outstretched, and her eyes dull and unblinking. The creature's agony touched every nerve in my body; I needed those antibiotics, no matter how bleak the odds.

I rushed through chores and hurried to Soldal for my first ride aboard the morning school bus to Øystese. Our downhill drive went quickly, while my walk back home seemed to take forever.

Nilsen arrived right after I did. He'd spent the night in Øystese and was back for another day of observing and interviewing. Now he helped administer the medicine, and he didn't make fun of me when I climbed in with the lamb to hold her head in my lap. I didn't do this because I was a soft-hearted city girl tending to a dying pet—at least I don't think I did—but from a practical stance. This young animal had spent her entire short life close to her fellow sheep. Since November she'd been penned up in even tighter quarters with six others. Surely the shock of being isolated in a cold pen without the comfort and warmth of these friends intensified her suffering.

The first time I held and stroked her, I could feel her body relax. After that, I climbed over the railing several times a day, trying to ignore the certainty that most any Norwegian farmer, Nilsen included, would consider my actions ridiculous.

On Saturday morning I offered my little lamb a handful of sweet, fine-stemmed hay. She took a few blades and started to chew. When she wobbled to her feet and ate a bit more that afternoon, I was filled with joy. This lamb was going to live, and I had a reporter to thank for it. Without Nilsen's advice to give her milk that first evening, I'm sure I would have found her dead the next morning.

Gunnar drove up from Øystese at the end of that long week, right after the final news team departed. He was here to pick up the spæl ram and return it to its owner. During my five weeks with the little fellow, we'd become fast friends. He was fond of me, because I provided him with—well—a lot of fun. He'd also grown accustomed to the scratching around the ears that I gave him several times a day. In return, I was fond of him not only for the many gifts he was bestowing on the farm but because he was also a joy to work with: an efficient machine who took his job seriously and did it well.

Gunnar assured me that a bright future was in store for the young animal. His lineage was excellent, and he had passed his first test with flying colors. If my ewes delivered healthy lambs in the spring, any farmer who kept spæl sheep in the region would be happy to pay for the services of this fine animal for years to come.

35

Mørketida

Norwegians have a word for winter's sunless months: *mørketida*, "the dark time." Strictly speaking, this term applies only to regions north of the Arctic Circle during those days and months when the sun never shows itself above the horizon. Suicide rates climb, people become irritable and tense, and therapists and social workers put in a lot of overtime.

But I felt the dark time at Hovland, too. In mid-January, the sun rose above the horizon at 9:30 a.m. and set at 4:00 p.m. For a couple of those hours the distant southern mountains hid the orb from view. On most days, clouds obscured it altogether. So more often than not, our long, dark nights were interspersed with short, gloomy days.

The unusually warm weather and raging storms that had melted away November and December snowfalls continued through January. Forecasters were predicting that this winter would end up being Norway's warmest on record.

These long weeks of wet storms made me yearn for snow, for I'd quickly learned that rain gave rise to seas of mud, soaked me when I ran to the barn and back, leaked through the barn roof, and created a tent city of wet clothes hanging to dry in the kitchen. Each time a snowflake or two fell in January, it had me hoping that I'd soon be able to step from the kitchen windows (on the second floor) onto a bed of snow, just as Johannes had done during a storied winter decades earlier.

In the depths of *mørketida*—after weeks of miserable weather, long dark nights, short dreary days, and one mishap after another—my mood began to swing up and down. Mostly down. The troubles began two days after I returned from Oslo, when Begonia rammed her nose into a grain bucket I was holding out for her. The motion was so forceful that it twisted me downward. Something seemed to snap in my back, and I sank to my knees. For an entire week, if I moved the wrong way a searing pain shot down my back into my right leg. Torkel came five days in a row to dig up silage for my animals. Inger made me meals and spent a few hours each day helping me get around while reporters and photographers followed my every move.

Two nights after that injury, I was alone in the hayloft when it finally happened. As I threaded my way over the floor, both legs suddenly broke through its rotten boards, and I dropped through the hole like a dead weight. I threw out my arms to arrest the descent, but my elbows merely smashed into floorboards without slowing me down. The eight-foot plunge left time for only one quick thought: would I break one leg or both? Miraculously, I landed upright atop a spongy pile of moldy silage directly in front of a very startled heifer.

Lying in bed that night, I wondered whether *hulder*s might have taken up winter residency in the barn. Who but one of those beautiful, mischievous women Øystein had told me about—the ones with tails who live inside mountains—who but one of them could have hatched a plot to have my own rotten silage save me from Johannes's rotten floor?

A week later, I was finishing morning chores when I noticed a ewe standing with head down and jaw quivering. As I approached, she lurched forward and fell to the floor, kicking her legs and shaking violently. When Torkel came to take a look, he guessed that she might have meningitis and advised that I administer the same medication prescribed for my lamb.

I found her dead in the morning, her body grotesquely bloated. Torkel once again came to my aid. Together we loaded her into the manure cart and drove across the field to my dumping site for rotten hay and silage. But the bare ground was frozen so deep that we couldn't penetrate it with our shovels. We continued on to one of the manure piles I'd carted out months earlier. We pitched it aside, dug a grave in the soft earth below, and laid the ewe to rest.

That evening as I sat at the kitchen table mourning her death, I was overwhelmed by a sensation that there was nothing left that could comfort me, nothing to make me happy, nothing to make sense of what I was doing in this big, cold house in this cold, dark place. Wouldn't it be nice, I thought, to be like Bella, calm and relaxed as she slept at my feet? I kneeled to run my hand along her soft side and around her ears and neck. She rolled onto her back and lay with feet hanging limply in the air.

A little jolt shot through me. Right here was something that made me feel better. And so did the sheep when I went into their pens with a can of grain and they came crowding against my legs, bleating and shoving. Why was I *skorfast* here in the house, letting myself sink into a pool of despair?

Bella jumped up when she saw that I was heading out and beat me to the barn like she always did. I followed her to the sheep pens, where I sat on the edge of a manger and closed my eyes. With long, deep breaths, I took in the familiar bouquet of lanolin, sweet hay, and manure and let myself be soothed by the soft cadence of ewes chewing their cud. Time slowed as my mind settled into their silence and my heart into their rhythm. Centered in this dark, still place, I felt the outside world recede until the only things left were these ewes and this peace.

During the first three weeks of January, Øystein had visited only once. At month's end, after Linda had left and reporters were no longer showing up on my doorstep, he started coming around again. If I was outside when he arrived, he joined me in work. If he couldn't find me outside, he searched for a task on his own, fixing a sheep pen in need of repair or recovering the axe that I sometimes embedded so deeply into a chunk of firewood that I could neither pull it out nor pound it further in.

I didn't like it when he did these things. Perhaps he was simply doing the work out of the goodness of his heart. But I suspected that—whether he was fully aware of it or not—he felt these favors entitled him to spend the rest of the day with me, whether I was hanging out indoors or working outside. And perhaps he *was* entitled. The guilt I still felt over opening my bedroom door to him made it impossible for me to suggest, or even hint, that I needed him to cut back on these long visits. What's more, in light of all the help he'd provided over the months, asking him to leave would make me feel like a particularly cruel ingrate.

Throughout the fall and into winter, he had spent so much time with me that I began to feel trapped. Yet I had never been able to bring myself to talk with him directly about my feelings. Instead, I just grew more and more glum and sharp tongued whenever he was around.

Crazily, though, during those first three weeks of January—when my behavior had finally appeared to keep him away—the relief I experienced was uneasy. I hated to hurt people's feelings, and I was sure I had deeply wounded his.

Now he was back. Hovering over me. Shadowing me in the kitchen during those few hard-won hours when I was free of work. I craved that time for my own, to use however I saw fit, without having to contend with a brooding presence at my side.

So I grew more sullen. And he did, too. He contradicted me all the time and criticized my performance of most any task. Instead of conversing, he instructed: delivering long lectures that I tried to ignore as they slowly drove me to resentment, anger, and despair.

Even then, even *then,* I couldn't find the nerve to ask him to leave. He was a strong man in his fifties. I was young, alone, and afraid. Afraid that he might respond with anger. Afraid that he would accuse me of beguiling him into spending so many hours helping out on the farm. Afraid, most of all, of hurting him. So I endured his presence, responding in monosyllables to anything he said, trying to make myself repellent enough that he would be repelled.

One day it rained and slushed so hard that water breached the barn's rock foundation and began running through two sheep pens. Set deep into the hillside, the foundation normally served as a subterranean barrier to groundwater flowing down from above. But the ancient bulwark was no match for the deluge unleashed by this storm.

Since I couldn't intercept an entire hillside of rainwater, all I could do was climb into the pens and dig channels through the manure to contain the flow to two or three rivulets. If the storm let up soon, at least portions of each pen might remain dry.

When I inspected my work the next morning, I found water running into yet another pen. The animals were dirty, wet, and miserable, and there was nothing I could do about it.

I didn't discover the huge hole in the silo's roof until just before dark. The wind had died down somewhat by then, but it was still raining, and the top layer of silage was soaked. When I clambered to the barn's upper story and trod across that treacherous floor to a little portal that provided access to the roof, my heart sank. The patchwork of corrugated metal sheets that Johannes had held in place by rocks and cinder blocks was all jumbled up. Two sheets had completely disappeared.

Back on the ground searching for them in the gloom, I considered giving up. Why not just go inside and make supper? The alternative was to find these two heavy pieces of metal, get them to the roof somehow, and do what I could to position and secure them—while the wind buffeted them like a sail. I envisioned them being ripped from my grasp, slicing my hand open, and pulling me over the edge or down into that gaping hole.

After a brief search, I found the sheets far apart, each of them about one hundred feet from the concrete tower. Night had fallen now, so to save my precious fodder, I'd have to work in the dark. As I carried the first one uphill, I could feel how even a little burst of wind gained purchase on its broad surface. At the bridge leading to the barn's upper loft, I put the sheet down and stood atop it to keep it from flying away while I gathered my thoughts.

It would be so much more pleasant, I told myself, to get into bed tonight—safe, warm, and dry—than to face the terror awaiting me in the dark on top of Johannes's flimsy roof. But unless the hole was repaired right away, rain would undoubtedly destroy all the rest of my silage, and Johannes would be forced to buy truckloads of fodder to replace it. For all I knew, that much hay and silage wasn't available for sale anywhere in the region. Without it, I'd have to send a good number of sheep to the slaughterhouse or watch all of them waste away in the months ahead.

Faced with this choice, a sudden rage washed over me. Johannes was completely blind to the mess he'd created here. I despised his arrogance, along with his self-righteous claims that his neighbors were his inferiors. They were not the ones squandering their resources on water lilies and exotic ferns while their animals ate wet hay and rotten silage, died of meningitis, and lived in barns with rivers running through them. And they were not the ones who would beat a horse, cram gentle ewes into squalid quarters, throw a puppy against a wall, or stand by doing nothing at all while a hayloft floor decomposed into a deadly pitfall.

I was done with Johannes. Done with this farm. I would let this big sheet of metal lie right here on the ground, and I would walk back to the house and write a letter to my mother to tell her about this storm and assure her that I was warm and safe. After all, my destiny was in my own hands.

Why, then, were my hands shaking?

The rain was still falling. The forecast was for at least another day of this weather. So I should just go inside and fix supper and drink a cup of tea. Read a book, perhaps. Go upstairs with Bella and get into bed. And then try to sleep—listening to the rain, picturing it falling through a big gap in the silo roof.

When I took a deep breath, I could feel moisture seeping through my rain jacket and all three layers of clothes to my skin. If I didn't get back to the house soon, I'd be drenched. Still, I stood *skorfast*, rooted to this sheet of metal beneath my feet, just as the three sheep Øystein and I rescued had been rooted to their mountain ledge.

The decision to stay at Hovland had been my own. No one else made it for me. I'd wanted to experience a real winter. See what the farm was like in this season. Live in the snow. Spend more time with friends I'd made over the summer. But above all, I was concerned for the animals.

And there was the rub. The animals, of course. The sheep, heifer, and horse penned up in this dark barn were in *my* hands. What did it matter how bad a farmer Johannes was or how angry he made me? He was in a convalescent hospital on the other side of the country. For me to let these creatures suffer to spite their owner was ridiculous and not just a little bit cowardly. If I didn't stop this storm from destroying the silage, they *would* suffer—and I wouldn't be able to live with myself.

With a sigh, I made my decision. To outwit the wind, I would need to suppress my fear of heights and that yawning black hole. And so I did, picking up the metal sheet and carrying on.

36

An Unbidden Guest

The letter was electrifying. I stood on the milk ramp in Soldal staring at a return address of Langvin Jordbruksskule, 6875 Innvik, and reading three short paragraphs over and over. Finally I convinced myself that this really was an offer of a scholarship to attend a ten-month course of study at a place called Langvin School of Agriculture. The school's principal and its chairman of the board wrote that they had seen me on Erik Bye's show and felt I was a good candidate for their program. The scholarship would cover tuition, books, and room and board. Plus, I could work on the school farm to earn pocket money. The duo enclosed an annual report and a detailed schedule of classes and signed off by saying they were looking forward to hearing from me.

I knew that Norway, like Denmark, maintained an impressive network of vocational education opportunities. But I'd always been on an academic track and had never given a second thought to anything but four-year colleges. Now, as I studied the two enclosures, I was astonished by how closely Langvin's program fit in with the kind of education I was looking for. The school was organized around morning classes that covered everything from animal husbandry and forestry to agricultural technology and economics. Each day after lunch, students headed to fields, barns, and machine sheds for hands-on instruction.

After spending a week gathering information and advice about agricultural programs like Langvin's, I sent a list of questions to Principal Norang. On February 19, I walked to the post office in Øystese to pick up a registered letter containing his answers.

The postmaster peered over his glasses as I ripped open the envelope and read down the page. Right then and there I made up my mind. With a huge smile, I looked up and told him that I was on my way to ag school. Classes would start on August 21 in the town of Innvik, located on the inner reaches of Nordfjord, a day's travel by ferry and bus north of Øystese.

It was a momentous decision that filled me with optimism and relief. For the first time since leaving home, I had a clear plan. Now, instead of continuing my bewildering search for a university program in agriculture—and a way I could possibly fund it—I'd be staying in Norway for at least another year, getting an education that would serve as a solid foundation for my career. It was exciting to think that I'd be living in a new region of the country, making friends with a group of young farmers who would be my classmates. As for my friends in Hardanger, I wouldn't be moving a world away from them—only a couple of fjords.

The postmaster had no inkling of the grand celebration taking place in my head, so I would forgive him for cutting it short.

"Seen the newspaper today?" he asked, holding up a copy of an Oslo daily. "They've written a big story about your boss. I guess he's just as famous as you are now, after that Erik Bye show."

Before I could check out the front-page headline, he flipped to an inside page and pointed to a paragraph midway down the column.

"Look here," he said. "Seems like you're going to be having company soon."

I read the lines twice. First in a whir with my heart racing, then more slowly, one word at a time.

Johannes was coming home. Not at some vague point in the future but soon. Perhaps in just a week or two. The only reason he wasn't on a train crossing the mountains this very minute was that he first needed to find a home-care nurse to live with him at the farm. As soon as someone turned up, he'd be on his way.

By rights, I should have felt joyful for the man who was finally coming back to his farm after nine months in the hospital. Instead, I was imagining how much of what I loved about living at Hovland was about to be swept away. No more solitude. No more independence. No more being the person in charge. No more hosting my friends for a cup of tea and homemade cookies late at night. Would I have to tell the farmer where I was going every time I walked out the door? What would he say if I wanted to strap on my skis and spend an afternoon in the mountains—would I have to ask his permission?

The postmaster was staring at me, so I finally looked up and nodded politely.

“Thank you for showing this to me,” I said. “I’m so happy that he’s finally coming home. It will be nice having him there.”

Six days earlier a storm had buried Hovland under twenty inches of snow, and this time the white stuff was finally sticking around. I’d taken on the job of plowing the road from Johannes’s barn to Soldal following December’s big snowfall, when Torkel and I hitched his homemade plow to Begonia and did the job together. We’d had so little snow since then that this February storm was only my second solo outing.

With Begonia straining under the load and me walking behind Torkel’s wooden plow—or sometimes sitting on it to weigh it down—we managed to push aside about ten inches of snow on our way out and another six on our way back. Cars couldn’t drive on the narrow lane we created with its six-inch base of nicely packed snow, but horses could pull sleighs and sledges over it, and it provided a good surface for walking or skiing.

When the sun had come out twenty-four hours later, I felt as if the world had opened up again. I strapped on the cross-country skis I’d bought in town and headed into the mountains. Since then, the weather had been indescribably beautiful, freezing every night and warming under bright sunlight to about 40 degrees every day.

For the rest of the month, I hurried through chores and other barn work as quickly as I could and went skiing almost every afternoon. One day, I made it all the way to Hyrting, the first time I’d been there since October. On February 27, Arne led me to the top of Manfjell, thirty-three hundred feet higher than Hovland. For a fledgling skier like me, the descent was both exhilarating and terrifying, ending with five days of exquisitely sore muscles in both legs.

Bella and I moved next door early in March to spend a week caring for Torkel and Inger’s boys and livestock. The couple was taking a rare vacation, first to Oslo to visit their daughter Solveig, then three hundred miles north to the city of Namsos to attend their daughter Brynhild’s graduation from nursing school. When Inger had hesitantly asked if I might take over for them, I jumped at the chance to help the friends who’d stood by me all year.

Each morning I got up at 6:30, started the fire, made coffee, set the table, got breakfast ready, woke Tormod and Arne at 7:00, ate breakfast with them and got them out the door to the school bus, went into Torkel's barn at 8:00, went into my barn at 9:00, came into my house at 10:30, went back to Torkel's at 11:30, made *middag,* ate *middag* with the boys when they got back from school at 2:30, did the dishes, went back to my barn at 5:00, finished at 7:00, went back to Torkel and Inger's, made sure the boys had done evening chores in their own barn and were doing their homework, made a little supper for the three of us, did dishes, and fell into bed at 11:30.

Whenever I had a free hour or two, I baked treats for the party Inger and I were going to throw on Saturday. That was the day she and Torkel would return, and it was also my twenty-first birthday.

I awoke that morning in a horrible mood. Saturdays were school days in Norway, affording no break from our daily routine. Outside, gray clouds were drizzling on eighteen inches of hardened snow. At 7:00 I hollered a wakeup call to the boys. My practice was to shout once, wait a few minutes, shout again, wait a bit longer, then run upstairs to shake them out of their beds. Before I could let out a second call, Tormod and Arne appeared at the head of the stairs with smiles on their faces and presents in hand. Catching sight of me, they burst out singing "Happy Birthday" in English as they descended to the living room. Suddenly the day felt brighter.

After our quick breakfast, I watched from a window as they ran off to catch the bus in Soldal. They had just disappeared over the rise behind Solveig's yellow house when Edvard appeared from the opposite direction, hunched over a shapeless green object as if protecting it from the rain. I hurried to clean up and was out the door just as he reached Torkel's stone stairway.

"No one should spend her birthday morning working alone in two barns," he said, looking up at me with a smile. "If you can spare a cup of coffee and a wee bit of breakfast, I'll lend you a hand."

At the top of the stairs, he held out a soggy mass of green tissue paper. "Sorry," he apologized. "They got kind of wet." I peeled away the wrappings, and a big bouquet of yellow daffodils and red tulips billowed forth.

How I wished I could thank my friend with a kiss or even a hug. Couldn't I be allowed to do that just once? Not romantically, of course. Just a long embrace to release this uncertainty and tension that hung over me when I was with him. We could simply stand there for three seconds, or ten, and keep each other warm and not have to worry or wonder about anything else.

Impossible, of course. In a place where no one touched anyone else, a hug would muddle up our friendship. So I shook his hand as was proper and told him how much I loved his gift. "They need to get into water right away," I murmured. "I'll find one of Inger's vases."

We wrapped up chores in both barns in under two hours. Edvard headed back to town, and I headed back to my neighbors' kitchen for a day of cleaning, baking, and cooking. Ingebjørg arrived at noon to lend a hand, and an hour later Inger—who'd insisted on hosting my party—pitched in when she and Torkel returned home from their long trip.

I'd invited eight close neighbors, along with Torkel's family of four. When Inger introduced me to her brother and sister-in-law, who had just given her and Torkel a ride home from Bergen, of course I extended an invitation to these two *bergensers*, as well. So fifteen people were settled into the living room right after dinner when a loud knock sounded at the door. Before anyone could answer, Øystein strode into the room, greeted us with a curt "Good evening," and thrust a small box wrapped with pink paper into my hands.

Crashing a formal party was a severe breach of etiquette. My first reaction was embarrassment for Øystein's sake that he'd shown up like this and then a feeling of guilt that I hadn't invited him. Yet a hostess's duty is to make every guest feel welcome. So I smiled and stood up, extending my hand to thank him for the gift. With no warning, this unbidden guest threw his arms around me, pulled me into a tight embrace, stepped back for an instant, then pulled me to his chest again and kissed me on the cheek.

My face burned bright red. What could he possibly be thinking? By now I was sure that the only people who would hug or kiss one another in this part of the world were either dating, betrothed, or already married. And, of course, they only did so in private.

"*Ja,*" Øystein said, looking around defiantly at the wide-eyed guests frozen in their seats. "This is the way Liese and I always greet each other."

My embarrassment turned to horror. We didn't "always" greet each other like this. We *never* did. My thoughts raced back to the last time he'd taken such liberty: that evening in August when Linda caught sight of him abruptly pecking me on the cheek. Why was he lying to all these people? Surely he understood that his actions would cause tongues to wag throughout the neighborhood and beyond. Was he trying to stake claim to me? Embarrass me? Disgrace me in some way?

My horror quickly transformed to rage. I wanted to shout "No we don't!" to let everyone know. But a fight could only make this awful moment far worse. So I kept quiet and sat down to unwrap the present, fearful that it might be another trap. It turned out to be a flower vase of Hardanger pewter, locally made and surprisingly thoughtful. I forced a wan smile and thank-you. The guests relaxed, the party continued, and I proceeded to avoid Øystein as best I could while we drank Torkel's wines, sampled all six desserts that Inger, Ingebjørg, and I had made, and filled the air with conversation and laughter. When the party broke up at two in the morning, Bella and I walked home to sleep in our own place for the first time in a week.

My anger over Øystein's dramatic performance died down a few days later. After trying all winter to make sense of his behavior, that evening opened my eyes. When he stood glaring at my friends, announcing that he and I always greeted each other with an embrace and a kiss, I saw a man in deep despair, grasping at something he felt he had lost. His own anger and resentment and, perhaps most important, his stubborn nature were surely part of the mix, as well.

Whether this elementary analysis was right or not, I finally understood how important it was that I have a talk with him. Yet when he showed up the next Saturday, something seemed to have changed for him, too. Instead of shadowing me, he spent the better part of three hours sitting in the living room leafing through a book.

Just before noon, he stuck his head into the kitchen where I was making *middag*—not for us together but for me alone.

"Well, I guess I'd better be going," he said. "I'm sorry if I've been a bother."

His eyes were suffused with sadness. And somehow I knew that this apology was sincere and that this was his way of putting an end to his visits.

"Øystein, it's okay," I said. "We can still be friends."

37

Homecoming

Two days later, on March 21, Torkel came over after morning chores to help me with Johannes's sledge. I'd first hitched Begonia to this vehicle in November to haul rotten silage over the snow to a dumping site. I'd been using it ever since, whenever there was too much snow for the cart's rubber tires.

While I swept all traces of manure from this low-slung box mounted on runners, my neighbor cut a piece of scrap lumber to fit across its heavy sideboards. I folded two thin wool blankets together and placed them atop our makeshift seat to complete the transformation of Johannes's winter transporter of firewood and cow dung into a ferry to shuttle people over the snow.

It was strange to think that at this very moment Johannes was crossing the mountains on a train, headed home. I'd made it through the worst challenges of a dark winter, and now on the vernal equinox, the first day of spring, I knew my life was about to change again. I just didn't know how.

In the south-sloping garden below us, hundreds of delicate snowbells blossomed above the snow in tight clusters of white and green, their sweet scent wafting over the yard. Fragile leaves, just beginning to unfurl, graced all of the garden's rambling honeysuckles. Here and there, snow gave way to brown patches of earth pierced by tiny green spires ascending from bulbs hidden below.

"The starling is back!" Arne had announced a week earlier. I'd heard this once before, when my friend Flemming in Denmark came running to find me during recess at school. He pulled me outside shouting, "Come listen! The starling has come! The starling has come!"

I spent the day splitting firewood for my two usual stoves and now a third—the one in Johannes's room—sweeping floors, tidying up the barn, and pondering what changes the farmer's arrival might bring.

Over the past year I'd grown to love living alone, being responsible only to myself and my barn menagerie. On the many days when I didn't see another human being, I wasn't bothered a bit. Now I was thinking about all the precious hours that would be lost on the simple matter of having to talk with my housemates each time we happened to cross paths.

All my favorite habits, I was sure, were about to be shattered. Those magic interludes when I came into the house after morning and evening chores to fix a little food, listen to the radio, read a book, write a letter—those would be impossible with someone else there. Instead of changing into my nightgown in the warmth of the kitchen, I'd have to do it upstairs in my freezing bedroom. My little companion Bella would soon be sleeping at the foot of Johannes's bed, not mine. I'd even have to give up Johannes's old overalls, which I'd worn every day since arriving at the farm.

Begonia trotted at a steady clip over packed snow that evening, drawing Bella and me along in our fine sledge. Pulling up at the milk ramp in Soldal, I surveyed the road ahead where it cut downhill through snow-covered fields to a plain ringed by brooding firs and bare-branched hardwoods. Soon a car emerged from those trees and slowly wound its way uphill through this quiet landscape.

The cab driver stopped in front of us and jumped out to open a rear door for one of his passengers. A woman emerged and nodded a quick hello before hurrying to assist Johannes in the front seat. She helped him swing his body around and lifted his weak left leg over the doorframe. Then she took the farmer under one arm while the driver took him under the other, and together they pulled him to his feet. Before he could straighten up, Bella was at his side wagging her body with the passion of a crowd welcoming the troops home.

While the driver unloaded half a dozen bags from the trunk and propped them around Johannes's legs for support, the woman and I shook hands and introduced ourselves. Her name was Klara, and she was seventy-one years old. Nearly my height but of a more slender build, she had a pleasant, finely wrinkled face framed by white curls. I noticed immediately that she was hard of hearing.

The journey had done her in, too, but the narrow seat could accommodate only one passenger. Determined to see his fares safely home, the driver walked at Klara's side behind the rig, offering his arm when necessary. I trudged through plowed-up snow beside the sledge, keeping firm hold of the lines to steady Begonia, who'd been on edge since Johannes sat down behind her. Perched beside her old master, Bella was the only one of us with no worries.

At the first of Hovland's three gates, Johannes directed me to stop. He sat quietly in the fading light taking in the vista of three snow-covered farms and the peaks beyond. Or perhaps he was looking only at his own place: the red and white house and weathered outbuildings at road's end, the largest and highest of these three farms, the only one with a sweeping view, the gatekeeper to mountains stretching north to Sognefjord, and the place where Johannes was king.

Down the hill some one hundred yards ahead, Solveig emerged from her barn and walked to the road. It had been ten months since she'd last seen her neighbor, a man three years her senior whom she'd known all her life and whose farm she had helped keep alive through his long absence. Now she stood with a smile on her face.

"Don't stop," Johannes commanded as we approached.

He turned away from his expectant neighbor and stared fixedly at nothing, his mouth set in a rigid line while Klara and the cab driver looked on in confusion.

The farmer said little and ate only a few bites of supper before asking Klara to help him to bed. She came out of his room half an hour later, anxious to talk.

"He told me on the phone that he could take care of himself," she said in a whisper, pulling her chair closer to mine at the kitchen table. "So I thought it was strange that the ad was for a nurse, especially after he said that he was only looking for someone to do a little personal care and a little cooking and cleaning."

Johannes's room was right next door, so I listened to Klara but didn't respond, for I'd quickly discovered that her hearing was so bad that even when I spoke in a normal voice, she missed much of what I said. If I raised my voice at all, Johannes would hear every word.

"He can't walk by himself or change into his night clothes or get into bed," she was telling me, shaking her head. "He wasn't truthful when he described his condition . . . or this house. He told me there was no toilet, but I didn't know there was no place to bathe."

I tried to convey that I was surprised by his condition, too. In his last letter from Sunnaas he'd bragged that he was now walking as well as before the stroke.

"At the train station he blew up at the cab driver," she continued in her whisper. "It took him a couple of minutes to find us—such a nice man. I had to help Johannes stay on his feet while we waited on the platform. When he finally appeared, Johannes laid into him and wouldn't stop. I was so embarrassed."

The first few days were not so bad. Johannes spent most of his time sitting up in bed. His door was usually closed to keep the stove's heat from escaping. With Klara's help, he came to the kitchen three times a day to eat meals she prepared for him. Each afternoon, he took a long nap. When he awoke, he would usually ask the nurse to help him to the barn for an inspection, followed by a walk along the road above the garden.

To get her attention, he rang an old handbell that he'd dug out of storage. He required her help for just about everything: getting into and out of bed, sitting down on a chair, standing back up, and making his way to the commode, which had been installed in the small room that housed his firearms collection.

Except for the meals we ate together, I rarely saw him. When I did, he usually seemed to be in a fairly good mood. I'd give him a report from the barn, and he'd ask questions about the garden. On days when he felt the best, he'd elaborate on his new landscaping ideas, always including his favorite scheme: the construction of his biggest pond ever, a full eighty feet long.

By the end of her first week, Klara was a wreck. Every time she caught me alone, she cornered me to whisper a long litany of complaints, adding new ones every day: Johannes's irrational demands; the cold house;

the lack of a bathroom, toilet, or outhouse; and, perhaps worst of all, no washing machine.

"He didn't tell me about any of this. And he certainly didn't say that he didn't own a washer! I would *never* have agreed to this job if I'd known I'd be washing clothes by hand." Her whisper was like a low, hot wind. "There's not a nurse in the country who would do what I'm doing here. In the state he's in, the only suitable place for him is a nursing home."

Before the end of that first week, I was a wreck, too. It didn't matter where I was or what I was doing, Klara would find me and air her complaints. These encounters were particularly vexing because they were so lopsided; I could say nothing in reply, for fear of being overheard by Johannes. Soon I started planning every step of the day to avoid running into either of them.

During our daily meetings, I did my best to ignore the deepening furrows on Johannes's brow and his dark looks of disapproval. I didn't care what he thought about my disappearances. I was still working hard every day and keeping the farm running better than he ever had.

I really did feel sorry for Klara, though, which was why her misery created a dilemma for me. I didn't want to be in the house with her and Johannes, but the less time I spent there, the more she suffered by being alone with him. Right from the start, I'd seen how poorly he treated her. This was in part due to her hearing loss. With his slightly slurred speech and Hardanger dialect, Johannes was particularly difficult for her to understand. I could see that it irritated him each time he had to repeat himself. I also sensed that the mere act of being forced to raise his voice was all it took to trigger his anger.

One day, Johannes told me that he thought Klara was "petty." I, on the other hand, was someone worth talking to, he declared, because I had some knowledge of botany and a broad view of the world. That probably explained why he addressed himself only to me during meals. He never spoke to Klara at all, unless to ask for something. If she interjected a comment, he ignored her, continuing his conversation with me as if she didn't exist. Stuck in the middle, I would just sit there simmering over his scornful treatment of this good woman.

38

Skiing to Valhalla

Facing a long Easter break in England, Linda sent a letter to Johannes asking if she could spend the holiday at Hovland. It would be a working vacation, she was quick to add. Just like her two previous visits.

Johannes readily assented. There would be plenty to do. Lambing season was rapidly approaching, and the heifer was due to calve in mid-April. As soon as a bit more snow melted, we could start clearing away wagonloads of branches that had fallen onto our hayfields over the winter from trees scattered across the hillsides. On sunny days when my mood was bright, I even contemplated hauling out the mountain of cow and horse dung that had been accumulating for years in the manure cellar.

So Linda again sailed across the North Sea, arriving at Hovland on April 3. Snow had been intermittently falling for four days and would continue for one more, burying the farm and obliterating spring. Because Linda and I were the only Californians in the area, we were the only ones surprised by this sudden shift back to winter.

In the days leading up to Linda's arrival, the mood in my little three-person household had grown increasingly tense. On April Fool's Day, just ten days into the job, Klara gave Johannes her notice, softening this bombshell by promising to stay until he could find a suitable replacement. In the meantime, I kept looking for ways to stay out of their reach: I prolonged my visits to the barn; walked or skied to Soldal every day for the mail; and spent as much time as I could at Torkel and Inger's.

Three days into Linda's visit, I was in the kitchen when I spotted Torkel walking up the road. As he slogged his way through a foot of new snow that had fallen overnight, it dawned on me that this was the first time since Johannes's homecoming that any of my friends or neighbors had made this journey.

Torkel was not coming for a visit, I knew, but to shear our flock. The day before, Johannes had given me permission to hire him. Spring shearing was an important task on these farms. Not only did it provide a welcome source of early season income, but by removing a ewe's scraggly, manure-tinged wool, it created a healthier and safer environment for the messy process of lambing. It also made it easier for a newborn to find its dam's udder instead of inadvertently latching onto a lock of grimy wool.

I rapped on a window and waved to Torkel as he passed by below. Seeing me, he veered from his course toward the barn and headed up the rock stairway. I beat him to the door before he could knock.

"I'm way overdue in welcoming your boss back home." His eyes lit up in a smile. "Would it be okay to come in and tell him hello?"

Ten feet behind me, the door to Johannes's room was ajar.

"I have no interest in seeing the man," Johannes shouted. "He's here to shear, not to visit, so tell him to get on with it!"

I flushed red with embarrassment, feeling as if I were somehow responsible for this vile remark. But when I turned to apologize, Torkel was trying so hard not to laugh that his face was red as a sunburn.

"Good morning to you, too, neighbor!" he managed to call out.

For the next few hours, while Begonia and I plowed a channel through new snow to Soldal and back, Linda helped Torkel shear eighteen ewes. By noon, his injured foot—the one crushed by a horse at the onset of World War II—had flared up so badly that it forced him to quit.

Those eighteen animals would be the only ones shorn that spring. Although Torkel claimed it was his foot and bad back that kept him from returning, I suspected the true cause was Johannes's raw contempt for him and the entire neighborhood. Try as I might over the coming days, I was unable to find anyone willing to finish the job for us.

On the afternoon of Torkel's visit, another ewe died, the barn's second death that winter. She had stopped eating three weeks earlier. During her final five days of life, she had lain on her side, pawing feebly at the air. When I asked Johannes for permission to put her down, he shook his head, declaring, "Where there's life, there's hope."

So I trickled water into her mouth half a dozen times each day and shifted her position morning and evening by taking hold of her outstretched legs to roll her over. After a couple of days of this, her pawing grew weaker, and she began to smell like rotting flesh, a stench that enveloped the entire barn as her misery dragged on.

The temperature had soared above 50 degrees under a bright sun when Linda and I loaded her carcass onto a sled. With its runners sinking deep into the wet snow, our little hearse felt like it weighed hundreds of pounds as we dragged it behind us. At the dumping ground, we pitched aside a broad circle of snow, dug three and a half feet into the earth, and laid my friend to rest.

Just past noon a few days later, Linda and I were approaching the house after a trip to the mailboxes when an unfamiliar noise stopped us cold. The noise—more like a roar—was issuing from a window ahead. In a heartbeat, we realized it was Johannes in his bedroom shouting at the top of his lungs. We bolted forward, tore past the cellar door and were bounding up the rock stairway when a single word stood out from the garbled stream.

"*Kviga,*" Johannes was yelling. "The heifer!"

Grabbing Linda's arm, I reversed direction and sped to the barn. Now a new clamor reached our ears; deep within that building's thick stone walls, the heifer was bellowing with all her might.

For two weeks I'd been checking on my pregnant black nemesis at least a dozen times daily. Eleven days earlier, her udder had grown large. When that happened, I was sure the calf would arrive momentarily. Two days later, her abdomen lost its barrel-like bulge that had been visible for months. This, Solveig told me, was a sign that the calf had dropped toward the birth canal. At that point, I was sure calving was *really* close. When nothing more happened, I began to pester all my neighbors for advice on how to read every change in the heifer's body, every nuance of her behavior.

"Relax," Inger said, when she'd finally had enough of me. "Your worrying won't help. The calf will be born when it's born. Now just stop thinking about it."

I'd taken a look at the heifer just before Linda and I left for Soldal. She'd flung her head at me with her usual request for an ear rub. Everything was perfectly normal. I had no idea that an hour was all it would take for a birth to start, proceed to the final stage, and—if I understood Johannes's yelling correctly—go bad.

As Linda and I sprinted through the barn's ponderous stone portal, we were greeted by another thunderous bellow. We headed toward the row of stanchions, and there it was, lying in a limp heap in the gutter between Begonia's stall and the heifer's rear legs: an enormous black-and-white calf smudged with manure and coated in a shiny layer of membranous goo. Begonia was pacing, flicking her ears nervously, while the heifer was pulling at her lead for all she was worth, trying to free herself to turn around to view this dark, motionless bundle.

I'd spent all these weeks worrying about the date of the birth, yet only now did I realize that I had no idea what I was supposed to do when it actually happened. I rushed to the calf and ran my hands over it, to feel what life might be within. It shuddered, a strong, healthy motion. And with that, I left Linda and ran in a panic back to the house for instruction.

"If it's moving, put it into its pen. Don't let her touch it!" Johannes shouted. "Milk her right away and give the calf as much as it can drink."

I ran back to the barn, where the heifer, tethered in her narrow stall, was straining even harder to get a glimpse of her offspring.

"I got a good look," Linda said breathlessly. "He's a little bull."

The revelation stopped me dead. For nine months I'd been hoping for a heifer. More than anything, this was what the farm needed—a little heifer to grow up and bear her own calf. Then there would be two cows in the barn, providing milk enough to sell, bringing in precious income.

As the little fellow raised his head for his first look at the world, Linda and I attempted to lift him off the cold concrete. But he was coated in the slime that had lubricated his passage down the birth canal, and his limp body slipped out of our grasp time and again. It was Linda who thought to grab him by the legs. She took his forelegs, I took the rear, and together we dragged him over the concrete into his pen. A barbarous welcome for a helpless newborn.

Weeks earlier, in preparation for the birth, I'd thrown a thick layer of hay into the empty pen. Now Linda and I each grabbed a handful and kneaded the little animal all over with gentle circular motions as he tried to stand for the first time. Eventually he managed to splay his rear legs far apart and push his hindquarters into the air while kneeling on his forelegs. He stood like that for a second or two, swaying dangerously, before toppling over. On his second attempt, he maintained this position a tad longer. He was a healthy little guy, no question about it.

Every once in a while during these exertions, he made a soft, low-pitched cry. And each time he did, his mother reacted as if possessed, which she was, of course: possessed with a burning desire to be with her newborn. Her mission was urgent, for she knew by instinct that she had to lick away the mucus and membranes enveloping his muzzle. If she didn't, his breath would be cut off. She needed to massage strength into her offspring's limbs with her rough tongue, to help him rise on those wobbly legs and explore her belly to find his first meal.

I hated myself for separating the two. It was the most depraved act of cruelty I could imagine inflicting on any creature under my care. The calf was enclosed in a pen less than ten feet from his mother. She could hear and smell him but couldn't touch or see him. Their anguish was heartrending.

I understood that if I allowed the calf to suckle, his mother's milk production would diminish considerably. Yet much later I would learn that many farmers allow mother and calf to spend up to twenty-four hours together before separation, which provides both animals with physiological and emotional benefits. Any longer than twenty-four hours makes their separation even more stressful than the immediate severance Linda and I were witnessing.

Even if the heifer had been in a calm state, I'd have needed reinforcements to milk her for the first time. I went back to the house and called the most accomplished milkmaid for miles around.

Solveig showed up a half hour later carrying a short chain with J-hooks at both ends. She fastened a hook above each of the heifer's rear legs just above the hocks, effectively tethering them together to limit their ability to shoot out at us. But the fiendish animal twisted, turned, and kicked with a power that more than made up for her limited range. After several attempts, Solveig gave up. It was simply too dangerous for her to be anyplace close to the explosive force of those limbs.

"I'll come back with Alv when he's done with chores," she said. "It won't be more than an hour or two. You and Linda will both need to give us a hand."

When brother and sister showed up, it took Solveig's chain plus all four of us to accomplish our mission. While Alv, Linda, and I pressed the heifer against the wall of her stall, Solveig stroked the new mother's flank and soothed her with a medley of words and song, all the while moving her hand closer and closer to the sensitive udder. When she reached it, she used firm, calm pressure to massage the taut bag, until finally her experienced fingers enveloped a teat and succeeded in getting the heifer to let her milk down.

That first milk, the colostrum, was so essential for the baby's health that Solveig worked one teat at a time. Instead of clenching the bucket between her legs, she held it wrapped in her free arm, ready to protect it at all costs. After a while, the once bulging udder hung flaccid. When I proffered the small bucket of colostrum to my little calf, he slurped it down with frenetic gulps.

For two days, Solveig did the milking morning and evening, just as she'd done when I first arrived at Hovland. After she turned the job over to me, I lived in fear of this twice daily task. The heifer was a beast, nothing like my gentle cow. Her mood shifted from one encounter to the next, ranging from nervous to furious. I never knew when the next blow might strike.

As early as the beginning of March, I'd begun to notice the word *påske*, "Easter," popping up more and more often. By month's end, I understood that Easter in Norway went far beyond the rituals of egg dying, egg hunts, and baskets of candy that I knew from home. Yet not until April 15, Palm Sunday, did I fully register that *påske* was not a *day* but rather a national concept: an entire week when the country shuts down and everyone who possibly can do so heads to a cabin in the mountains to ski, relax, and make merry.

With dozens of Hovland's and Soldal's far-flung children flocking home for the festivities, it felt to Linda and me like Christmas all over again. Even the weather cooperated, with the sun shining brightly almost every day for a week. Of course, there was no time off from the barn. And now with a baby calf to care for and a cow to milk twice a day, chores required three hours each morning and evening. Without Linda's help, I would never have been able to break away.

Yet when time was available, break away we did. We hurried through chores—finishing in under two hours—dashed inside for a quick breakfast, then headed uphill, with Bella in the lead. It took half an hour to reach Blomseter's two cabins, and there the forest disappeared, replaced by a landscape of snow undulating outward and upward, as if a pure white cumulus had dropped from the sky to cover the earth.

It was an incredible feeling to ascend into this dazzling new cosmos that stretched as far as the eye could see or the mind could imagine. I rejoiced in the physical strength that a year on the farm had bestowed on me and in my budding skills on skis that made it possible to explore this foreign world.

Linda and I soon discovered that there were one or two people ensconced in each of the small clusters of cabins above the farm, where, as near as we could tell, custom and etiquette required that these hardy souls provision their abodes with an overabundance of food, coffee, and beer, offering all of this—along with a bed, if needed—to anyone who passed by. The obligation of a skier to drop in and say hello seemed at least as strong as the host's obligation to offer sustenance.

Visits in these lofty outposts were a time for talking about the mountains. All that was tedious or worrisome was left behind. We traded information about skiing conditions and weather forecasts, reported on sightings of reindeer and ptarmigan, gossiped about goings-on at each cabin, and boasted of summits conquered. Never mentioned was the world below or the poor souls down there leading their sorry lives, unwilling or unable to ascend into our Valhalla.

Two days after Easter Sunday, I released the fourteen yearling ewes that hadn't been bred in the fall. Much of the snow was melted away now, and new grass had inched up just enough to sustain a few animals. That afternoon Linda and I watched our happy young sheep lying in a group on the hillside, with their heads tilted toward the sun and eyes half-closed, enjoying their first day of fresh air since November.

The next morning we got up at six, hurried through breakfast, and rushed outside to hitch Begonia to the cart. We said our goodbyes driving down the road, which was still too slushy for any car to traverse. At the milk ramp in Soldal, Linda transferred her backpack into a waiting taxi and departed for England. My heart sank as the car drove off. My good friend was gone, leaving me alone with a man I could barely tolerate, just as I was heading into lambing season, the year's most grueling period of work.

I made the same trip the following afternoon, this time with Klara as passenger. After five weeks of caring for Johannes, she was going home. During these last three weeks while Linda had been visiting, I'd seen the nurse only once or twice a day, usually in the barn, where she came to visit the animals. Her complaints never stopped, yet I'd come to admire her professional handling of a difficult boss in the face of so many hardships.

Klara's replacement was due to arrive the following morning. So I was caught off guard that evening when a car eased its way up the road, which no locals had the nerve to drive on. It stopped at the house, and a tall, handsome woman emerged from the driver's seat. She didn't introduce herself using her first and last names but called herself *fru* Schreiner, that is, "Mrs. Schreiner": only the second woman I'd met in Norway who expected to be addressed in this formal manner. But it fit her well, and it never crossed my mind to call her anything else.

"Johannes told me nothing about any of this," *fru* Schreiner told me after supper that evening. "He said that he could take care of himself and that the only personal assistance I would have to provide was tying his shoelaces."

In the morning, she sought me out in the barn.

"The conditions here are untenable for a man in his state," she proclaimed. "Surely the health authorities in Øystese are already aware of this. I'll be contacting them this morning to request that they secure a room for him in the nursing home as soon as possible."

39

Lamb Spring

When a ewe starts pushing her lamb into the world, what you want to see first are the tips of the little animal's front toes. If all is well, the next thing to appear is a delicate snout nestled atop tiny knees, a streamlined arrangement that allows a slippery little body to exit the birth canal and slide safely into life on the outside.

That was not how it happened when my fourth ewe went into labor. As I monitored her progress, the first thing to pop out was the lamb's snout, no toes in sight. For just a moment I had an overwhelming urge to run from the barn to fetch Torkel. But I knew more now than I did a year ago, I reminded myself. And Torkel had actually described a presentation like this and instructed me on how to deal with it.

Another contraction revealed no sign of toes, which almost certainly meant that both legs were pointing backward; that is, they were positioned alongside the lamb's belly. A configuration like this makes the lamb's shoulders splay out, so the little guy was now stuck in the birth canal like a cork in a bottle. My job was to find those legs and pull them forward into the proper position, one at a time. I was glad that I'd been watching this ewe so closely, because the job would be far more challenging if the head had already emerged into daylight.

Settling onto a bed of hay I'd thrown down for the laboring ewe, I took a deep breath and gently pushed the tiny snout back into the birth canal. That was the easy part. Now I carefully slid my hand into the canal and began to ease it inward, farther and farther, in search of a missing leg. Yet this was my first exploration into those warm, wet crevices, and by the time my arm had been swallowed nearly to the elbow, I had no idea what I was feeling or even whether the tissues under my fingers belonged to the lamb or its mother. The task was made more difficult by the ewe's frequent contractions, which tightened around my arm with a vengeance and seemed to rearrange whatever it was my fingers were exploring.

I glanced at a lamb in an adjacent pen, trying to imagine how its legs would look if they were drawn back. A thrill went through me when I recognized that it was a slender crease I needed to find. Keeping my eyes on the roadmap next door, I traced my fingers back and forth, descending from what I now imagined was the lamb's shoulder. And suddenly I found it: that crease that told me I'd reached the intersection of the lamb's body and leg—a leg that I could slide my hand along as I pushed just a little bit deeper into the darkness.

The ewe groaned with such a strong contraction that my arm went numb. But the moment her muscles relaxed, I found what I'd been looking for: the inside joint of a knobby little knee. I clenched two fingers around it and pulled. My heart, already pumping fast, ramped up when I felt the knee unfold. Torkel had told me to pull a leg forward with my hand cupped around the foot, which would prevent it from bruising the birth canal. I found the foot a second later and drew it toward me. It seemed like a miracle that it was actually coming my way and an even greater miracle when my hand emerged clutching a pair of tiny, slimy, pointy, white and purple toes.

The second leg was easier to locate, and in just a minute or two I had it positioned alongside the first. At the ewe's next contraction, I kept hold of both legs and gently pulled them outward. Now the little snout reappeared right where it was supposed to be. With me pulling and the ewe pushing, on her third contraction, a long, limp, and gooey body glided out onto the hay.

I wanted to jump up and scream with victory. I'd done this! I'd actually done this all on my own! The lamb was fine, the ewe was fine, and I hadn't bothered Torkel or anyone else to bring the little critter into the world. A delivery like this would have been a ho-hum task for my neighbors, but as I stood by watching the new mother nuzzle and lick her wobbly newborn to its feet, I was filled with a mixture of pride and joy that knew no bounds.

That same day, ten inches of wet snow buried the wild anemones on the forest floor and washed golden pollen from a stand of pussy willows along the creek. The next morning, fourteen yearling ewes, the ones who had been so happy when they first gained their freedom a few days earlier, huddled miserably together with nothing to eat but the hay I carted out to them.

This was precious food indeed, because we'd run out of our own hay and were nearly out of silage, too. In the week before Easter, Torkel had lent me his hay wagon and accompanied me down the hill and past Skårsvatnet to a farm about the size of a postage stamp that belonged to a couple in their seventies. Although they kept only four ewes—half as many as in their younger days—they still cut all the grass on their small holding, curing it to hay on short, orderly *hesjes*.

Johannes had negotiated to buy their surplus, and together Torkel and I loaded it up and drove it back to Hovland. He and I made three trips on that sunny day, and Linda and I made two more the day after. When I surveyed this bounty in the hayloft, I figured it might be just enough to squeeze by on until spring's new grass grew dense enough to support my fifty-three sheep, cow, calf, and horse, plus the flood of lambs on their way. Now this new snowfall was delaying spring once again, and I was desperately close to running out of feed.

In the first nine days of lambing, twenty ewes gave birth. In one frenzied twenty-hour period, ten lambs were born. Johannes's big-headed dala sheep had been bred for size, not easy births, so problems were rampant. I had to reposition the limbs of four or five more young ones that were hung up in the birth canal. And I found myself dashing down the road for Torkel's assistance twice, once in my nightgown at four o'clock in the morning. But unlike my panicked midnight run to his house a year earlier—when I was so young and callow that it felt like a lifetime ago—this time my ewes and their lambs really did need his help, without which all of them most likely would have died.

For three weeks, I tried to be everywhere at once, keeping watch over ewes in all stages of labor and on lambs that were small enough to slip out of their pens whenever they felt like venturing into the wider world. One evening I found a ewe happily licking the membranes off newborn twins. The only problem was that the lambs' real mother was still lying on her side recovering from labor. When I moved the kidnapper to another pen, she went berserk trying to get back to the newborns. She calmed down only after delivering her own set of twins the next day. Another lamb, a fine coal-black ram with tight curly wool, was born so weak that he never rose to his feet, dying an hour after birth.

When a young ewe rejected one of her two lambs, I shackled her into a small stall with both of them. Even then, she could stamp and kick hard enough to prevent her unwanted twin from nursing. One evening the little waif squeezed out of her pen and stumbled to the stall next door, where she got trampled under the hoof of my very annoyed cow. I kept her alive with bottle feeding, but given that she was both injured and rejected, her plight seemed hopeless—until a week later, when I found a baby ram dead in his pen for no apparent reason.

Torkel showed up later in the morning to sculpt my new lambs' ears with Johannes's earmark. He couldn't miss the carcass—which I'd placed outside—or the dead ram's inconsolable dam, who was pacing in circles and bleating without stop.

"It's a good thing I brought my knife," he said, holding up a sharp blade. "Let's see if we can use this poor little fellow's hide to save your bottle lamb."

Soon we were tying the flayed hide of a dead lamb around the body of an abandoned one. Drooping nearly to the floor, this ungainly white pelt made my little waif look even more pathetic. But that was not what the grieving mother saw when we tied her up in a small pen along with the hungry little reject. Within an hour, she accepted the foundling cloaked in the scent of her own lamb. I stole a glance at Torkel while we stood watching the adoptee nursing to her heart's content: his eyes, like mine, were beaming with happiness.

On her sixth morning at Hovland, *fru* Schreiner searched me out in the barn to tell me that she had just received a call informing her that in a few hours a room would be ready for Johannes at a nursing home in town. She would be leaving as soon as she finished packing for herself and for him.

She drove away that afternoon. An hour later, a cab ferried Johannes down the hill to Øystese.

"Johannes is gone! I feel so much better now!" I wrote in a letter to my family, without so much as a word of sympathy for the man who was forced from his home a second time. Now I could cook my meals and relax in the house rather than planning my days around avoiding him there. I would no longer have to endure the dark glances he threw my way from time to time or his rants about our neighbors. And I wouldn't need to bite my tongue at the illogical pronouncements he frequently made during our daily meetings. Surely Johannes was devastated. But I had only enough time and energy to care for his farm, with nothing left over for him.

Soon after his departure, a new group of lambs began to grace the barn: the delicate-looking offspring of my little black spæl ram and his sturdy white dala mates. These lambs had finer features than their large-boned mothers. And unlike the crimped white wool of their full-blooded dala siblings, they had long wavy hair that came in every imaginable color: black, brown, gray, white, and even blue and orange. One of the first to arrive was the coal-black ram that died at birth. But after that, the others proved to be scrappy little creatures, finding their mother's teats even before rising to their feet.

With so little sleep and so much work, my mood was swinging from one extreme to another. When the sun came out for three days after Johannes left, I was ecstatic. Spring, this wonderful and expectant season, had finally arrived! The temperature rose to 60 degrees, and I wore short sleeves for the first time since August.

Then rain and snow returned, falling for eight days without stop. My livestock were enduring horrific conditions. The sheep I'd released into the field couldn't find enough grass to eat and were suffering from the cold and wet. Inside the barn it was even worse. I'd cut down on rations for all the animals, even Begonia and the cow. This dark, dank, manure-filled environment itself was growing unhealthier by the day. After being shut inside for six months, my charges needed to get outside into clean air and open space as soon as possible. Not being able to fix any of this was tearing me apart.

Swaddled in misery as I sat at the kitchen table on the evening of May 13, I wrote to my family that I was on the verge of a nervous breakdown. I was desperate to be in a place that was warm and safe. More than anything else, though, I needed to get away from the agony of watching my animals suffer and not being able to do anything about it no matter how hard I tried. So I made up my mind and reserved passage to San Francisco on a June 9 flight from Bergen. By then, I reckoned, lambing would be finished and there would be more than enough grass in the meadows and pasture to sustain my beloved four-legged menagerie.

On May 16, the sun finally came out again. I opened the barn door and released every animal but the calf, a half dozen ewes with newborns, and those still pregnant. Within hours my emancipated lambs were racing across the hillsides, punctuating their joyful sprints with jerky little leaps into the air. If I'd been a lamb, I would have raced with them, for spring's sweet promises filled my senses, too. A few hours of sunlight was all it took to sweep away my misery.

This weather was merely a trial run for the sizzling 68 degrees the thermometer registered the next day, May 17—*syttende mai,* Norway's Constitution Day—and the anniversary of my arrival in the country. With magnificent snow-covered mountains rising from the fjord's far shore and spring-green hillsides all around, the setting for the day's festivities could not have been more beautiful.

In the morning, I went with neighbors to Øystese, where hundreds of people had gathered for the holiday's parades: first a procession of young children, then everyone else from high school up. Flagbearers waving Norway's beautiful blue, white, and red standard led the way, with a couple of marching bands providing music. This parade was nothing fancy, just people dressed in their very best, walking together along the town's main drag, where "very best" for most women and a handful of men meant Hardanger's stunning *bunad*s.

In Oslo a year earlier, I'd stared in wonder at a parade hundreds of times larger than this one. Then I was an outsider who could barely understand Norwegian. In Øystese I stood with friends, speaking a Hardanger dialect I loved and dressed in the resplendent *bunad* that women of this region had been making and wearing for generations.

In the afternoon a more intimate gathering took place when everyone from Hovland to Soldal and all the way down to Fyksesund assembled at the community hall by Skårsvatnet for coffee, cake, ice cream, music, games, and socializing. The party adjourned at five, when most of us headed home for evening chores before returning for the *real* party, a big dance in the hall that started at ten.

At the Christmas dance five months earlier, Linda and I had watched in envy as *bunad*-clad women swirled over the floor with their black pleated skirts billowing around them. Now I spent the night doing the same. At times, the dance floor was so crowded that our swirling skirts collided. Other times, we womenfolk sat in chairs lining the walls, while our menfolk huddled together in the basement or out in the parking lot guzzling whatever it was they'd filled into their pocket flasks. When I walked back up the hill at two in the morning, May's full moon was glowing pale yellow and birds were starting up their dawn chorus.

Three days later, I was staked out in the barn keeping an eye on a ewe in labor when Edvard showed up. He'd heard that I was leaving, he told me, and had come to say goodbye. He was in the midst of studying for finals and would be staying in Bergen until finishing his last exam in mid-June. After that, he would find a job as a ship's mate and head to sea. We stood side by side in the barn watching the birth of twins and waiting until both had latched onto a teat and their long tails were wriggling in that sure sign that milk was flowing into their tummies.

In the kitchen, I made us a cup of tea and set out some food. Neither of us ate much as we talked about the future—a future in which the chances of our paths crossing again were dim. He could be at sea for months, while I might only be able to travel back to Øystese from my school in Innvik two or three times during the year.

We stayed in the kitchen together until midnight, and when he stood up to leave, I started to cry. He looked at me in distress. And at that moment, through tears that I couldn't hold back, I told him how much I cared for him. He had been my best friend throughout the year, I said, the only person I felt entirely comfortable with. I didn't know how I could have kept going at the farm without his companionship and support, and I'd missed him whenever he'd been gone.

He told me much the same. That he cared for me deeply and had missed me, too. We hugged each other there in the kitchen, a long and loving embrace. And then we walked side by side across field and pasture to the forest trail, where I stood alone in the night's dusky light, watching him disappear into the woods.

40

Onward

I leaped up, terrified, and ran out the door. How could I possibly have forgotten? It had been days since I'd last fed the calf, and the poor little critter was still locked in his pen. I sped to the barn, praying to find him alive. But when I got there, everything looked different: more pens and stalls than I remembered and a huge network of passageways. I ran down all of them, searching and searching until—I woke up. At home. In my own bed. Warm. Clean. Comfortable. Happy.

I was having dreams like this once or twice a week during my first month back home in Mill Valley. But rather than upsetting me, they filled me with bliss the moment I awoke to the realization that I'd done nothing wrong, my calf was fine, and I could stay under the covers without worrying about rushing to the barn for chores. When I did get up and go downstairs, my mother was usually there to give me a hug and sometimes even make breakfast for me.

While these dreams weren't troubling, I spent days coming to grips with a real-life nightmare. On Sunday morning, May 27, Johannes had shown up at the farm unannounced. "I have some questions you need to answer," he declared, while a man I didn't recognize helped him out of the car.

I'd heard nothing from Johannes since the day four weeks earlier when *fru* Schreiner had departed, forcing him to leave, too. Now I shuddered at his words, for they held no hint of warmth. After supporting Johannes up the trail and settling him into a chair in the kitchen, the driver took his leave, saying that he'd be back in an hour.

I sat down opposite my boss and looked him in the eye.

"So, Liese, tell me, why did you let my farm and garden fall to ruin even though you had all the help you needed?" His tone was patronizing, as if this accusation was self-evident. "You could have at least kept the weeds down. But you didn't even do that."

I'd stopped breathing at his first words. Now I sat frozen, my mind racing to comprehend and respond. Screaming at him won't help, the voice in my head was telling me. Stay calm. Pretend this is a normal conversation.

"Well, I don't understand what you mean. You can see for yourself that the farm's in better shape now than when I got here."

"I know quite well what you and your friends did with your time last summer." His tone was sharper now, his eyes narrowed to slits. "Off you went to the mountains, hiking and drifting about, while my garden, my beautiful garden, was growing over with weeds."

And so it went for half an hour: this angry man accusing me of turning his farm and garden into a pigsty, cheating him out of money, making life hell for Klara.

I did my best to parry each accusation, forcing myself to remain calm and rational. Talking over each of his interruptions. Reminding him of all that I'd done through the year, culminating with five weeks of lambing, when I'd barely had time to sleep.

"And you know it wasn't just me who's been working here, but your neighbors and Gunnar and Ola and Ingebjørg and so many others," I went on. Now it was impossible to remain calm. "Altogether they've put in hundreds of hours helping out . . . helping *you* out. So, yes, like you said, I had plenty of help. And all of us together got much more done than you ever could have managed by yourself!"

"Then how do you account for what Klara told me?" he seethed. "She said you were the worst housekeeper she'd ever met. She couldn't live in this house with you. It was easy to see that you were trying to drive her away, because you thought that as soon as she left, I'd have to go, too. Shame on you for making me leave my own house!"

Of everything he'd said, this was the worst. Had Klara really told him that I tried to drive her away? Did he really believe this? Was it possible that she had been going to Johannes day after day complaining to him about me, just like she'd been coming to me with stories about him? These were horrible accusations, piled one atop the next. Suddenly, instead of wanting to yell at Johannes, I had to stop myself from breaking into tears.

"Johannes, look around you," I pleaded. "Your house is fine. The garden is fine. You're not making sense. The evidence is right here. Just look at your sheep! I kept them alive through the winter, even when the barn was flooded. Since lambing started, I've been in the barn all night, too. You know what lambing's like. You can see for yourself that I've done a good job of it."

"Yes, you kept the animals alive," he replied. "But that's the only thing you've done. Otherwise you were just having a luxury vacation at my expense for a year! I even paid for Linda's food at Easter when both of you spent your time gallivanting around. You know it was fraudulent, asking me to pay her."

My head was spinning and my heart was beating so fast I thought it would explode. I needed something to hold on to, a foil to his madness. I reached down to Bella, who was lying on the floor between us. As I stroked her head, she looked up at me with big-hearted eyes. In that quiet second I understood that I was leaving—not in two weeks but today. And after I left, I could never return to the farm that I'd grown to love with all my heart.

I straightened up to confront him. Over his shoulder I could see the faraway line of snowy mountains capped by the hazy white saddle of Folgefonna Glacier. If rain had been falling or if clouds had shrouded my view, this passage would have been easier. But the day was as beautiful as no other, and the dazzling white peaks were framed between a brilliant blue sky and a deep green forest. I wanted to go out there, get away from Johannes's poison, stand under that sky right now. But I couldn't let his charges go uncontested.

A luxury vacation. The declaration was so absurd that it wasn't worth wasting my time on. My mind flailed around for a way of freeing myself from this vile man. If it was money he wanted, so be it.

"Linda did good work every day she was here, and you agreed to pay her. But if you think we took that money from you, I'll give it back right now. How much do you want?"

"I gave you a hundred kroner for her." His face was rigid, his gray eyes steely.

I jumped up and grabbed my little bag of cash from a cupboard above the sink, counted out the bills, and whipped them across the table.

"There you have it," I said. "What else do you want? Tell me now, because I'm going to leave as soon as I can pack. And I don't want you to ever say that I took anything from you."

"You never paid me for the phone calls you made in January," he said flatly. "That's 140 kroner."

I counted out seven more bills, stood up, and slapped them onto the table in front of him. "What else do I owe you?"

"Nothing more. That's all."

"Are you sure?"

He took up a red pen that was lying on the table. "Give me a piece of paper," he said. "I'll put it in writing."

I fetched a piece of lined paper and watched as he composed a single long sentence in his strange mix of dialect and written Norwegian.

Receipt

The undersigned hereby witnesses that Liese Greensfelder is leaving me in May June '73, that everything between us relating to economic matters and work-related things is settled, I have nothing more to demand of her.

Hovland 27/5–73

Johs. Hovland

I was exploding inside, overwhelmed by fury and sorrow, but I almost laughed when I read this sweeping declaration that he had nothing more to demand of me, as if I were indebted to him for my year of work on his farm. But there was something more that I wanted from *him*. So in my own strange mix of Danish and Norwegian, I took the pen and wrote a note for his signature.

27.5.73

I have received 100 kr from Liese Greensfelder for food for Linda Jolly for the time she was here during Easter 1973. I have also received 140 kr from Liese for the telephone bill of January 1973.

He signed the paper and flung it back at me.

During this writing exercise, Johannes had time to think about the consequences of my leaving so soon, and I had time to start wondering what was going to happen to the animals when I left: a moment of clarity that took some of the wind out of both of us.

Calling to Bella, I stood up and headed outside. Before slamming the door, I turned back for one last look. If I'd seen any sign of confusion, sadness, or regret, or as much as a hint of reflection in his countenance, even then, I think, I would have given him another chance. But the dead anger in his eyes held no quarter.

Bella trotted at my side as I looked around for the animals I'd been keeping an eye on: a ewe who'd been limping; two underweight lambs; and the heifer, who was still breaking through fences every day. When we reached my lookout point halfway up Johannes's steepest hill, I stopped to take in Hovland's three farms and the broad view beyond. To my left, the magnificent peaks rising above Fyksesund were so close I reached out to bid them farewell. The thought of leaving them was more than I could bear.

"Fagraseteggi, Klyvenuten," I said aloud, "*farvel.*" Farewell.

Thirty yards above us, a ewe lifted her head. With a throaty baa, she jogged our way, her two lambs trailing behind. I recognized her as one of my favorites, or perhaps one of the greediest, for she was always first in line when I made my rounds carrying a can of grain. Pulling up just beyond reach, she craned her neck toward my outstretched hand and gave it a hopeful nibble.

And that was all it took. A sob came on so hard I couldn't breathe. Then another and another. I doubled over, clutching my arms to my chest, and cried for so long that when I finally stopped, the grass at my feet glistened with snot and tears.

For the rest of the afternoon I walked from house to house, beseeching neighbors to watch over my four-legged charges. They had no desire to come to Johannes's aid, for he had turned his back on all of them since returning home, never offering a single thank-you for the extraordinary help they had provided during his absence. Now when I told them of the accusations he had leveled against me, they were even more upset. Like me, though, their anger toward Johannes did not extend to his animals. And they agreed to take on this extra burden.

The next morning, right after chores, I picked up the phone and rescheduled my June flight to Wednesday, two days away. To arrive at the airport in time, I'd need to leave Hovland on Tuesday afternoon. A mountain of work faced me, with little more than a day to do it in.

I spent two months in Mill Valley enjoying time with my parents and siblings, working at my old job in the Danish bakery, and trying to make sense of Johannes's accusations. They had hit me so unexpectedly and with such intensity that I had to tell myself time and again that the man was crazy and to remind myself that my neighbors, when they heard my story, had told me to laugh it off. After all, almost every one of them had been targets of his vitriol at some point in their lives.

On the first day of August, I returned to Hovland. Not to Johannes's farm this time but to Torkel and Inger's. I'd come to help with haying for a couple of weeks before heading north to agriculture school in Innvik.

There was plenty of news to catch up on when I arrived. Solveig and Inger reported that all six of the pregnant ewes I'd left in their hands had produced a total of nine healthy offspring with no problems. I was not nearly as happy to learn that Magnar had made off with Begonia and my little black calf. He'd also taken the calf's mother, and from all accounts that accursed black beast had been breaking through his fences just as she had broken through mine. I should have felt sympathy for the old farmer, but I regarded his bovine misfortunes as nothing short of poetic justice: my malevolent heifer for his incompetent ram.

As for Johannes, he'd returned to the farm with a new caregiver in tow just two weeks after I left. That person hadn't lasted more than a few weeks, and neither had his replacement. Since then, Johannes had been living alone with Bella. How he managed to survive without assistance was a neighborhood mystery.

By the middle of September, just three weeks into classes, I knew that Langvin School of Agriculture was the perfect place for me. Six mornings a week, classroom teachers packed us with information about everything from animal husbandry and forestry to agricultural technology and economics. Five afternoons a week, instructors took us to the school's fields, forests, greenhouses, barns, and machine shops for demonstrations and hands-on training. At the same time, I was forging friendships with fellow students from around the country.

The knowledge and practical experience I gained during my year there provided a solid foundation for working with Norwegian agriculture: from small fruit and vegetable operations to large dairy, sheep, or pig farms. Much of what I'd learned was transferable to agricultural settings around the world, as well.

Those months at school opened my eyes to just how isolated Hovland and other mountain farms had been from the rest of Norway. From my limited vantage point at the end of a long dirt road, I'd seen neighbors working with horses, fertilizing their fields with manure, and using scythes to harvest grass that their cutting machines couldn't reach.

Of course, I did have hints during that time that the use of draft horses in Norway was on the wane. If asked, I may have ventured a guess that only 50 percent of the country's farmers still worked with them. So it was a shock to learn that tractors outnumbered horses by five to one on Norwegian farms and that most of the remaining steeds were not working under harness but being ridden under saddle, for fun.

As to manure, our agronomy teacher employed tables and graphs to demonstrate that the use of cow pies and sheep droppings was a drop in the bucket compared with the amount of artificial fertilizers that Norway's farmers were spreading over their fields. And scythes? Tut-tut! The only suitable place for such an ancient tool was in a museum display case.

I spent a total of two and a half years in Norway before returning to California to pursue a bachelor's degree in agronomy. Six months into my studies, I fell in love with a young man within an hour of meeting him. Bob was a woodworker who had built a small shop on a large, forested parcel in the Sierra Nevada foothills. He'd bought the land with a group of like-minded friends who aimed to establish a community and forge independent careers away from suburbs and cities.

Early on, I told him of my life plan to work with farmers in developing countries. It would be a challenge to live in South America or Africa, he said, but he was willing to try. Two years into our relationship, he realized that the challenge would be too great. But by then, I couldn't imagine a life without him.

A year after I obtained my degree, we built a house with our own hands four hundred feet from his shop. A few months later our son was born. When Tor was two, the three of us moved to a university town, where I obtained a master's degree in orchard science. After that, I spent four years as a University of California farm adviser in a county where I focused my work on helping relatively small growers produce fruit and vegetable crops and market them directly to restaurants and consumers.

Since then, I've changed careers a time or two: sometimes working from home, sometimes taking jobs so distant that I commuted on weekends. Several years ago, when I took over the care of my aged father, I finally settled down at home.

Meanwhile, Tor has become a furniture maker himself, joining Bob in designing and making stylish chairs and stunning tables. Now I help both of them manage the business side of their craft.

I've returned to Hovland many times over the years as a guest of Svein Hovland, Gunnar's son, who took over the farm after his uncle's death in 1986. Svein and his partner, Marian Bolstad, have taken pains to preserve much of Johannes's garden and to restore the farm's buildings, retaining all that they could of those structures' splendid rock foundations and walls and preserving the barn's expertly crafted timber framing. From the outside, the buildings still look much the same, but now the barn has a solid roof and red-painted siding that even the most ferocious winter storms can't penetrate.

Now when I stand at Hovland and regard this landscape shaped by hundreds of years of toil and care, my thoughts invariably fly back to the day I first met Johannes, when, lying in a hospital bed, he entrusted me with everything he owned.

"I give you my full authority," he told me. And throughout the twelve months that I cared for his house, garden, and farm, he stood by his word.

That covenant opened up a new world for me, a world layered with tradition where neighbors relied on one another for survival; crafted local materials into houses, barns, tools, and other necessities of life; utilized mountains beyond the borders of cultivation; grew their own food; and employed centuries-old methods to preserve it.

The covenant bonded me to a community with ties that have remained strong through the intervening decades and that bestowed on me yet one more extraordinary gift: my own place in that long, unbroken line of Hovland farmers stretching back more than four hundred years.

For all this, I am forever grateful.

Acknowledgments

I will begin these acknowledgments from the beginning, that is, with my parents, Robert and Jean Greensfelder, who raised my siblings and me to be independent and taught us the value of critical thinking, two gifts that gave me strength throughout my time at Hovland. I'm also grateful for their careful preservation of the hundreds of pages of letters I wrote home—and that they didn't freak out when those pages described hair-raising adventures and, during winter's darkest days, my dips into depression.

I could not have made it through the year without the boundless help, instruction, friendship, good humor, and terrific meals that my closest neighbors, Torkel, Inger, Tormod, and Arne Hovland, showered on me. My next closest neighbors, the siblings Solveig and Alv Hovland, were excellent and careful teachers who came to my rescue time and again.

Ola and Ingebjørg Mæland regularly drove up the hill from Øystese to lend a hand. On various celebratory occasions, they drove me down the hill to their house on the fjord, where Ingebjørg treated us to her exquisite homemade *rømmegraut,* sour cream porridge. During my first week on the farm, they lent me their daughter, nine-year-old Martha Johanne, who did a great job as my guide and language instructor.

I extend my gratitude to many others who toiled beside me in Hovland's fields and barn, including Edvard Heggland, Øystein Hovland, Linda Jolly, Gunnar Hovland, Einar Flatebø, *snille* Alfred Flatabø, Johan Flatabø, Jon Teigland, Knut Soldal, Anne Liv Soldal, *vetle* Nils Soldal, and Torgeir Hovland.

A host of neighbors provided other kinds of support, both while I lived on the farm and for years afterward. In addition to their friendship and good cheer, they dispensed enlightening information about local history, customs, land ownership, inheritance practices, and much more—details that have diffused their way into the pages of this book. Notable among them are Bjørg *Kampen* Flatabø, Leiv and Gudrun

Soldal, Nils and Solveig Flatabø, Aslaug and *store* Nils Soldal, Alis Soldal Bjotveit, Tord Øverland, Ola and Amanda Flatabø, and Nils Årekol.

On my many sojourns and fact-finding missions back to Hardanger, big-hearted friends have generously provided living quarters. Thank you, Bjørg Skåre, Arne Hovland, Vigdis Tangen, Nils and Solveig Flatabø, Torunn Øvsthus and Nick Christensen, and Ingunn Teigland Hildonen and Morten Hildonen Teigland. On my visits to Bergen, Karen and Kaare Gundersen, Britt Hysing-Dahl, and Steiner Døsvik never failed to welcome me, no matter how often I turned up on their doorstep.

Marian Bolstad, Arne Hovland, Alis Bjotveit, and Svein Hovland, your unending support and willingness to dig up answers to my countless esoteric and arcane questions about language, people, places, and more have been of tremendous value. Marian, your photographs of Hovland and the mountains beyond are breathtaking.

Steiner Døsvik, Erik Berglund, and Linda Jolly, *tusen takk,* a thousand thanks, for your marvelous photographs. Camilla Flaatten, you instilled me with confidence while championing publication of this book.

I am forever indebted to Inez Fung and Jim Bishop for providing me with unlimited use of a writing retreat like no other: a lovely studio shaded by wisteria vines and lemon trees. To Mesa Refuge and Blue Mountain Center, thank you for granting me writer's residencies in your gorgeous and peaceful surroundings. Nathanael Johnson, you have been more than generous in sharing your insights on publishing and referring me to agents.

To the many readers and editors who plowed through various drafts of this work (and especially those of you who read more than one draft), I treasured each of your comments, critiques, and encouragements. Every one of you has contributed to making this book better. Please accept my gratitude, Don Losure, Anne Greensfelder, Ben Greensfelder, Sarah Miller, Diane Stockwell, Gary Snyder, Lindsey Alexander, John Wilkes, Tanya and Wendell Berry, Kate Dwyer, Torunn Kveen, Cynthia Erickson, Joe McCabe, Mark Kane, Marilyn Mociun, Nancy Lorenz, Susanne Rockwell, Leslie Guinan, Jennifer Rain, Carole Koda, Jonathan Keehn, Les Whipp, Kaaren Wiken, Elisabeth Maurland, Mary Street, and LSE '65 book club members Joel Babb, Gretchen Garlinghouse, Dale Guilford, Milo Alexander, Mary Kay Zabel, Gregg Wright, Denise Fourie, and Nancy Horn.

And to eagle-eyed copy editor Anne Taylor: I'd been dreading this process, but you made it interesting and fun. Thank you for making *Accidental Shepherd* shine!

Annette Dunklin, Mary Losure, and Tavia Cathcart, you are my tireless readers and pillars of support! I can't find words to express how much your help has meant to me. Tiina Nunnally, magnificent translator of Scandinavian literature and fellow AFSer from our year in Denmark, heartfelt thanks for presenting my story to your editor at the University of Minnesota Press, Erik Anderson.

And thank you, Erik Anderson, for the confidence you placed in this work, your gentle and perceptive editing suggestions, and your professional guidance. Emma Saks, your unwavering assistance has been invaluable in keeping this project on track. It has been a true pleasure working with both of you.

My deep appreciation goes out to the others at the University Minnesota Press who have done so much for this book: to Rachel Moeller, for the gorgeous cover and design; Shelby Connelly, Heather Skinner, Maggie Sattler, and Matt Smiley, for working so hard to get *Accidental Shepherd* into the hands of readers; and Laura Westlund, for shepherding it through all its stages.

I reserve my deepest gratitude for my husband and son, Robert and Tor Erickson, who somehow managed to put up with me through the yearslong evolution of this book. Thank you for your razor-sharp comments on of each of the many drafts I pushed into your hands and for your bottomless well of patience, encouragement, and love throughout.

Glossary

Thanks to its formidable and isolating landscape of mountains and fjords, Norway evolved as a country of localized dialects—hundreds of them. By 1814, when a nearly three-century-old union of Denmark and Norway came to an end, the Danish language had also crept into the country. Not only was it used as Norway's official written language, but it had also rooted itself into the upper classes, the church, government, courts, and universities.

In the mid-1800s, Ivar Aasen, a brilliant, self-taught farmer's son from northwest Norway, took it upon himself to develop a written language based on the dialects and grammar of rural Norwegians. Today, his creation, which has been modified into *nynorsk* ("new Norwegian"), is recognized along with the Danish-derived *bokmål* ("book language") as one of Norway's two official standards of written Norwegian.

I've chosen to use *nynorsk* for all of the Norwegian words scattered through this book, for I'm wedded to this older form of the language and its dialects that are spoken in western Norway's fjord districts. I could have attempted to use *kvammamaol,* the dialect that my neighbors at Hovland spoke, which I tried my best to learn. But I would most certainly have botched the spelling of many words or, worse yet, gotten them completely wrong.

Due to myriad factors, less than 15 percent of Norwegians are now using *nynorsk,* down from about a third of the population in the 1940s. Yet, to the great joy of all *nynorsk* and minority language speakers around the world, the 2023 Nobel Prize in Literature was awarded to Jon Fosse, who composes his work in *nynorsk* and who still lives in the small town where he grew up, just twelve miles across the mountains from Hovland.

bokmål: One of two official standards of written Norwegian, essentially a lightly modified Danish (*bok* = book, *mål* = language).
budeie (plural, *budeier*): A woman or girl who spends summers in the mountains tending cows and sheep (*bu* = livestock belonging to a farm, *deie* = woman, maid).
bunad: A traditional Norwegian folk costume. Varying greatly in style from region to region, these outfits are worn on certain holidays and celebratory occasions, especially on May 17, Norway's Constitution Day.
eldhus: An outbuilding that has an open fireplace for baking (*eld* = fire, *hus* = house).
fjell: High-elevation areas dominated by bedrock; mountain.
fru: Mrs.
fullmakt: Power of attorney (*full* = full, *makt* = power).
god dag: Good day (greeting).
god morgon: Good morning (greeting), often shortened to *god morn.*
gymnasium: A three-year secondary school that focuses on preparing students for higher education.
hå: Regrowth of grass and other plants in a field after the first hay harvest.
hesje: A long fence-like structure on which grass is hung in layers to allow it to dry into hay.
hov: Heathen temple. This Old Norse word stems from the Viking Age.
hulder: *Hulder*s are beautiful women, with a tail like a cow's, who live deep inside mountains and in dense forests. Some will take a man as a husband. If treated well, *hulder*s have the ability to keep a farm's livestock healthy and well fed.
ja: Yes.
kraftfôr: Energy-rich feed supplement (*kraft* = power, *fôr* = fodder).
kvammamaol: The dialect spoken in and around the municipality of Kvam in Vestland County (*maol* is the dialect's spelling and pronunciation of the word *mål* = language).
kvige/kviga: Heifer/the heifer.
lefse: A soft kind of flatbread, often spread with butter and sugar, then folded or rolled together.
middag: *Middag* has three meanings: noon, midday, or dinner. On most farms in Norway, dinner was traditionally eaten at noon.
møkk: Manure.

mørketida: The time of year above the Arctic Circle when the sun never rises above the horizon (*mørk* = dark, *tida* = the time).

NIU: A former Norwegian organization that made arrangements for young people from abroad to live and work on Norwegian farms "like a member of the family."

nynorsk: One of two official standards of written Norwegian, *nynorsk* is based on dialects that were spoken in rural districts of Norway in the 1800s (*ny* = new, *norsk* = Norwegian).

pinnekjøt: Salted, smoked, and cured rack of lamb (*pinne* = wooden stick, *kjøt* = meat).

potetkaker: A soft Norwegian flatbread made with potatoes, salt, and flour (*potet* = potato, *kaker* = cakes).

rømmekolle: Fermented sour milk with soured cream on top (*rømme* = sour cream, *kolle* = a low wooden vessel without handles in which milk is stored).

sauesleppet: The release of a herd of sheep from its home pasture into unfenced areas such as mountains or forests (*sau* = sheep, *sleppet* = the act of releasing something).

skorfast: Stuck on a mountain ledge/in a bind (*skòr* = a narrow ledge on a mountain wall, *fast* = firmly fixed, stuck).

snill: Kind, nice.

spælsau: One of several traditional breeds of short-tailed sheep found in Northern Europe, the *spælsau* is thought to be the original sheep breed of Norway (*spæl* = short tail, *sau* = sheep).

spekekjøt: All forms of cured meats; when I was at Hovland it referred specifically to cured and smoked leg of lamb (*speke* = cured, *kjøt* = meat).

støl, seter (plural, *stølar/setrar*): Grazing grounds with a cabin or cabins on uncultivated land (usually in the mountains or forest) where cows, sheep, and goats were sent during the summer to be cared for by a *budeie*.

stutagalen: An expression used to describe a cow in heat (*stut* = bull, *galen* = crazy, mad).

syttende mai: May 17, Norway's national holiday commemorating the signing of its constitution in 1814 (*syttende* = seventeenth, *mai* = May).

utmark: Uncultivated land (*ut* = out, *mark* = field, cultivated ground).

Liese Greensfelder is a freelance writer who focuses on biology, medicine, and agriculture. She has worked as a farm adviser for University of California Cooperative Extension and as a science writer for UC San Francisco and UC Berkeley. In the 1990s, she spearheaded an agricultural development project in the Guatemalan highlands. She is coeditor of *The Nature of This Place* and author of a 1975 Norwegian bestseller, *Hardanger—her kjem eg!*, an account of her first months on the Hovland farm. She lives in rural Nevada County, California, on the western slope of the Sierra Nevada.